The Partition of Ireland

Partition represents the most fundamental revolution in modern Irish history. By 1925 the country had been divided into two states embodying rival religious and political identities, an outcome unthinkable only a decade before. While often analysed through the lens of elite high politics, partition was by definition a mass participation event, where decision-making was shaped by elections, propaganda and savage acts of violence in defence of, or in opposition to, the new settlement. By examining the complex interaction of nationalism, religion and politics, Robert Lynch seeks to understand how partition was constructed and imagined by Irish people themselves, arguing for a relocation of partition at the centre of historical understandings of events in Ireland which spanned the First World War. Lynch highlights the deep confusion and expediency which lay behind the partition plan, and how it failed to provide answers to the complex and enduring problems of Irish identity.

Robert Lynch has worked, taught and researched at the universities of Stirling, Oxford, Trinity College Dublin, Warwick and Queen's University Belfast. He has published numerous articles and books on the early history of Northern Ireland and the partition era, including *The Northern IRA and the Early Years of Partition, 1920–1922* (2006) and most recently contributing to *The Irish Revolution* (2017). He has also published a number of articles in journals such as the *Journal for British Studies* and *Irish Historical Studies*.

The Partition of Ireland
1918–1925

Robert Lynch

CAMBRIDGE
UNIVERSITY PRESS

CAMBRIDGE
UNIVERSITY PRESS

University Printing House, Cambridge CB2 8BS, United Kingdom

One Liberty Plaza, 20th Floor, New York, NY 10006, USA

477 Williamstown Road, Port Melbourne, VIC 3207, Australia

314–321, 3rd Floor, Plot 3, Splendor Forum, Jasola District Centre, New Delhi – 110025, India

79 Anson Road, #06–04/06, Singapore 079906

Cambridge University Press is part of the University of Cambridge.

It furthers the University's mission by disseminating knowledge in the pursuit of education, learning, and research at the highest international levels of excellence.

www.cambridge.org
Information on this title: www.cambridge.org/9781107007734
DOI: 10.1017/9781139017619

First published 2019

Printed in the United Kingdom by TJ International Ltd, Padstow Cornwall

A catalogue record for this publication is available from the British Library.

Library of Congress Cataloging-in-Publication Data
Names: Lynch, Robert John, author.
Title: The partition of Ireland 1918–1925 / Robert Lynch.
Description: United Kingdom ; New York, NY : Cambridge University Press, [2019?] |
Identifiers: LCCN 2018057272 | ISBN 9781107007734
Subjects: LCSH: Ireland – History – Partition, 1921. | Ireland – History – 1910–1921. | Ireland – History – 1922–
Classification: LCC DA962 .L964 2019 | DDC 941.5082/1–dc23
LC record available at https://lccn.loc.gov/2018057272

ISBN 978-1-107-00773-4 Hardback
ISBN 978-0-521-18958-3 Paperback

For Michael Hopkinson, a dear friend, and a true gentleman

Contents

Chronology

1912	11 April	Third Home Rule bill introduced in the House of Commons
	28 September	Ulster's Solemn League and Covenant signed on 'Ulster Day'
1913	31 January	Ulster Volunteer Force (UVF) founded
	24 September	Ulster Unionist Council calls for the creation of the Ulster provisional government if the Home Rule is enacted
	25 November	Irish Volunteers founded at Rotunda in Dublin
1914	20 March	Curragh 'mutiny'
	24 April	Weapons landed at Larne to arm UVF
	25 May	Third Home Rule bill passed for third time by the House of Commons
	26 July	Weapons landed at Howth for Irish Volunteers
	15 September	Third Home Rule Act suspended for duration of the war pending an amendment for special treatment for Ulster
1916	24–29 April	Easter Rising in Dublin
	1 July	36th (Ulster) Division decimated on the first day of the Somme offensive
	23 December	Remaining internees released from Frongoch internment camp and Reading gaol
1917	5 February	Count Plunkett wins by-election victory in North Roscommon
	16 June	Remaining prisoners released
	10 July	Eamon de Valera wins by-election in East Clare
	25 July	Irish Convention opens in Dublin
	26 October	De Valera elected president of Sinn Féin

1918	9 April	Military Service bill introduced, clearing the way for the possible extension of conscription in Ireland
	18 April	Anti-conscription conference held in Dublin
	11 November	Armistice ends the First World War
	14 December	Sinn Féin wins seventy-three Irish seats in the general election
1919	21 January	Dáil Éireann convened at Mansion House in Dublin
	1 April	Eamon de Valera elected president of Dáil
	28 June	Treaty of Versailles signed
1920	25 February	Government of Ireland Act introduced in the House of Commons
	4 April	Irish Republican Army (IRA) launches attacks on over 300 unoccupied Royal Irish Constabulary (RIC) barracks across Ireland
	June	Sinn Féin and the nationalists make substantial gains in local elections following on from victories in urban elections in January
	21 July	'Shipyard expulsions' in Belfast lead to three days of rioting
	6 August	Dáil instigate the Belfast Boycott
	1 November	Recruitment started for new Ulster Special Constabulary
	23 December	Government of Ireland Act becomes law
1921	24 May	Unionists win substantial victory in elections to the new Northern Ireland parliament
	22 June	Northern Ireland parliament opened by King George V
	9–14 July	Sustained sectarian rioting in Belfast
	11 July	Truce implemented, ending War of Independence
	11 October	Anglo-Irish negotiations begin in London
	22 November	Security and policing powers transferred to the new Northern Ireland government
	6 December	Anglo-Irish Treaty signed
1922	7 January	Dáil approves the treaty
	21 January	First Craig–Collins Pact
	12 February	Violence erupts in Belfast after IRA shootings along the border, leading to almost thirty deaths in three days

	30 March	Second Craig–Collins Pact
	7 April	Northern Ireland government introduces the Civil Authorities (Special Powers) Act
	May	Ineffectual IRA offensive launched in Ulster
	23 May	Mass internment of hundreds of Republicans in Northern Ireland
	31 May	Royal Ulster Constabulary (RUC) established
	28 June	Provisional government troops open fire on the Four Courts, thus initiating the Irish Civil War
	12 August	Arthur Griffith dies
	22 August	Michael Collins is killed in an ambush in west Cork
	11 September	Proportional representation for local government elections abolished in Northern Ireland
	28 September	Dáil votes to create special military courts
	17 November	First executions of Republican prisoners takes place
	7 December	Northern Ireland parliament votes to opt out of the Irish Free State
1923	27 April	Suspension of the IRA campaign, effectively ending civil war in the south
	10 September	Irish Free State admitted to the League of Nations
1924	10 May	Northern Ireland government refuses to nominate candidate for the Boundary Commission
	6 November	Boundary Commission convened following the Labour government's legislation allowing the British government to appoint a representative for the Northern Ireland government
1925	7 November	Leaked Boundary Commission report is published in the *Morning Post*
	20 November	Eoin MacNeill resigns from the Boundary Commission
	3 December	Final settlement of boundary and financial arrangements between the British and both Irish governments in London

Map

Map showing major areas to be transferred under the Boundary Commission, 1925

■ Proposed areas to go to the Free State

▨ Proposed areas to go to Northern Ireland

Introduction: The Tragedy of Two Lunatics

You remember that village where the border ran
Down the middle of the street,
With the butcher and baker in different states?
Today he remarked how a shower of rain
Had stopped so cleanly across Golightly's lane
It might have been a wall of glass
That has toppled over. He stood there, for ages,
To wonder which side, if any, he should be on.[1]

'The Tragedy of Two Lunatics'

During the early evening of Thursday 3 December 1925, the British prime minister, Stanley Baldwin, made a hurried address to the House of Commons to outline his government's response to the worrying political situation in Ireland. Although he spoke for barely twenty minutes, he was able in that short time to assure the house that, after ten years of violence and political upheaval, the outstanding issues of the divisive Irish question, which had dogged British politics for two generations, had finally been settled.

The ink on the brief agreement he read was barely dry, having been signed a short distance away in his Westminster office less than an hour before. Joining him at that meeting had been his chancellor of the exchequer, Winston Churchill, the only senior British political figure remaining in office from the days of the Ulster Crisis thirteen years earlier.[2] Also in attendance were the premiers of the two new Irish states; Northern Ireland's James Craig and William Cosgrave, the leader of the recently established Irish Free State. By 1925, the two men headed exhausted and deeply compromised regimes. Both had recently steered their embryonic states through the trauma of bitter civil wars, and now faced the monumental task of building effective

---

[1] Paul Muldoon 'The Boundary Commission', in *Why Brownlee Left* (London, 1980), p. 15.
[2] Churchill's pivotal role in the Irish policy of successive British governments has been explored insightfully in Paul Bew's recent *Churchill and Ireland* (Oxford, 2016).

1

governments in their impoverished states in the face of strident opposition from political and religious minorities. That afternoon in Baldwin's office would be the last time they, or any two Irish leaders, met face to face for the next forty years.

The presence of the final two individuals at the impromptu conference, Richard Feetham and Joseph Fisher, had been demanded by the latest crisis to beset the ailing partition settlement. Feetham, a senior South African colonial judge, had been appointed chairman of an Irish Boundary Commission the previous year. Along with representatives from the two new Irish governments, Feetham, who had never set foot in Ireland before, was handed the formidable task of deciding how best to adjust the new three-year old border so as 'to reflect the wishes of the inhabitants, as far as economic and geographic conditions'[3] would allow. For months, they, and their tiny retinues of staff, had toured around the frontier, taking soundings at public meetings and poring over a bewildering array of maps and statistics in order to come to their decision.

However, four weeks prior to the meeting in Baldwin's office, as they prepared the commission's report for final publication, its confidential findings found their way into the right-wing British press. Unbeknown to those attending the meeting, it was Fisher, erstwhile newspaper editor and the Belfast government's de facto representative on the commission, who is now believed to have been the source of the leak. The fact that he had been parachuted in at the last minute when the uncooperative unionist government refused to nominate its own member of the commission, added to the surreal atmosphere which pervaded the whole affair.

The most damaging aspect of the subsequent scandalous news report, published in the *Morning Post* on 7 November, was the inclusion of a hand-drawn map which, although crude, was uncannily accurate in reflecting the commission's final decision. It showed that, despite suffering some slight trims at the edges, Northern Ireland would remain largely as it had been envisioned in 1919, even unexpectedly gaining some territory from the Free State in the shape of a significant chunk of Donegal to the west of the majority Catholic city of Derry.

To southern nationalist eyes this was not the way the commission had meant to play out. For years Irish nationalist propaganda had poured scorn on the perfidy of the northern state and the injustice of the border, enclosing as it did hundreds of thousands of Catholics within its jurisdiction. Even in its most conservative estimates, the expectation had been that the commission

---

[3] 'Final Text of the Articles of Agreement between Great Britain and Ireland', London, 6 December 1921, www.difp.ie/docs/1921/Anglo-Irish-Treaty/214.htm.

would award them the majority-Catholic counties of Fermanagh and Tyrone (what Herbert Asquith once called 'the Alsace-Lorraine of Ireland'), Derry city and large southern sections of the counties of Down and Armagh.

In response to the leaked report, all hell was let loose in the South. Public opinion, mediated through a vociferous nationalist press, was outraged. Not only would the Free State not gain the third of Ulster territory that they had expected, but would actually lose significant areas of the north-west, further impoverishing and isolating the region. Feetham, it appeared, had viewed his remit to be one of shortening and rationalising the sprawling border between the two states, rather than attempting any wholesale dismemberment of the new Northern Ireland. The Dublin representative on the body, Eoin MacNeill, who was not present at the December meeting, resigned from the commission on 17 November. One week later, the humiliated minister of education would resign from the Free State government all together. Even so, Feetham and Fisher technically had the power to publish the report regardless, a situation which Cosgrave felt would have led to the collapse of his government and potentially the Free State itself.

In response, a frantic series of meetings were organised at the prime ministerial residence at Chequers to hammer out some form of compromise, with the Dublin government calling forcefully for the report to be supressed. Kevin O'Higgins, the uncompromising Free State minister for justice, who himself was to be assassinated eighteen months later in Dublin, excoriated the commission's methodology and pro-unionist bias, while an exasperated Cosgrave requested that the report be 'buried or burned'.[4]

Finally, after much debate, a hasty trade-off was agreed. The border was to remain unchanged, circling six of Ulster's nine counties, just as it had been envisioned in the Government of Ireland Act of 1920. To sweeten the pill of partition, the Free State government was to be alleviated of its responsibility for paying off the British war debt, as had been outlined in Article 5 of the 1921 Anglo-Irish Treaty. O'Higgins was well-aware that his government would be open to accusations of selling the Northern Catholic minority, which he described candidly as 'more than a half truth'.[5] However, he also suspected that any areas transferred would prove to be a constant source of dissent whichever side was awarded them, so perhaps would be more trouble than they were worth. To this end, the Council of Ireland, part of the original partition act and

[4] G. J. Hand, Report of the Irish Boundary Commission 1925 (Dublin, 1969), p. ix.
[5] 'Draft notes on a conference held in the Board Room, Treasury, Whitehall, London, 1 December 1925', National Archives of Ireland (NAI), Department of the Taoiseach, S4720A.

once painted as an embryonic all-Ireland government in waiting, was to be abolished. Its powers were devolved to the two new administrations and this last gesture to Irish unity quietly discarded.

It was decided that the findings of the Boundary Commission itself should not be made public, much to the chagrin of Feetham who never got over the disparagement of his lovingly prepared report which he had gone at with such conservative diligence. Churchill, however, ever the historian, expressed the opinion that the report should be retained for posterity, at the government's discretion, 'as it may prove of interest to later generations'[6]. In the end, it would not be made public until 1969, just in time for the irrationality of partition to once again play out in the violence of the 'Troubles'.

It was perhaps fitting that the final act of the partition drama should end in such confusion and farce. The crisis of November 1925 was not the first time the agreement looked to be on the verge of collapse. Far from it. Since its unveiling by the then-prime minister David Lloyd George in December 1919, the partition plan had gone through numerous crises and hasty amendments. Behind the myriad of calculations loomed the deep confusion and expediency of the plan, to get out of Ireland with as little trouble or cost as possible. In every sense this was an attempt at partition on the cheap. In the end, the process of dividing Ireland would cost a fortune. Due to the poor fundamentals of the plan, money would be poured into Ireland in the intervening six years merely to hold the fragile settlement together, both from the threat of violence and to compensate or subdue forgotten and marginalised groups.

Baldwin ended his impromptu speech by expressing the hope that the agreement be passed by the three governments as soon as possible, 'before anyone could change their mind again', according to the *Guardian*.[7] He was not to be disappointed. The new settlement and the dissolution of the Boundary Commission was accepted and passed within two weeks. As he was leaving the Commons, a backbench Tory MP expressed the opinion that news of this final resolution 'will have been heard with relief and pleasure by the whole of the English-speaking world'.[8] The chaotic and bloody process of partitioning Ireland was finally over.

*

The failure of those who instigated and sustained the partition project to grasp the crucial role it would play in shaping the social, political and cultural character of modern Ireland has been mirrored to some extent in

---

[6] Hand, *Boundary Commission*, p. xi.   [7] Editorial, *Guardian*, 27 December 1925, p. 19.
[8] Hansard, HC vol 122, cols 875–979 (25 December 1925).

popular and academic reconstructions of the period. Historical understandings of partition have remained as ambiguous as those which pervaded the minds of the partitioners back in the early 1920s. While the division of the island into two antithetical states represents the most fundamental change in twentieth-century Ireland, partition as a topic sits very much on the periphery of historical scholarship.

There are very few dedicated histories of partition amid the healthy abundance of modern Irish historical writing on the revolutionary period, and the subject remains a notably under-researched area. This is particularly striking, as the partition experience of other postcolonial states has inspired a rich and vigorous historiography. For example, the partitions of Palestine and India, especially the latter, have been the subject of reams of historical analysis and inspired the creation of several schools and research centres devoted to their study. Much like these other instances in Asia and the Middle East, partition seems to define the Irish experience in the twentieth century. As a historical process they share many similarities: a rapid postwar decolonisation set against the backdrop of nationalist 'revolution', followed by an ill-conceived and clumsy attempt to transfer power, and midwifed by a cynical and war-weary British establishment. All of these partitions were made workable only through repeated short-term modifications to the plan and unspeakable acts of violence, leaving behind embittered minorities and a legacy of acrimony and political instability. While the recent 'Troubles' in Northern Ireland has played a key role in shaping the agendas and perspectives of a whole generation of modern Irish historians, this has not led to any subsequent sustained analysis of the causes, course and consequences of partition.

Indeed, rather than any sustained analysis of partition, historians have discovered amid the chaotic political and social changes which engulfed Ireland during the decade which spanned the First World War, an 'Irish revolution', a period which saw the rise of advanced forms of nationalism and the subsequent violent upheavals of separatist rebellion. The foundation myths which emerged to shape the new southern state were firmly based around nationalist sentiment and the perceived historic evils of British rule. Partition was both subsumed within and oddly sidelined in this process.

For all the concern of the current generation of Irish historians to understand the origins and dynamics of communal conflict in Northern Ireland, partition has escaped convincing assimilation into broadly accepted narratives. By its very nature, partition, much like the frontier itself, sits in a no-man's land between competing national histories. As a topic, it challenges objective statist accounts and the homogeneous communal identities they demand. It is often allowed to metaphorically fall between these emerging cracks, or, as one Indian historian has written, partition 'folds into a black impenetrable line ... and simply disappears'.[9]

Partition certainly occupies an uncertain place in historical narratives of the period, even for historians whose primary focus is on the north-east. Although the creation of Northern Ireland retains a relatively more significant profile in the narrative of Ulster Protestant history, its link with that broader context remains deeply ambiguous. Recent centenary commemorations in Ulster, for example, have focused on the earlier Ulster Crisis and First World War, with its mass mobilisations of Ulster Volunteers and Covenanters, or the sacrifice of the 36th Ulster Division at the Somme, rather than the foundation of the six-county state itself. The fact that the establishment of Northern Ireland entailed a partition, not only of Ireland, but also Ulster itself, not to mention the overall Irish Protestant population, has confounded simplistic narrative categorisation. The experience of the 'Troubles', subsequent power-sharing, development of cross-border bodies and the open borders implicit in European Union membership, not to mention Brexit, have made this historiographical placement all the more problematic.

Certainly, in retellings of the period there has been a tendency to reduce modern Irish history to a teleological biography of the southern nation state, focusing in particular on the growth and inner workings of the nationalist movement, its triumphs and failures, and the conversion experiences of its leaders and adherents.[10] The repeated revisiting of iconic events such as the Easter Rising demonstrates how dominant this nationalist narrative remains.[11] Historians themselves have inadvertently fuelled popular misconceptions by using nationalist frameworks and periodisation to place partition safely within the broader national story. Of course, without partition, the narrative presents a more straightforward and relatable story; a typical nationalist triptych of suffering, struggle and deliverance, followed by a focus on the challenges and achievements of state formation.[12] However, as Lindsay Crawford, the Canadian unionist wrote in 1920:

---

[9] Vazira Fazila-Yacoobali Zamindar, *The Long Partition and the Making of Modern South Asia* (New York, 2007), p. 1.

[10] See, for example, Roy Foster's recent book *Vivid Faces: The Revolutionary Generation in Ireland, 1890–1923* (London, 2015).

[11] The two most prominent major studies of the Easter Rising are F. McGarry, *The Rising: Easter 1916* (Oxford, 2011) and C. Townshend, *Easter 1916: The Irish Rebellion* (London, 2015).

[12] Notable, for example, is the periodisation of the Irish Revolution which ends in 1923 with the end of the southern civil war, rather than with the more logical 1925 with the final settlement of the boundary issue. Popular portrayals of the period are similarly southern-centric. See, for example, the recent RTÉ documentary based on the *Atlas of the Irish Revolution* (Cork, 2017) ends in 1921 with the termination of the War of Independence, thus avoiding more ambiguous and divisive topics such as the Irish Civil War and partition itself.

'The Irish Question is an Ulster Question. If there were no Ulster, the Irish question could be solved overnight.'[13]

While the history of partition would become in subsequent decades largely a battle between contrary narratives of revolutionary deliverance and resistance, for much of the partition period itself, both Irish unionism and Irish nationalism were themselves only works in progress and remained in a state of flux.[14] These two dominant revolutionary parties of the partition period would be responsible for constructing the states which emerged. Often themselves merely a bundle of assumptions and prejudices in search of legitimacy, they further distorted or evaded key questions as to how and why the island was divided. Indeed, successive governments in both new Irish capitals have worked hard to instil statist narratives and set limits to their new empires through the control of historical archives and in the institution of a host of political and cultural symbols. In 1928, D. A. Chart, the deputy keeper of public records in Belfast, felt already well-enough equipped to write a full biography of the new Ulster state entitled *A History of Northern Ireland*, despite it's having existed for barely six years. This ambitious feat was achieved by ranging back centuries to uncover an 'old country', a historic Ulster which, through the use of historical slight of hand, Chart made co-terminus with the recently and arbitrarily drawn boundary line. Indeed, ironically, despite the book's title, little mention was made of Northern Ireland's recent history and the opposition and violence which had threatened unionist hegemony or the use of state-sponsored coercion and discrimination to maintain it.[15]

Hindsight has done much to lessen the dramatic impact of partition. Looking back, the division of the island and the creation of a separate state in Ulster has become for many almost a historical inevitability. To this end, historians have scoured the pre-partition landscape for evidence to confirm the development of 'two nations' in Ireland, both shaped by

[13] L. Crawford, *The Problem of Ulster* (Toronto, 1920), p. 1.

[14] Compare, for example, the two radically contradictory takes on the period from Brian Follis in his *A State under Siege: The Establishment of Northern Ireland* (Oxford, 1995) and Michael Farrell's, *Arming the Protestants: The Formation of the Ulster Special Constabulary and the Royal Ulster Constabulary 1920–1927* (London, 1983).

[15] D. A. Chart, *A History of Northern Ireland* (Belfast, 1928). A similar partitionist assumption has underlain many works from southern historians writing modern histories of 'Ireland'. A good example of this is Dermot Keogh's *Twentieth Century Ireland: Revolution and State Building* (Dublin, 2005), which, despite its avowed aim of writing a history of *Ireland* and offering a 'narrative of inclusion', goes on to state in the next line, 'This book does not deal with the politics of Northern Ireland except in so far as they impinge on the life of the Saorstat2' p. 15. For a good summary of the problems posed by two-nations history see Paul Bew's 'Against Partitionist History' in his *Ideology and the Irish Question: Ulster Unionism and Irish Nationalism, 1912–1916* (Oxford, 1998).

incompatible social, cultural and political trajectories. Such arguments view Irish history through a rear-view mirror. There was as much difference between Leinster and the west of Ireland in terms of culture, economy, history and language as there was between Ulster and the rest of Ireland, making, with the use of identical criteria, three 'nations' in Ireland. This dangerous historicist interpretation has influenced some of the most iconic historical works of modern Irish history, many of which have been implicitly partitionist in their assumptions. In his seminal 1962 monograph, *The Irish Border as a Cultural Divide: A Contribution to the Study of Regionalism in the British Isles*, Dutch historical geographer Marcus Heslinga shaped much later scholarship with his contention that the Irish border represents an extension of a deeper millennium-old cultural divide in the British Isles. In the words of one of his admirers, Heslinga painted the border and the 'Ulster' it contained as 'a cross channel extension of the Scottish border, marking off ... the *scoticized* part of Ireland from the most anglicized part', with, in the author's own words, 'the intervening seas ... only a geological creation of yesterday'.[16] During the following decade, A. T. Q. Stewart's *The Narrow Ground: Aspects of Ulster, 1609–1979*, arguably the most influential contribution to the study of Ulster distinctiveness, expanded on Heslinga's work by drawing 'on the hidden patterns of the past' to highlight Ulster's singular historical destiny.[17]

Writing in the shadow of the Northern Irish 'Troubles', Stewart and many subsequent historians, presented a paradigm which saw Ulster as a place of enduring and endemic sectarian strife, and partition less its cause than its result. As such, it was obliquely suggested that partition rather than exacerbating violence and division, actually acted to hold these darker forces of division at bay. As Stewart himself wrote: 'Whatever the "Ulster Question" is in Irish history, it is not the question of partition.'[18] In a broader sense, they were keen to challenge nationalist shibboleths about the island's assumed political unity which saw partition as, in the words of John Redmond, 'an unnatural abomination and a blasphemy'.[19] As such, they presupposed the existence of two distinct

---

[16] M. W. Heslinga, *The Irish Border as a Cultural Divide: A Contribution to the Study of Regionalism in the British Isles* (Assen, 1962). For an admiring overview of the work and influence of Heslinga, see A. Green, 'Homage to Heslinga' in *Forging the Smithy: National Identity and Representation in Anglo-Irish Literary History* (Amsterdam, 1995) pp. 145–9.

[17] A. T. Q. Stewart, *The Narrow Ground: Aspects of Ulster, 1609–1979* (London, 1977).

[18] Ibid, p. 157.

[19] Quoted in John Bowman, *De Valera and the Ulster Question, 1917–1973* (Oxford, 1982), p. 14.

pre-partition national entities in Ireland.[20] However, the inherent paradox of such arguments against an illusory nationalist historical geography was that they were achieved by the championing of a similarly imagined portrayal of unionism in the six north-eastern counties of Ulster. As Mary Burgess has insightfully observed, such perspectives must be seen in the light of 'a long and complex effort by unionists to manufacture a sense in which the Northern Irish state has always "really" existed . . . the myth of the always-and-ever separateness of Ulster'.[21]

Such pro-partitionist arguments are nothing new. They have had a long and well-rehearsed history in the political discourse surrounding the Irish Question, stretching back to the failed attempts to introduce Home Rule to Ireland in the late-Victorian era. Indeed, many of these arguments were employed by leading politicians seeking support for the idea of dividing Ireland during the genesis of the partition plan itself. In 1912, Liberal MP Thomas Agar-Robartes, the first politician to seriously propose a partitionist answer to the Irish Question, claimed in the House of Commons:

I think everyone will admit that Ireland consists of two nations different in sentiment, character, history, and religion. I maintain it is absolutely impossible to fuse these two incongruous elements together. It is as impossible as to try to reconcile the irreconcilable.[22]

Similar assumptions were expressed by most of the leading government figures of the day, including Lloyd George who, in the spring of 1917, made a comparison worthy of Heslinga, claiming in a Common's speech that the Protestant population of Ulster were, 'as alien in blood, in religious faith, in traditions, in outlook from the rest of Ireland as the inhabitants of Fife or Aberdeen'.[23] From Thomas McKnight's *Ulster as It Is*, published in 1896 shortly after the collapse of the Second Home Rule

[20] A good example of such presuppositions can be found in M. Laffan, *The Partition of Ireland, 1912–1925* (Dundalgen, 1983), which sets out its stall on the first page with the sentence, 'Ulster had always been different from the rest of the country' (p. 1). See also Ian Adamson, *The Identity of Ulster: The Land, the Language and the People* (Belfast, 1982) and D. G. Pringle, *One Island, Two Nations: A Political Geographical Analysis of the National Conflict in Ireland* (Letchworth, 1985). See also F. S. L. Lyons, 'Ulster: The Roots of Difference', in *Culture and Anarchy in Ireland, 1890–1939* (Oxford, 1979). Stewart's work should also be viewed as a response to a rise in nationalist anti-partition apologetics in the 1950s inspired by the work of the Anti-Partition League. See, in particular, Denis Gwynn's seminal, *The History of Partition, 1912–1925* (London, 1950). Other similar works include A. J. Rose, *Partition and Ireland* (Dublin, 1955) and F. Gallagher, *The Indivisible Island* (Cork, 1957).

[21] M. Burgess, 'Mapping the Narrow Ground: Geography, History and Partition', *Field Day Review*, vol. 1 (2005), p. 124.

[22] Hansard, HC vol 39, cols 744–824 (11 June 1912).

[23] Hansard, HC vol 38, cols 424–42 (7 March 1917).

bill, through to William Moneypenny's *The Two Irish Nations*, written in the summer of 1913 during the increasingly polarising atmosphere of the Ulster Crisis, such arguments, much like those made by Stewart and his contemporaries, cannot be divorced from the political context in which they were voiced and the central role they played in the virulent unionist propaganda campaigns against the threat of resurgent Irish nationalism.[24]

The power and longevity of the 'two nations' perspective has led to partition being portrayed as the logical, if crude, conferral of statehood on already homogeneous communities. As such, much of the dynamism has been taken out of the process itself. Historical writing on partition has largely focused on the pre-partition Ulster Crisis or the high politics of the period, a top–down process centred on Westminster and Whitehall.[25] While there is much value in this high politics approach, it has inadvertently led to a tendency to reduce partition to a dry and dusty act of administrative chicanery. While backs were turned and more momentous events occurred elsewhere, Ireland was partitioned from afar almost by stealth. The recent trend in Irish historical scholarship to examine the revolution from the bottom–up has made limited impact on the study of Ulster during the period and remains largely a twenty-six–county phenomenon.[26] While the focus of this study is on Ulster and the creation of Northern Ireland, it should be remembered that partition saw the founding of two states, not one. It was in the words of one contemporary journalist 'the tragedy of two lunatics'.[27] Historical narratives which continue to view the political upheavals which occurred in places as different as the mountains of Kerry and the grubby backstreets of West Belfast as part of subdivided national stories must be put aside. So central was partition to the Irish experience that it couldn't help but affect people right across the island, even those living hundreds of miles from the new

---

[24] T. McKnight, *Ulster as It Is* (London, 1896); W. Moneypenny, *Two Irish Nations* (London, 1913).

[25] See, for example, Laffan, *The Partition of Ireland, 1912–1925*; T. Hennessey, *Dividing Ireland: World War One and Partition* (Abingdon, 1998); G. Lewis, *Carson: The Man Who Divided Ireland* (London, 2004); A. T. Q. Stewart, *The Ulster Crisis: Resistance to Home Rule, 1912–14* (London, 1969); G. Boyce and A. O'Day, eds *The Ulster Crisis, 1885–1921* (London, 2005) and A. Jackson, *The Irish Party: Ulster Unionists in the House of Commons, 1884–1911* (Oxford, 1989).

[26] The most notable of the many recent local studies of the period are P. Hart, *The IRA and Its Enemies: Violence and Community in Cork, 1916–1923* (Oxford, 1998); D. Fitzpatrick, *Politics and Irish Life, 1913–21: Provincial Experience of War and Revolution* (Cork, 1998); M. Farry, *Aftermath of Revolution: Sligo, 1921–23* (Dublin, 2000); M. Coleman, *County Longford and the Irish Revolution, 1910–1923* (Dublin, 2000).

[27] P. W. Wilson, 'The Irish Free State', *The North American Review*, vol. 215, no. 796 (March 1922), pp. 322–30.

border, not to mention its deep and abiding impact on the character of diaspora communities in Britain and North America.

This book seeks to interrupt these dominant and long-running narratives. In reality, partition was a chaotic, confused and, at times, surreal process, far removed from the 'natural' conferral of statehood on pre-existing homogeneous populations imagined by the partitioners and later historians. As such, this study looks to differentiate itself from earlier scholarship by going beyond the irredentist claims of all governments and examining the way partition was constructed and imagined by Irish people themselves. It was by definition a mass participation event where political decision-making was shaped by elections, demonstrations, popular refusal to participate in the new states' institutions and the direct experience of savage and unprecedented acts of violence in defence or opposition to the new settlement. Partition was a period of deep contradictions, where idealism and self-sacrifice were intermingled with brutality and coercion. Dividing Ireland entailed a series of ill-conceived and ad hoc responses to unpredictable and unprecedented political developments, ushering in a human tragedy. Indeed, violence was to be the constant background noise to partition. Far from being a necessary evil reluctantly embraced by all sides to drive on the more enlightened goals of freedom and democracy, partition was, in a very real sense, brought about through violence and the threat of force.

Ireland is notable for the diversity of its violence; guerrilla ambushes, vigilante punishments, reprisal killings, political assassination, mass protests and urban rioting were all features of the Irish experience. Until relatively recently there has been a tendency by historians to favour examination of certain types of violence over others. While the minute details of provincial ambushes and the genesis and workings of revolutionary guerrilla warfare have been analysed in excruciating detail, this has been achieved at the expense of a focus on more unsavoury incidents such as mass rioting, communal expulsions and intimidation. Contained within these were numerous stories of murder, mutilation, arson and sectarian massacres which did not sit well with state foundation myths and their martial pretensions. Only recently, with the move towards local and county studies, have what Gemma Clark has dubbed 'everyday violence' in her recent study of the Irish Civil War been more fully explored.[28] However, there has been less extensive study of such experiences in Ulster, where this type of popular mass violence predominated. The vast majority of the violence of partition remains murky and largely forgotten and the memories of its victims uncollected, unlike those of the many paramilitaries who received the blessing of the new partition states.

[28] G. Clark, *Everyday Violence in the Irish Civil War* (Cambridge, 2017).

As such, this book also focuses on the too-often forgotten losers and victims of partition. The new settlements of 1922 saw the victory of the two most authoritarian parties in Ireland: Ulster unionists and pro-treaty Sinn Féin, both of whom asserted their new state power by coercion and force of arms, instilling their own statist narrative on events. This shared winner's history left many losers in its wake in the shape of political and religious minorities: Northern Catholics, Southern Protestants, socialists, republicans, moderate Home Rulers, refugees and a whole host of others who simply found themselves on the wrong side of the border or fell by the wayside in the rush to narrow Irish identity to a simple for or against duality. They are thus the great leftovers from partition and can also be considered its chief and most troubling legacy. Partition swept away a vast array of traditional institutions, mentalities and certainties. With partition, the Ireland people had known effectively ceased to exist and was replaced by two other entities. How people made sense of these changes and the way in which the new states communicated their legitimacy and asserted their new power over them is the chief aim of this study.[29]

By 1925, Ireland had been split into two oppositional states embodying rival religious and political identities, a state of affairs unthinkable only a decade before. All of these changes took place in the midst of desperate confusion and uncertainty, long before the states and their historians had managed to construct a meaningful narrative which could be sold to ordinary Irish people. The narratives which emerged, of nationalism and mass support in elections and political organisations, have proved the simple building blocks for the two versions of Ireland and their claims to legitimacy. Placing an X on a ballot paper, haranguing a speaker at a rally or lighting a candle for a dead martyr have been used simplistically to demonstrate that it was the people who demanded partition and turned it into an earthly reality. For people themselves, however, partition was not a final settlement, but rather the start of a far more disquieting journey which saw them decide how to rebuild their old familiar identities anew in the states which emerged in its aftermath.

---

[29] Some attention has begun to turn to minority groups in Ireland of late. See, for example, R. Bury, *Buried Lives: The Protestants of Southern Ireland* (Dublin, 2017); M. Elliott, *The Catholics of Ulster: A History* (London, 2000).

Part I

The Origins of Partition

1   Where Is Ireland?

In the spring of 1902, the itinerant Irish journalist William Bulfin, recently returned from seventeen years of self-imposed exile in Argentina, undertook a 3,000-mile bicycle journey around Ireland. The aim of this 'pilgrimage' was to find the 'soul of Ireland' and the 'essence of Irishness'. Decrying the use of 'West Briton' guide books, he set out from Dublin on his trusty 'Wexford wheel' to write his own, and for the next seven months toured the highways and byways, scribbling down his opinions and experiences on the roadside. Like many Irish-Irelanders of the day, Bulfin's accounts were full of maudlin longing for a lost rural idyll. Judgemental in the extreme, he intermingled his mawkish observations with vicious polemic railing against Anglicisation, landlordism and the 'loss of the true Gaelic virtue', while, at the same time, saluting the 'sturdy suffering' of the Irish peasants who he sought out at every opportunity. In a small hamlet in Offaly, he recalls after a day spent toiling in the fields where he blistered his hands, 'broke fork handles, made tramp cocks, and grass cocks and fork cocks, drank oatmeal water, and buttermilk' he and his new friends relaxed at the end of the day.

We sat on the golden-tinted cocks near the road when the work was finished, and they told me about the harvest prospects, and about hares and foxes and many other things while the west grew rosy and shook out purple swathings to welcome the homing sun. They were fine hearty fellows, stronglimbed, clear-complexioned, bright-eyed, and as for their health, it seemed to come to them out of every stubble and grass-blade in all the magnificent country-side. They were hurlers, they told me, forwards in the local team, and were proud of the fact. They were splendid children of the soil, and they were worthy of it. Their native sod could scarcely have been fairer.[1]

Such scenes were repeated across the length and breadth of Ireland. In Limerick, he was transfixed by the 'purple hills that loomed beyond the Shannon'; in Longford, he paid tribute to 'strong fighting men and the splendid days gone by when there was battle in the wind'; 'saw some very

---

[1] W. Bulfin, *Rambles in Eireann*, vol. 2 (Dublin, 1905), p. 56.

15

fine cattle in Kildare'; stood in silent reverie on the 'sacred grounds at the hill of Tara' and 'sniffed creamy honeysuckle' in the Wicklow hills.

However, when Bulfin reached the north-east of Ireland his mood darkened and his sentimental style changed abruptly. Standing in the burgeoning urban sprawl of the Lagan Valley, Bulfin was appalled by what he saw. 'The noise of wheels and hoofs and cranks and spindles and steam hammers filled my ears and made my head ache ... I saw thousands of well-dressed people hurrying to and fro with no flash of humour in their glances and no bloom of health in their set and earnest faces' (p. 9). The atmosphere was 'foreign in its origins and meaning, cruel, corroding, unfathomable' and he searched in vain for 'some signs of Ireland'. The streets were 'filled with monuments to men for which I could find no place in the story of my country ... Money, money, money, Trade, trade, trade, business, business, business ... where is Ulster and where is Ireland?' (p. 10).

The city which Bulfin stood in, 'a freak of parochialism and fanaticism', as he called it, was Belfast.[2] More than any other factor it was the rise of Belfast which would shape both the fact and character of partition. It was in this city that the real battles of partition would be fought with over 450 people losing their lives in less than two years, almost 200 of these in the first six months of 1922 alone. During the negotiations that led towards the Anglo-Irish Treaty of December 1921, Arthur Griffith, the deputy-leader of the predominant nationalist party Sinn Féin, confided to Assistant Under Secretary Thomas Jones that 'the "Ulster" Question was in reality the Belfast city question'.[3] In 1919, James Winder Good left a memorable description of nationalist perceptions of the city on the eve of partition:

Belfast is to Ulster what Paris is supposed to be to France. Many visitors have been tempted to dismiss it as no more than a Scottish or English industrial centre dumped by some freakish chance into an Irish setting. This view is common among South of Ireland folk ... who resent its existence as not only an anomaly but as an offence. The cocksure perkiness of its red-brick houses jars on their nerves; its monstrous array of factory chimneys, flaunting volumes of smoke above the diminished spires of churches, symbolises commercialism exulting in the overthrow of all that is simple and comely in life. I know many to whom the most fitting symbol of the town is the appalling chorus of steam-whistles, buzzers, and hooters that startles the stranger from sleep in the small hours of the morning. It is a Futurist fantasia: to more sensitive folk it sounds as if

[2] The sense of foreignness that Bulfin had noted in 1902 has been echoed down the ages by generations of Irish nationalists. Tim Healy, the Cork nationalist, recalled a day trip to Belfast during 1914 as 'the most unhappy twenty-four hours I ever spent'. Tim Pat Coogan refers derisively to the city as a 'red bricked Mancunian capital'.

[3] Quoted in S. Lawlor, *Britain and Ireland 1914–1923* (Dublin, 1983), p. 124.

factories and workshops were roaring, like lions at feeding time, for their daily tribute of human bodies.[4]

It was the process by which Belfast came to be perceived as what Bulfin referred to as an 'un-Irish' city which is really the story of partition itself.

By the time Bulfin made his visit, Belfast, fired by linen and shipbuilding, had developed into the most important industrial and commercial centre in Ireland. Three quarters of all Irish exports originated in east Ulster and its banks, most notably the Ulster Banking Company, Belfast Banking Company and Northern Banking Company, held a similar proportion of business deposits. The population of the city had also seen a dramatic rise, increasing from a mere 75,000 in the 1840s to 387,000 by 1911, making it more populous than Dublin, until then the largest city in Ireland. As one impressed American visitor explained in 1912:

Belfast, which is the headquarters of Ulsteria, is a city of inexhaustible industrial marvels. It has the largest shipyard, the largest linen-mill, and the largest rope, tobacco, and mineral-water factories in the world. Perhaps nowhere on earth do 390,000 people produce so much wealth as in Belfast or produce it, since every ton of coal they use has to be imported, under greater disabilities. It is the Chicago of Ireland, and its industrial record constitutes one of the greatest and most inspiring achievements in the history of world commerce.[5]

In the words of a later Free State official, 'Belfast was a sort of commercial octopus with tentacles stretching out in all directions.'[6]

The growing class of industrial and commercial elites who precipitated this economic revolution in Belfast would increasingly come to dominate the political direction and priorities of Irish unionism. Through the organ of the influential Belfast Chamber of Commerce, this formidable alliance of political and business interests viewed Belfast prosperity as wholly dependent on Ireland retaining strong links with both Britain and its empire. Any attempt to loosen the political connection between the two countries was felt would have a calamitous and degrading effect on the economic fortunes of east Ulster. Edward Harland himself had stated during the Home Rule debates of 1885 that if devolved government were granted to Ireland he would move his shipyard lock, stock and barrel to Glasgow.[7] To some extent such arguments made sense. It was clear that Belfast prosperity had only been possible due to the strong commercial

---

[4] James Winder Good, *Ulster and Ireland* (Dublin, 1919), p. 253.
[5] Sydney Brook, 'The Problem of Ulster', *The North American Review*, vol. 198, no. 696 (November 1913), pp. 617–29.
[6] 'Customs barrier: Irish Free State and Northern Ireland', January 1923–June 1951, NAI, TSCH/3/S1955A.
[7] P. Buckland, *The Factory of Grievances: Devolved Government in Northern Ireland 1921–39* (Dublin, 1979), p. 125.

ties which had developed between east Ulster, the west of Scotland and the north-west of England. Ireland's shortage of essential industrial raw materials such as coal and iron was filled by imports from Glasgow, Barrow and Liverpool, which also offered broader access to the world-wide markets of the empire.

While it would be wrong to dismiss the genuine economic fears which underlay unionist resistance to Home Rule, it is also clear that many saw the success they sought to protect as due in large part to their distinctive Protestant character and culture. Contrasting Belfast's modernity and prosperity with the evident poverty and perceived backwardness of the predominantly Catholic south and west, many argued that their achievements were a reflection of their unique culture and innate racial supremacy. Awarding Home Rule to a Dublin government in such circumstances would, in this view, be not only economically disastrous, but almost a sin against natural order. As one American journalist commented in 1913, in such understandings, unionists in Ulster viewed Home Rule:

as a white planter in Texas would regard a proposal to hand over the administration of his State to the negroes. It is not merely an insult; it seems to him positively unnatural, something that involves him in a personal degradation, and that aims at lowering him to the level of an alien and abject civilization.[8]

Such views were depressingly prevalent among many unionist political leaders. In 1912, one member of the Chamber of Commerce commented, 'We have proven that through hard work and eschewing the profligacy of our neighbours that the Ulsterman is the highest form of Irishman,' while Fred Crawford, the Ulster Volunteer Force (UVF) gunrunner, confided bluntly in his diary: 'I am ashamed to call myself an Irishman. Thank God I am not one. I am an Ulsterman, a very different breed.'[9] Andrew Bonar Law, the Conservative Party leader and later prime minister, saw the 'Irish', typical code for Catholic nationalists, as an 'inferior race'.[10] While reflecting, to some extent, contemporaneous understandings about the Protestant work ethic, such opinions long predated Max Weber. However, there remains no compelling evidence for a more significant level of entrepreneurial ability in Ulster than the rest of Ireland. Indeed, the vast majority of the most effective business talent in the province originated from outside Ireland. It was a combination of fortunate timing and the changing imperial context, rather than any innate aptitude, which accounted for Ulster prosperity. In the fifty years prior to the First World War, demand for shipping in Britain grew

[8] Brook, 'The Problem of Ulster', p. 621.
[9] P. Buckland, *Irish Unionism 1885–1921* (Dublin, 1988), p. 176.
[10] Thomas Jones, *Whitehall Diary* (Oxford, 1969), p. 50.

dramatically alongside the empire it was designed to service. Between 1860 and 1914, the value of merchant shipping rose from £375 million to £1.5 billion.[11] Along with other British port cities, such as Newcastle, Glasgow and Barrow, which experienced similar dynamic growth, Belfast would benefit from this increase in demand, as it did from a wider shift of heavy industry and engineering away from the south and east of England to the north and west. Perhaps most tellingly, far from being reflected in Protestant Ulster as a whole, the industrial miracle of the north-east was confined almost wholly to Belfast and its environs. Most of Ulster remained largely rural in character, agriculture consuming over two-thirds of the working population, and little different from other parts of Ireland outside of the major urban centres. False as these perceptions were, it was clear that on the verge of the partition decade unionist leaders had managed to convince the vast majority of Irish Protestants that their economic prospects looked bleak in any kind of nationalist-controlled Ireland.

The evident uniqueness of Belfast and the increasing forcefulness of its political and business leadership created a widening gulf between, not just Belfast and Dublin, but Belfast and the rest of Ireland. Indeed, what one journalist called 'the fact of Belfast' would define the eventual partition settlement in the most profound sense.[12] From the 1890s, Irish unionism became increasingly dominated by east Ulster priorities in terms of both its ideology and its geographical focus. The partition settlement which would eventually emerge in the shape of Northern Ireland would amount to Belfast and its own self-defined hinterland. This is demonstrated markedly by the decision to keep the cities of Newry and Derry within the Northern area despite their being cut off almost completely from their natural markets. The former was retained largely for its economic benefits, while the latter's historical importance, being the site of the famous Jacobite siege of 1689, was retained largely due to its sacred place in Ulster Protestant foundation myths. Indeed, Northern Ireland remains almost unique among partitioned countries in having four of its major urban centres (Derry, Newry, Strabane and Enniskillen) lying only a matter of a few miles from the border. Furthermore, the three other Ulster counties of Monaghan, Donegal and Cavan, whose minority Protestant communities had played a prominent role in the Ulster unionist campaign against the Third Home Rule bill in 1912–1914, would be jettisoned by its own Belfast leadership from the eventual territorial limits of the partition settlement. The maintenance of its heartlands in the east

---

[11] L. Kennedy and P. Ollrenshaw, eds, *An Economic History of Ulster, 1820–1939* (Manchester, 1995), p. 71.
[12] *Northern Whig*, 15 October 1912.

of the province and the retention of symbolic and economically important towns at its eastern and western extremities meant that the predominant industrial and commercial leadership in Belfast allowed the Ulster of the 1912 Covenant to fray at the edges in order to reinforce its own predominance.

It was the damaging impact of Belfast's rise on the nature of Irish unionism though that would be perhaps most significant in making partition a viable political option. Even prior to the crisis over the Third Home Rule bill in 1912, it was clear that unionism as a force in the new age of mass party politics was increasingly becoming an Ulster phenomenon, with power shifting from the old, landed southern unionist elites who had held the leadership of the movement since the 1860s to the commercial middle classes of Belfast and the Lagan Valley. The shift was also one towards the Presbyterians of Ulster. While Protestants of all denominations made up almost a quarter of the entire population of the island, amounting to some 1.1 million people, this number was divided almost equally between Anglicans, in the shape of the Church of Ireland and Presbyterians. Of the almost 440,000 Irish Presbyterians, 95 per cent of them lived in the province of Ulster, 90 per cent of them in the future six counties of Northern Ireland, while almost half of the 575,000 Church of Ireland Protestants lived in the twenty-six counties which made up the future southern state.

In a broader sense, this process, the so-called Ulsterisation of Irish unionism, symbolically reinforced with the creation of a separate Ulster unionist council in 1906, reflected a number of longer-term developments. As elsewhere in Europe, the power of the landed gentry was on the wane in the second half of the nineteenth century, giving way to that of urbanised industrial and commercial elites. In Ireland itself, the gradual lessening in intensity of land grievances after the Irish Land acts of 1870 and 1881 and the subsequent Land Purchase acts of 1885 and 1903 shifted over half of Irish land from the old Anglo-Irish elites into the hands of small tenant farmers. This was particularly notable in Ulster, where by 1914, 73 per cent of farmers were tenant owners, a higher proportion than in any of the other three provinces. In such an environment it appeared that southern unionists had lost not only their powerful hold on Ireland's land, but also their principal political purpose.

Furthermore, in an age of increasing mass popular politics, southern unionists lacked the sheer numbers to make a notable impact. It was only in Ulster that unionism could mobilise a significant enough level of support which came close to matching the electoral power of Irish nationalism. Faced with an almost inevitable future in a self-governing Ireland of some form, many southern unionists were divided over which was the better strategy to pursue. For some, perhaps the majority, staunch and continued opposition was the favoured option. Indeed, throughout the period many southern unionists were among the most vocal supporters of the Ulster unionist's confrontational strategy, which until 1917 at least remained one of using the Ulster question as a way of wrecking the whole Home Rule project. Few, even then it seemed, had considered partition a viable solution, or one that Ulster unionists would ever accept. It was not until Carson's flirtations with notions of Ulster 'special treatment' or 'exclusion' from the Irish settlement that these diehards finally accepted they were backing a lost cause, many of them choosing emigration rather than accommodation. The replacement of Dubliner Edward Carson by the Belfast-born Presbyterian James Craig in 1921 as the head of the Irish unionist movement and first prime minister of Northern Ireland was the final symbolic act in this shift northwards. The smaller minority of southern unionists who did choose the latter option of accommodation chose to lobby not their fellow unionists in Belfast, but the British government in order to win concessions and keep Ireland as close to Britain politically as possible. While the growing dominance of the Belfast leadership was greeted by some in unionist circles as a significant victory, giving them an opportunity to promote and articulate a more populist and homogeneous Ulster identity, for others it was inherently illogical, taking as it did the cherished notion of Irish unity out of Irish unionism itself.

By contrast, the generation of Irish nationalists who would shape the political trajectory of the separatist movement in the partition period consciously articulated themselves against everything they believed Ulster and Belfast represented; one polemicist styling the city as 'a creeping disease . . . a home to prostitution, gambling, materialism . . . ugliness, exploitation'.[13] Similar views had long been expressed more generally by nationalists over the perfidious and corrupting nature of low British culture on Ireland's moral character. During the First World War, the presence of thousands of British soldiers on leave in Dublin and the accompanying black markets, prostitution and lewd music hall reviews which rose up to service them reinforced in the minds of many this impression of moral degeneration.[14] From the 1880s, a whole host of Irish cultural movements emerged within the wider nationalist fold which sought to halt what they perceived as this creeping degradation and Anglicisation of Irish life. Typical of many late–nineteenth-century nationalist movements, those in Ireland both sought out and attempted

---

[13] Anonymous pamphlet entitled 'Ulster and Home Rule' (Dublin, 1893).

[14] P. Yates, 'Oh What a Lovely War! Dublin and the First World War', *History Ireland*, vol. 19, no. 6 (November/December 2011), pp. 22–4.

to engineer an appreciation of what they viewed as a more authentic nativist culture unsullied by the corrupting influences of British imperialism. The most widespread and popular movement, the Gaelic Athletic Association (GAA), formed in 1884 by a tweedy Clare school teacher, Michael Cusack, pitched its appeal especially to young Irish men, a generation it was felt which was in danger of losing its innate Celtic virility; Cusack himself styling the movement as 'an effort to preserve the physical strength of [the Irish] race'.[15] Through the promotion of what it defined as 'native', 'real' or 'natural' Irish sports, such as Gaelic football, handball and hurling, the GAA spread across the south and west of Ireland with incredible vibrancy. By 1908 it had well over 800 local parish branches with hundreds of thousands of active members. The darker volkisch undertones of the organisation were affirmed by campaigns against 'alien' or 'garrison' British games such as rugby, football and cricket, until then the most popular sport on the island. A similar campaign was launched when it came to the Gaelic language, with the creation of the less popular, if more distinguished, Gaelic League in 1893. The League, whose founding moment can be pinpointed to an address given by its first leader Douglas Hyde entitled 'The Necessity for De-Anglicising Ireland' at an Irish National Literary Society meeting in November 1892, sought to protect, teach and promote the language. Through a range of newspapers, teaching tours and publications its activists sought to 'keep the Irish Language spoken in Ireland ... to live on the lips of Irishmen'.[16] They sought and found an authentic Irish cultural heartland in the west and would make summer pilgrimages to Gaelic-speaking areas to study their traditions, record folk memories, wear traditional costume or sketch the landscape and its people. The stated aim of the League, the compulsory inclusion of Gaelic in the Irish school syllabus, would be achieved with the founding of the Irish Free State in 1922.

The phenomenon of the so-called 'new nationalism' was notable for its diversity. Despite its archaic pretensions, its origins were as modern and its influence just as dynamic as the economic transformation which had gripped north-east Ulster. While there is little doubt that many of those who participated in Gaelic games or learnt a few stuttering Gaelic phrases were driven less by its romantic nationalist pretensions than by a way of escaping the lethargy of small town Irish life, the 'new nationalism' did allow for the communication of a crude and potentially dangerous nativism. Although both the Gaelic League and the GAA began as apolitical,

---

[15] Marcus de Búrca, *The GAA a History* (Dublin, 1980), p. 12.
[16] Gaelic League Advertisement, *Gaelic Journal* (June 1894), p. 13.

the League stridently so, they acted as a magnet for the most committed nationalists who became increasingly prominent in the ranks of their leadership, and thus of the later independent Irish state itself.

One nationalist journalist poured barely concealed scorn on the rural sentimentalism of the 'simplifiers' which characterised much advanced nationalist thinking:

While Ulstermen are prone to make a fetish of material prosperity ... a vast amount of nonsense, and pernicious nonsense too, has been talked about the advantages which the peasant enjoys over the city worker. The title 'Irish' being reserved for one-horse enterprises which, as often as not, use the catch-cries of patriotism to enable them to underpay their workers and overcharge their customers. The working-class quarters of Belfast are mean enough in all conscience, but those who denounce them to exalt the transfiguring influences of nature on the mind of the countryman conveniently forget that the most beautiful districts from the poet's point of view are, as a rule, from the human point of view, appalling agricultural slums. Its inhabitants await the opportunity to follow other generations into exile ... driven abroad to work out its destiny in the blast-furnaces of Pittsburgh or the coal-mines of the Black Country.[17]

The reality which lay behind this campaign for an 'Irish Ireland' was an attempt to explore and define a more homogeneous and ultimately chauvinistic form of Irishness. While many professed themselves to be little interested in politics, much like the pan-Slavist and populist movements in Russia and eastern Europe, they shared a reverence for native culture and a broad political impulse which rejected the conservatism of Irish unionism and the stagnant dominance of the Home Rule Party.

Certainly, one cannot judge the Irish situation as exceptional or separate from the powerful influences of what was also occurring elsewhere in Europe. Instead, the Irish found themselves influenced by the wider patterns of social, political and economic change that characterised the continent in the interwar period. As such, the radical shifts which took place in both Irish unionism and Irish nationalism in the first decade of the twentieth century must be viewed as part of the ethnonationalist challenge to empire which had become all pervasive across the European empires by 1914 as a means of resisting political and cultural consolidation. By the turn of the century, nationalism had become a ubiquitous phenomenon across Europe, challenging continental empires from Ireland to Asiatic Russia. Both as a set of ideas and a prescription for action, nationalism was viewed as largely self-evident, an almost organically given form of identity in which nations were ranked hierarchically in terms of their cultural and civilisational achievements. Fired by modernity, nationalism would emerge as a response to the growth of a

---

[17] Winder Good, *Ulster and Ireland*, p. 246.

more sophisticated and integrated civic society fostered through mass literacy, industrialisation and urbanisation. These new ethnonationalist movements of which Ireland was to serve as an important model, unlike earlier large-scale movements in Germany, Poland and Italy, emerged among small ethnic groups such as the Czechs, Bulgarians and Armenians – the so called submerged peoples – often with little history of independence or native self-government. Based on a long list of grievances stretching from an alien landlord class, political and religious subjugation and the attendant degrading of unique native cultural and linguistic identities that imperialism entailed, the commitment gave many of its advocates almost a religious dedication to the struggling nation. In the context of impersonal modernity, individuals, by ascribing to these ideals, could not only root themselves within a historic communal identity, but also place themselves at the nexus of an age-old struggle now finally coming to fruition, giving their efforts for some an almost cosmic significance. While still largely confined to small, educated elites, its appeal would grow with the communication of its core ideas of self-government through the medium of popular cultural, sporting and literary pursuits during an age of increasing mass politics.

Indeed, it was on the political front that change seemed most imminent. The most rapid transformation was especially evident in the wake of the Easter Rising of April 1916. Led by a heterogeneous and marginalised group of radicals, it would lead to a shift in nationalist opinion in a more advanced separatist direction. While taking it on an unexpected trajectory, the Rising was the most evident outworking of the paramilitarisation of Irish politics which had characterised the Ulster Crisis. Within two years of the Rising, Irish nationalist politics had been transformed. A new movement, Sinn Féin, emerged to represent a whole range of advanced nationalist groups. Tying itself closely to the martyred leaders of the Rising and raging against what it perceived as the pernicious nature of British rule in Ireland, within the space of two years this party had grown to 100,000 members in over 1,200 local organisations across the country. More a movement than a political party, Sinn Féin became a repository for all kinds of idealistic political and cultural aspirations. Made up of an incongruous amalgamation of socialists, militant republicans, Gaelic revivalists and political opportunists, smaller parties were swallowed up and local and regional particularism subsumed by the uncomplicated fanaticism of the new movement. Avowedly anti-partitionist, the heterogeneous nature of Sinn Féin demonstrated just how unclear and fluid the political situation of Ireland was in the aftermath of the war.

The Home Rule Party watched these changes with growing fear. Formed in the 1860s, the party had become the established voice of nationalist Ireland. Steeped in the political traditions and cultures of constitutional nationalism, it honed its programme around the repeal of the Act of Union of 1801 and the creation of a devolved legislative assembly in Dublin. Prior to the Easter Rising, and for a time after, advanced forms of nationalism were firmly in the minority. The party dominated almost all aspects of Irish national political life. Strongly allied with the Catholic Church, it had become by 1914 an effective all-embracing political machine through the use of well-established patterns of local patronage and the ability to co-opt and thus effectively neutralise factionalism. This was achieved by control of a myriad of affiliated pseudo-political social and cultural organisations which acted as a malleable popular movement, providing campaign funds and grass roots activism particularly during election campaigns. Tory journalist, A. A. Baumann, characterised the party's electoral support derisively as,

contented with their material, if not their political condition ... they vote for their Nationalist members of parliament because ... they have a hazy idea that there are still some slices to be cut from the British joint. But Home rule is purely the policy of the Machine, which is run by the priests and politicians.[18]

The party leadership itself reflected the rigidity of the organisation it headed. Drawn from an ageing cadre of academics, lawyers and career politicians, it had become increasingly dominated by family dynasties and drew in little new blood. Even more sympathetic nationalist voices grew wary of this remote oligarchy:

we have been told ... not to criticize our leaders, to trust our leaders, and so intellectual discussion ceased ... The nation was not conceived of as a democracy freely discussing its laws, but as a secret society with political chiefs meeting in the dark and issuing orders.[19]

At Westminster, the parliamentary party was regimented and obedient. This rigidity, and its commitment to evolutionary rather than revolutionary methods, meant it lacked the flexibility to adapt to sudden shifts in the political culture or react to fast-paced crises. The party was particularly hamstrung by its strong links with the Liberal Party with whom it had moulded an informal alliance back in the 1880s. With Ireland heavily over-represented at Westminster, providing over eighty members of parliament, their voting power could not be ignored by either major political party. The fateful decision made by Parnell to ally with the Liberals in 1885 left the Conservative opposition little option but to align itself more closely with Irish unionists. Thus, the issue of Irish Home Rule had become strongly tied to the vagaries of British party politics and it was

[18] A. A. Baumann, *Persons and Politics of the Transition* (London, 1916), p. 93.
[19] G. Russell, *The Inner and Outer Ireland* (Dublin, 1921), p. 9.

London, as opposed to Dublin or Belfast, which became the principal forum for debates over the future political fate of the island.

Having dominated nationalist political culture for so long, there was little room for the respectable constitutionalism of the Home Rule Party in the new post-Rising political atmosphere. Its ageing and conservative leadership were unable to rouse themselves to face the quixotic utopianism of the new Sinn Féin, which *The Leader* newspaper characterised as a curious mixture of 'protest' and 'national resurrection'.[20] Nationalist politician Tim Healy likened the new movement to a ship 'with no safety valve ... manned by inexperienced engineers' who promised 'to bring the ship safely to port in El Dorado'.[21] Faced with this volatile and unpredictable Sinn Féin movement, the party's principles of non-violent constitutionalism appeared outmoded in the new polarising atmosphere.[22]

While the new Sinn Féin movement was evidence of a major shift in Irish nationalist political opinion, its electoral performance was patchy and to many appeared to have reached its peak. Having won a number of significant by-election victories in 1917, by the following spring it suffered some notable reversals and many felt that the new movement was running out of steam. Its popularity was only sealed when in the spring of 1918 the British government threatened to introduce conscription in Ireland. This radical move had been contemplated due to the collapse of Russia and the German offensive on the western front. Lloyd George did not feel the Irish could sit out the war any longer, but the political effects of the decision were devastating. The Irish question had matured eighteen months too early for the British. Sinn Féin took the lead in using the crisis to further their own radical agenda. Such anti-conscription protests were not untypical in other parts of the empire during the later stages of the war, but the volatile and uncertain nature of Irish politics at the time gave the campaign an added edge.[23] The Home Rule Party, along with other major Irish institutions such as the church, joined this uneasy coalition and, much in line with Sinn Féin's as yet unpractised ideas of abstention, the party's MPs walked out of parliament, the principal forum which it had operated in since its foundation, in protest. The renunciation of the core principles of constitutionalism and parliamentarianism meant Irish

---

[20] *The Leader*, 27 September 1917, p. 24.

[21] Tim Healy to William O'Brien, 4 November 1918 (National Library of Ireland (NLI), O'Brien Papers, 8556/21, 22).

[22] For the Home Rule Party during the Ulster Crisis, see P. Bew, *Ideology and the Irish Question* (Oxford, 1994). The most comprehensive biography of John Redmond is D. Meleady, *John Redmond: The National Leader* (Merrion, 2018).

[23] See Martin F. Auger, 'On the Brink of Civil War: The Canadian Government and the Suppression of the 1918 Quebec Easter Riots', *Canadian Historical Review*, vol. 89 (2008), p. 4.

nationalism was cast adrift from the old certainties, to be replaced by mass political forces peddling simple answers to complex political questions.

Indeed, the most notable feature of post-war Irish nationalist politics was the blending of a diverse range of ideologies and campaigning organisations under one banner. Disgruntled Home Rulers, Gaelic revival enthusiasts, constitutional democrats, socialists and militarists, to name but a few, all found a home in the new Sinn Féin movement. At base, all shared a demand for change and articulated their wishes through the prism of a growing sense of anti-imperialism and anti-Britishness. The strength of this message lay in its simplicity and that of its ultimate aim, with most groups able to subsume their wider sectional aspirations beneath a drive for the fullest separation achievable.

While nationalists were divided on the extent of the independence they demanded, they shared a deep antipathy to the unionist project and consciously articulated their rhetoric against everything that Belfast and east Ulster had come to represent. Home Rule politician Tom Kettle, in line with mainstream nationalist political opinion of the partition period, poured scorn on the authenticity and indeed sanity of Ulster unionist resistance:

If the policy of Ulster Unionism is unreal there is no word in any language that can describe the phantasmal nature of the grounds on which it professes to fear national freedom. Home Rule, declare the orators, will obviously mean Rome Rule. The *Ne Temere* decree [*the papal ruling on mixed marriages*] will de-legitimise every Protestant in the country. The Dublin Parliament will tax every "Ulster" industry out of existence. One is told that not only do many people say, but that some people even believe things of this kind. But then there are people who believe that they are made of Dresden china, and will break if they knock against a chair. These latter are to be found in lunatic asylums. It is indeed particularly worth noting that when a man begins to see in the whole movement of the world a conspiracy to oppress and injure him our first step is to inquire not into his grievance but into his sanity. One finds the same difficulty in discussing Irish politics in terms of the three hallucinations specified that one finds in discussing, say, Rugby football with a Dresden-china fellow-citizen. It is better not to make the attempt, but to substitute a plain statement of obvious facts.[24]

Of course, part of the process of defining what Ireland was involved defining what it wasn't and Irish unionists were easy targets for Gaelicist suspicion. The fact that they showed little interest in the Gaelic project, and some were openly hostile to it, meant that they became objects of distrust. One Ulster Protestant author noted in 1921: 'The Gaelic Revival has not touched us.

---

[24] T. M. Kettle, *The Open Secret of Ireland* (Dublin, 1912), p. 109.

[It] is too airy and unsubstantial for our Northern imaginations. It was but the other day that I was reproached with the scarcity of book-shops in Belfast, and could only retort irrelevantly with the output of our linen.'[25] In the same year, Hugh Pollock, Northern Ireland's first minister of finance scoffed that 'Southerners are too full of sentimental ideas about nationality'.[26]

To nationalists, their refusal to identify themselves with the newly imagined Irish nation smacked, ironically, of disloyalty. One nationalist polemicist noted in 1912:

It is again surely unique that people should live in a country for 300 years, and derive their sustenance therefrom, and yet not consider themselves as belonging to the country. This is to the looker-on the most astounding feature of the Ulster question. It has no parallel in the South or West, where the Protestant Unionists are proud to consider themselves Irish, and not "Munster Scots," "Connacht English" or "Leinster Welsh," on the strength of a remote Scotch, English, or Welsh progenitor![27]

The sheer intoxication of ethnonationalism led to a number of dangerous conclusions, chief of which was the belief that unionist opposition was at base 'unnatural', 'irrational' and fed by sectarian ignorance, crudely manipulated by Belfast elites. While there was some truth to the appeal of popular Orangeism, the notion that unionist opposition had shallow roots was fundamentally flawed and was to have a profound impact in hastening the division of the island into two antithetical states. While Eamon de Valera, later president of Sinn Féin, emphasised in speech after speech sentiments to the effect that,

to maintain their nationality men and women will endure as much as to maintain their religion ... to prevent the assimilation or absorption [they] will fight to prevent the assimilation into another Nation,[28]

it never seemed to strike leading republicans that this was the exact all-or-nothing struggle unionists in Ulster felt they faced. J. L. Garvin, the editor of *The Observer*, noted in late 1922 how detrimental the radical nationalism of Sinn Féin was to the prospect of Irish unity:

The atavistic chinoiserie of the Gaelic Revolution can never unite any part of Ireland but can only organise the real and lasting partition in a way that is going on now.[29]

[25] L. Doyle, *An Ulster Childhood* (Dublin, 1921), pp. 12–13.
[26] W. Ewart, *A Journey in Ireland, 1921* (Oxford, 1922), p. 174.
[27] 'The Denial of North-East Ulster', *The Irish Review (Dublin)*, vol. 2, no. 17 (July 1912), p. 230.
[28] Bowman, *De Valera and the Ulster Question, 1917–1973*, p. 38.
[29] J. L. Garvin to Stephen Gwynn, September 1922, quoted in P. Bew, 'Moderate Nationalism and the Irish Revolution, 1916–1923', *Historical Journal*, vol. 42, no. 3

Irish nationalism would thus undergo a similarly fundamental shift to that of Irish unionism in the years preceding partition. However, both of these new radical political movements, while ideologically opposed, shared some things in common. Both sought to motivate mass movements based on simple rhetorical slogans and shared an unhealthy millenarian view of the future if the other side were victorious. During the elections to the first Northern Ireland parliament, one Belfast unionist candidate claimed that 'failure means handing our bodies and souls over to Sinn Féin and the Roman Catholic Church'.[30] Similarly, a nationalist polemicist spelled out a nightmarish vision of the future for Ireland's Catholics if the independence movement failed:

We shall witness the final and fatal decadence which will make of the Emerald Isle a dying land, empty of inhabitants, reduced to the position of a ranch for England, and a poorhouse; that will be the end of the Celtic race, the proscription of the children of Ireland, condemned to wander the world, like the Jews, in an eternal exile.[31]

They also shared an ambivalent relationship with violence and physical force methods. Along with most Europeans by the end of the nineteenth century, the Irish viewed war less as a human-made tragedy, but rather as a test of national worth and communal cohesion. While Parnell had flirted unconvincingly with the threat of Fenian extremism in the 1880s, much of Sinn Féin's popularity was drawn from its association with the dead leaders of the Easter Rising. Participation in, or association with, the Rising would prove to be a key badge of honour and define the southern state's political elites for generations. It would not be until Albert Reynolds in the 1990s that a Taoiseach did not have a direct or familial link with the Easter Rising. The conspiratorial Irish Republican Brotherhood and openly paramilitary Irish Volunteers, later to morph into the Irish Republican Army (IRA), continued a watching brief on events in the wake of the Rising, reorganising, rearming and remaining wary of perceived backsliding on behalf of the political side of the movement and any compromise on the sacred aim of the martyred leaders of the Rising for a thirty-two–county all-Ireland republic.

(September 1999), p. 748. For a thorough exploration of the attitudes which underlay the attitudes of the nationalist revolutionary generation to the issue of Ulster, see Foster, Vivid Faces.

[30] Ewart, A Journey in Ireland, 1921, p. 158.

[31] P. J. Sheridan, 'At the Irish Junction', The Irish Review, vol. 4, no. 37 (March 1914), pp. 12–15.

Ulster unionism had a more dramatic, if equally ambivalent, relationship with paramilitarism and armed insurrection. The Ulster Crisis (1912–1914) had seen the mobilisation of Ulster unionism in resistance to the imminent passing of the Third Home Rule Act at Westminster. This mobilisation was both a resistance to, and manifestation of, the influence of mass political forces in Ireland and the increasing need for elites to incorporate their populations within the dynamics of political action. In response to the threat of Home Rule, Ulster unionism had mobilised. Orange and Ulster unionist clubs were revived and a massive propaganda campaign was launched on the British mainland. Demonstrations and marches became familiar sights, as did fierce speeches against attempts to place Ulster under a southern parliament. When the bill was finally introduced in 1912, unionists did all they could to upset its smooth passage through parliament with bitter speeches, delaying amendments and various stunts in order to force the Liberal government to back down. In September 1912, a theatrical signing of a 'Solemn League and Covenant' was held, eventually receiving over 500,000 signatures. Worse still for the stability of Ireland, unionism began to militarise. Early in 1913 the scattered units of men who had begun drilling in rural areas the year previously were concentrated into a single paramilitary group, the UVF, which imported 25,000 rifles from Imperial Germany, to defend Ulster should Home Rule ever become a reality. Almost 90,000 men had joined this unionist army by the middle of 1914.

Most concerning was the response of southern nationalists who decided to act in imitation of the UVF and formed their own paramilitary organisation, the Irish Volunteers, whose aim was to prevent the government reneging on its commitment to Home Rule under the threat of the UVF. Even the British army became involved when, in March 1914, sixty British officers refused to obey orders to reinforce British garrisons in Ulster in opposition to the UVF. It would only be with the arrival of the First World War that this confrontation between Irish nationalism and unionism would be averted, or at least delayed.

While there is little doubt that Ireland had changed, the British state had not. The twin revolutions within Irish nationalism and Irish unionism had created tension in the archaic constitutional arrangements in Ireland which had changed little since the Act of Union in 1801. The Union itself was a flawed and confused piece of legislation, more a short-term recipe for dealing with the 1798 Rising and French expansionism under the Directory and later Consulate than a blueprint for sustained state building and good government. Politically, the partial union saw Ireland sending a disproportionately large number of MPs to Westminster, while at the same time its native government remained largely colonial in character. The

Lord Lieutenant, a colonial viceroy in all but name, ruling through a series of chief secretaries, presided over a confusing array of branches of government and local boards and departments based in Dublin Castle, the nerve centre of British rule in Ireland. One Dublin journalist characterised the arrangement as follows:

The Chief Secretary exercises despotic powers over multitudinous boards, all working in separate compartments without regard either to the economy of force or the prevention of wasteful friction . . . the classical example of autocracy masking itself behind a threadbare pretence of constitutional forms.[32]

Ireland certainly lacked the distinctive legal basis of Scotland's union, with power instead being maintained by an extensive and armed paramilitary police force in the shape of the Royal Irish Constabulary (RIC). Indeed, British authority in Ireland had been maintained since the 1830s by an ongoing series of coercive emergency legislation, which, while managing to subdue Irish protest, was hardly a good base for progressive government reform, a fact Sir William Harcourt, William Gladstone's home secretary would candidly admit:

We hold Ireland by force and by force alone as in the days of Cromwell, only that we are obliged to hold it by a force ten times larger than he found necessary . . . We have never governed, and we never shall govern Ireland by the good will of its people.[33]

What Irish laws there were reflected developments in the rest of the UK, and were implemented by their full or piecemeal application to Ireland through a series of boards tacked on to existing ministries. Even though many of these laws were warmly welcomed, such as the 1909 extension of national insurance and old age pensions to Ireland in the wake of the Liberal welfare reforms, they tended to reflect British concerns rather than specifically Irish ones and the lack of any control of indirect taxation and customs duties left it constantly prey to economic uncertainty.

Attempts to redress these archaic structures and the grievances that many felt underlay them led to a series of government initiatives. During the almost two decades of unionist-dominated Conservative government, British policy would be marked by an attempt to address Irish economic grievances which underpinned political support for Home Rule. The policy which emerged, variously titled 'Constructive Unionism' or, more informally, 'Killing Home Rule with Kindness' sat easily within

---

[32] Winder Good, *Ulster and Ireland*, p. 202.
[33] Harcourt quoted in Vernon Bogdanor, *Devolution in the United Kingdom* (Oxford, 2001), p. 21.

contemporary thinking in British evolutionary conservative circles which saw change as an essential principle of preservation. One aspect of these initiatives was to rationalise Irish administration and this was carried through with the passing of a Local Government Act in 1898. Other more symbolic measures were also implemented, most notably with the creation of a much demanded Catholic National University of Ireland in 1908. The most notable achievement of these heterogeneous sets of political initiatives was its settlement of the deeply divisive issue of the ownership of Irish land, which had lain at the root of agrarian militancy and the creation of the hugely popular Irish National Land League in the 1880s. Addressed in a series of increasingly progressive pieces of parliamentary legislation, culminating in the Wyndham Land Act of 1903, the issue was effectively neutralised as a source of dissent in Irish nationalist political circles. By 1914, the government's system, which enabled native tenants to purchase land through the procurement of cheap government loans, had transferred over half of all Irish land from their Anglo-Irish owners into the hands of native tenant farmers. There was certainly a fond hope in government circles that this prosperous class of newly created Catholic landowners would prove more reluctant in the future to risk their material prosperity by supporting Home Rule and its uncertain economic implications.

Above all, therefore, it was the ambivalence of the relationship between Britain and Ireland, rather than its occasional coercive character, which fed the insecurities of political elites on both sides of the Irish Sea. Irish people were strongly represented in British political, military and colonial services and enmeshed within the wider British world. Perspective was therefore vital. Depending on where one stood, Ireland was either an archaic colony of Britain or an integrated partner; the union either an excuse for coercive government nakedly representing power and control or an opportunity for evolution and involvement in the most dynamic and economically prosperous state in the modern world. By the end of the war, this curious arrangement had already started to unravel.

Britain needed to discover a formula for the transfer of power. However, in this shifting, unstable political context it was not easy to discern who the representatives of Irish opinion were. Efforts had been made by the new British prime minister, David Lloyd George, to address the impasse by calling an Irish Convention in 1917. Announced in June of that year, the Convention was on the surface a brilliantly devious solution to the Irish political situation. By inviting delegates from all shades of Irish opinion to devise their own solution, Lloyd George hoped to shift responsibility back on to the Irish themselves, diverting ultimate responsibility from his government, who could take the role of both honest broker and legislative enabler.

Furthermore, those who refused to participate risked not only being labelled as obstructionist, but also being frozen out of any eventual solution. When the Convention's 100 delegates met at Trinity College on 25 July, hopes were high. A whole batch of internees who had been rounded up in the wake of the Easter Rising were released to soften the atmosphere and all shades of opinion were present including trade unionists, church leaders, representatives from each of Ireland's thirty-two counties and Gaelic Leaguers, including writers such as George Russel and Edward Lysaght who were felt to be favourable to advanced nationalism. However, ominously, Sinn Féin refused the five seats it had been allotted, stating, not unreasonably, that without a popular mandate the Convention was illegitimate. Indeed, the fact that delegates were appointed rather than elected was a source of constant criticism, leading many radicals to paint the Convention as, in the words of William O'Brien, leader of the small radical All for Ireland Party, nothing but a 'hateful bargain for the partition of the country under a plausible disguise'.[34]

It was certainly very clear right from the outset that the Convention was dominated by the old nationalist and unionist politicians of the Ulster Crisis who had failed so miserably to come to an agreement in 1914. Making up almost 90 per cent of all delegates, debates soon fell into their accustomed channels and well-rehearsed arguments. While the early stages of the Convention saw the emergence of a number of innovative ideas, it was clear that all sides shared wildly differing goals. The Home Rule Party itself was floundering under the assault of the advanced nationalism of Sinn Féin, a situation underlined by the victory of Sinn Féin leader Eamon de Valera in a by-election in East Clare and the popular nationalist protests which erupted after the death of republican prisoner Thomas Ashe who was on hunger strike. Ulster unionists stuck to their goal of ensuring Ulster exclusion from any proposed settlement, while southern unionists demanded safeguards for minority interests within any future settlement. Indeed, if the Convention achieved anything, it was to finally cement the division between northern and southern unionists. The moderate wing of southern unionism had sought a constructive plan for moderate all-Ireland devolution under the imperial umbrella, with Irish Protestant interests bolstered by a significant unionist population in Ulster and elsewhere. In the end, this compromise solution foundered due largely to its failure to deal with the reality of Ulster

---

[34] R. B. McDowell, *The Irish Convention, 1917–18* (Abingdon, 1980), p. 83.

opposition, appealing as it did directly to senior political figures at Westminster, resulting in an unlikely alliance of Ulster unionist, Northern Catholic and clerical resistance. The frustration of these moderate southern unionists led to the formation of the breakaway Anti-Partition League (APL), which emerged in January 1919 as a response to the increasingly confrontational and regionalist demands of Ulster unionism. Despite Carson's assurances that threats of Ulster exclusion were merely a political tactic to derail the Third Home Rule bill, the support of the Ulster unionist council for the Government of Ireland Act fed southern unionist suspicions that they were to be abandoned by their co-religionists in the north-east. Led by St John Broderick, First Earl of Midleton, former Tory cabinet minister and hailing from one of the oldest and most prestigious landowning families in Ireland, the APL failed to mobilise mass support, despite being bolstered to some extent by disaffected unionists from the three south Ulster border counties. For the rest of its existence, it remained an elite lobbying group for minority rights and constitutional safeguards for Irish Protestants. In 1922 it was able to contribute its constructive ideas to the new Free State Constitution, by which time its brand of southern unionism had become a largely decorous relic from a bygone pre-partition age.

While the Convention drifted on for almost eighteen months, its musings were increasingly irrelevant to Ireland's changed political circumstances. The continuing rise of Sinn Féin, the death of John Redmond in March 1918 and the threat to impose conscription on Ireland led to the British government becoming further enmeshed in the workings of the Convention, a process that would bring the Irish question once again back to the benches of Westminster. There was little difference, however, between this attempt to create a cross-party consensus and those already tried over the previous five years. Reflecting on these insoluble divisions, one journalist employed a colourful and, not untypical, post-war military metaphor to explain the failure of the plan:

It was very soon apparent that the offensive had taken place on too narrow a front, and the position so far gained was at once attacked on all sides. The Irish Unionists continued their resistance in front; many Nationalists and the machine-guns of the *Irish Independent* opened an enfilading fire; the *Morning Post* carried on its bomb-dropping on the lines of communication; and eventually the complete break-down came with a split in the attacking force itself, disagreement in the Cabinet as to the terms of settlement. With this final blow there was no other course open but a retreat to the original trench line.[35]

---

[35] Unificus, 'The Quest for an Irish Settlement', *The Irish Church Quarterly*, vol. 9, no. 36 (October 1916), p. 253.

Midleton gave a more ominous assessment, calling the Convention, 'the last endeavour to have the Irish question settled on constitutional lines'.[36] That the British would be leaving Ireland was not in doubt by 1918. How and when this withdrawal would be facilitated was the big question and the more they vacillated the more extreme the heterogeneous demands for the nature of the settlement would become.

[36] Joe Devlin to Plunkett, 26 December 1917 (Plunkett Papers, DEV 4/1).

2 Half a Revolution

On 14 November 1918, only twenty-four hours after the signing of the armistice ending the First World War, the British government announced its plan to hold a general election before the end of the year. This was the first election for almost eight years and much had changed. Four years of total war had shaken the political and social economy of the state, and while some saw this as a great opportunity, others were more dubious over the decision to go to the country in the immediate aftermath of such a profound upheaval. Herbert Asquith, the former Liberal prime minister, called the decision 'bewildering and potentially dangerous' while his Liberal colleague Donald Maclean found in it a 'recipe, if not for disaster, then certainly dismay'.[1]

While the election would indeed prove disastrous for the Liberal Party, and Asquith personally, who would lose his seat in East Fife, the unparalleled changes wrought by the war meant few were able to predict the outcome. David Lloyd George, Asquith's old ally turned bitter rival, led his version of the Liberal Party into a questionable electoral pact with the Conservatives, while the Labour Party fielded an unprecedented 388 candidates, compared to only fifty-six in the previous election eight years earlier. *The Times* editorial on the day after the announcement, noted that forecasting the result of the hard-fought election of December 1910 had been 'child's play' compared to this new contest:

The electoral position has been completely revolutionized by the war and the Reform Act. The war has broken up parties and led to political changes which cannot yet be fairly estimated. The Reform Act has more than doubled the electorate, enfranchised women and soldiers, brought about a wholesale redistribution of seats, and entirely remodelled the law relating to elections. It is a clean slate in electioneering, and the polls next month will mark the opening of a new epoch in the long political history of this country.[2]

---

[1] *Glasgow Herald*, 15 July 1918.   [2] *The Times*, 15 November 1918.

There was nowhere where this sense of uncertainty was more evident than in Ireland. The poll, set for 14 December 1918, would be the first election in Irish history to take place on a single day. It would also be the last time all Irish people voted together before the division of the island into two separate states.

The unprecedented one million Irish people who turned out to participate in this first postwar election were living in a country unrecognisable from that which had entered the conflict four years earlier. As elsewhere, the departure of thousands of men to the front opened up jobs in industry, many of them filled by working-class women who took their places in the increasing number of munitions factories sprouting up in and around Dublin and Belfast. These changes would set the context for the hasty partition solution of the following decade. While Ireland suffered from notable shortages in fuel and food in the latter stages of the conflict, overall, economically, the war came as a blessing for Ireland. With the closing off of competing European markets, Irish products of all varieties were in high demand. The predominant economic activity, however, remained agriculture, employing over 50 per cent of the male population. Even with government controls, the sheer demand for Irish food meant that prices far outstripped such restrictions. UK reliance on home-grown produce meant that all over Ireland farmers, especially those producing beef and butter, prospered in this sellers' market. Irish linen was also much in demand, with 80 per cent of its capacity employed for military purposes, making such things as rucksacks, aeroplane fabric and tents. Similarly, shipbuilding boomed with demand to replace lost shipping, leading to employment at the Belfast shipyards rising by a third. The wartime boom, however, was felt across the whole island in numerous ancillary industries. As in Britain, a system of mediation was introduced to deal with workplace and trade union disputes which had blighted Ireland prior to the war with the militancy of the 1913 Dublin Lockout.

Partition thus emerged from a period of unprecedented prosperity. It was indeed ironic that the most affluent years of the union were those immediately prior to its ending. Its outworking, however, would play out in a far more uncertain political climate. Wartime prosperity was to prove fleeting. As the economic situation began to normalise, demand for products began to crumble. In one year, from July 1920 to July 1921, demand for arable produce fell by almost 40 per cent, while that for animal products was down 17 per cent (the decline in prices were even more startling with 57 per cent and 38 per cent, respectively). Ireland's industries also went into sharp decline, with shipbuilding only recovering (again temporarily) with the onset of another world war in 1939, while the linen industry never recovered. Taken all together, Ireland's brief and unprecedented wartime boom and subsequent economic depression would coincide with the political radicalisation that led to partition.

Many political movements saw in the war the possibility of restyling Irish political culture in line with their own aspirations. It was certainly clear to all that in this new postwar, world politics would become a collective popular event. On the ground, the war offered a variety of new avenues for ordinary Irish people to articulate their own aspirations for a reshaping of the constitutional position of Ireland which would furnish their heterogeneous demands for political and social change. Socialists saw the conflict as a way of gaining political and social reform as rewards for the participation of their urban constituencies in the war effort, a view espoused most ably by the Labour minister of education, Arthur Henderson. While many saw the war as a way of furthering progressive social measures, the two radical ideologies who would come to dominate the politics of the partition period saw the war as a way of turning back the clock. Unionists saw the war as a watershed in its attempts to halt the movement towards Irish self-government, which had grown steadily since the 1860s. They saw this reversal as a way of returning Ireland to a more hierarchical, ordered and loyal past embedded deep inside the prosperous and liberal British imperial system, a past largely of their own invention. Similarly imagined was the world view of advanced nationalists who looked back even further to an idyllic pre-modern Gaelic utopia unsullied by colonialism and reflecting a purer form of authentic Ireland.

More pragmatically, for British politicians the war offered a way of breaking the political deadlock over the Third Home Rule bill and arresting the polarisation of Catholics and Protestants around increasingly incompatible political aspirations. The leadership of the main Irish political parties certainly showed little reluctance in mobilising their supporters to fight in the war, at least initially. Most of the Home Rule leadership felt it was unseemly to haggle for concessions while the Empire itself was fighting for its life and threw their weight behind the British war effort, as did the populations of the other dominions and colonies. They painted the war as one not for empire, but humanity, a fight for the rights of small nations, typified by Belgium, which they themselves were soon to become. While the Irish were no strangers to participating in British wars, the army which served in the First World War was the largest the island had ever fielded. Around 210,000 of the estimated 2.5 million men who volunteered to join the British army during the war came from Ireland. However, this was the lowest percentage of any of the four nations of the UK, representing only 11 per cent of eligible fighting men compared to over 27 per cent in Scotland. Conscription, although threatened, was never introduced in Ireland, and, although volunteering continued throughout the war, it declined enormously after the spring of 1916. On taking office in December 1916, Lloyd George confided to Home Rule MP T. P. O'Connor his concern that the number of Irish recruits had dropped to barely eighty men per week.[3] There were also distinct regional differences, with Ulster providing almost half of all recruits. These included both Northern Catholics and Protestants, although the latter represented across Ireland almost half of all volunteers despite making up only a quarter of the population. G. K. Chesterton left a memorable summary of the divisions which grew up in Ireland over participation in the conflict:

For some reason or other, there had been a very hopeful beginning of Irish volunteering at the beginning of the war; and that, for some reason or other, this had failed in the course of the war. The reasons alleged differed widely with the moods of men ... The different factions gave different explanations of why the thing had stopped; but they all agreed that it had begun. The Sinn Feiner said that the people soon found they had been lured into a Saxon trap, set for them by smooth, subservient Saxons like Mr. Devlin and Mr. Tim Healy. The Belfast citizen suggested that the Popish priest had terrorised the peasants when they tried to enlist, producing a thumbscrew from his pocket and a portable rack from his handbag. The Parliamentary Nationalist blamed both Sinn Fein and the persecution of Sinn Fein. The British Government officials, if they did not exactly blame themselves, at least blamed each other. The ordinary Southern Unionist (who played many parts of a more or less sensible sort, including that of a Home Ruler) generally agreed with the ordinary Nationalist that the Government's recruiting methods had been as bad as its cause was good.[4]

Of those who did volunteer, a staggering 40,000, almost 20 per cent of the total, lost their lives.[5] Almost half of these casualties came from the six north-eastern counties of the future Northern Ireland and represented 12.6 per cent of all adult males between the ages of 18 and 40. In early July 1916, the 36th Ulster Division, in many ways the prewar UVF in arms, were decimated during the Somme offensive, suffering over 5,500 casualties in two days.[6] Their bravery and noble sacrifice in the face of the enemy, much like that of the Easter rebels in Dublin, became a key foundation myth of Ulster unionism. Wilfred Spender, later to become the head of the Northern Irish civil service, after observing the attack,

[3] Letter from T. P. O'Connor to Joe Devlin, 22 January 1917 (Dillon Papers, 6730/176).
[4] G. K. Chesterton, *Irish Impressions* (London, 1918), p. 43.
[5] The most commonly quoted figure for casualties is 49,000. However, this erroneously includes non-Irish recruits in Irish regiments, a growing phenomenon in the second half of the war as native Irish recruitment dropped away. For an insightful analysis of these figures see K. Myers, *Ireland's Great War* (Dublin, 2014).
[6] C. Falls, *The History of the 36th Ulster Division* (London, 1922), p.58.

wrote the day after: 'I am not an Ulsterman, but yesterday, the 1st July, as I followed their amazing attack, I felt that I would rather be an Ulsterman than anything else in the world.'[7]

As such, the war presented Ireland with its greatest demographic catastrophe since the Famine. While volunteering had been proportionally higher in Ulster, volunteers came from all across Ireland, three-fifths from the future twenty-six counties of the south, and was made up of both Catholics and Protestants. Many fondly believed that serving together in the trenches, as thousands of Irishmen did from both communities, would act to soothe the enmities which had grown alarmingly during the prewar Ulster Crisis.

Such hopes, however, were to prove largely illusory. In the months preceding the proposed December election, as thousands of these soldiers returned home, most noted a profoundly changed political atmosphere.[8] The suspicion and hostility they received in the nationalist south on their return contrasted sharply with the heroic response of northern Protestants to their veterans. The different treatment soldiers received on their return to the two polarised Irish communities showed how far the two dominant radical ideologies were already shaping their own oppositional foundation myths. This new populist politics had become confrontational and worshipful. The poet George Russell wrote that 'Sinn Féin is fighting for freedom to manifest the Irish genius' and preserve the 'incorruptible spiritual atom of nationality in the Irishman'.[9] There was little room for moderates or the respectable constitutionalism of the old Home Rule Party or the paternalistic elitism of southern unionism. Indeed, within two months of the end of the war both these visions had been swept away.

Hanging over the forthcoming election was the more fundamental issue of Ulster. However, tellingly, the issue was to play a shadowy role in the campaign itself. None of the parties included the idea of partition in their manifestos. Indeed, British political parties spared only a few lines to the issue of Ireland, which were given over to general principles rather than concrete policy. The Conservatives came closest to addressing the notion of a geographical division of the island, standing firm against both complete separation and the 'forcible submission of the six counties of Ulster'. Liberals retained an almost quaint faith in the moribund Third Home

[7] See P. Orr, *The Road to the Somme: Men of the 36th Ulster Division Tell Their Story* (Belfast, 2008), p. 194.
[8] For a fascinating analysis of soldier's experiences in the south, see P. Taylor, *Heroes or Traitors?: Experiences of Southern Irish Soldiers Returning from the Great War 1919–1939* (Liverpool, 2015).
[9] Russell, *The Inner and Outer Ireland*, p. 7.

Rule bill, while the Labour Party struck the most radical note, promising not only 'freedom for Ireland and India', but also self-determination for 'all subject peoples within the British Commonwealth of Free Nations'.[10] Most surprisingly, perhaps, the Irish parties themselves failed to address the potential threat of partition or any way of avoiding it. Instead, they moved to rally support behind emotive appeals to avenge past sacrifice or crude tribalistic rallying cries, where they treated, in the words of James Winder Good, 'differences of national character as innate and inexplicable, and national crimes and virtues as the materials for mere party eulogy or party invective'.[11] In line with the besetting anxiety of the age, these appeals instilled an acceptance of conflict and competition as a way of bringing progress, the alternative to which would be national degeneration and de-civilisation.

Vague as these amorphous visions were, the cries of 'Ulster' or the 'Republic' proved to be dramatically effective, mobilising hundreds of thousands of Irish people in their support. Sinn Féin called on the electorate to follow them on 'the path to national salvation', blaming the British for everything from emigration to economic exploitation: 'The enforced exodus of millions of our people, the decay of our industrial life, the ever-increasing financial plunder of our country.'[12] By contrast, the Home Rule Party styled its manifesto as a passionate apologetic for its gradualist approach and past achievements. During the war, John Redmond noted in a speech in Dublin:

To-day, the people, broadly speaking, own the soil. To-day the labourers live in decent habitations. To-day there is absolute freedom in local government and local taxation of the country. To-day we have the widest parliamentary and municipal franchise. The congested districts, the scene of some of the most awful horrors of the old famine days, have been transformed. The farms have been enlarged, decent dwellings have been provided, and a new spirit of hope and independence is to-day among the people. In towns legislation has been passed facilitating the housing of the working classes – a piece of legislation far in advance of anything obtained for the town tenants of England. We have a system of old-age pensions in Ireland whereby every old man and woman over seventy is safe from the workhouse and free to spend their last days in comparative comfort.[13,14]

[10] Frederick Craig, *British General Election Manifestos, 1918–1966* (London, 1970).
[11] Winder Good, *Ulster and Ireland*, p. 13.
[12] Dorothy Macardle, 'The Manifesto of Sinn Féin as Prepared for Circulation for the General Election of December, 1918' in *The Irish Republic: A Documented Chronicle of the Anglo-Irish Conflict and the Partitioning of Ireland, with a Detailed Account of the Period 1916–1923* (London, 1937), pp. 919–20.
[13] *Irish Times*, 23 July 1917.
[14] Ronald McNeill, *Ulster's Stand for Union* (New York, 1922), p. 298.

Despite the fact that many of these practical achievements were largely Conservative and, later, Liberal initiatives at Westminster, they allowed the Home Rule Party to offer voters a 'practicable and attainable object', which John Dillon characterised as a stark choice between 'futile revolution and anarchy and the maintenance of the constitutional movement'.[15] It was in their handling of the Ulster issue that the nationalist parties most differed. When it came to the north-east, Sinn Féin used the Home Rule Party's acquiescence in a scheme for temporary Ulster exclusion to criticise their opponents, mercilessly attacking the Home Rule Party for contemplating the 'mutilation of our country by partition' a policy that will lead to 'national ruin'.[16] Typically, they provided little in the way of an alternative policy. One moderate nationalist critic pointed out this glaring omission in the radical republican vision:

The fundamental weakness of Sinn Fein is that not only have its leaders failed to evolve an Ulster policy, but they act as if such a policy were a minor detail as compared with eloquent arguments about the rights of small nationalities. Once they have settled the main point about England's right of intervention, all other difficulties, so they suggest, will solve themselves automatically, a contention which might carry weight if one could forget that it is exactly because Ulster blocks the way that English intervention is possible. Sinn Feiners would do well to remember that were this country an independent Republic tomorrow the covenanters would still be here.[17]

Even those who accepted the inevitability of a partitioned Ireland and the authenticity of the Ulster unionist claim tried to paint the idea as a chance to realise an ethnically homogeneous Gaelic homeland. Arthur Clery, Sinn Féin judicial officer and republican envoy to the Vatican, called almost uniquely for his countrymen to embrace partition:

Of course they [i.e., Ulster Protestants] love Ireland – as a country. After all, it's their country. It has always struck me that the attitude of Ireland towards the Ulsterman is not a little like that of the English towards ourselves. We both endeavour to gloss over the existence of the horrid thing, and hope without reason for a more united future ... Now, in reality the chances of our absorbing Ulster under Home Rule, and of England absorbing us if we do not get it, are about equal. It may be done, but it will take some doing, and just men will prefer not to see that doing. That they are sincere in their opposition it is mere futility to deny ... They have adopted precisely the same methods of propagating their opinions that we have ours. The press, the platform and the ballot-box have all borne witness to their national faith, and it seems to me that if these persons demand their national independence, and if they are, in truth, distinct in nationality, it requires a strong

[15] John Dillon to T. P. O'Connor, 18 August 1918 (Dillon Papers, 6742/515).
[16] Macardle, 'The Manifesto of Sinn Féin'.
[17] Winder Good, *Ulster and Ireland*, p. 250.

reason not to prevent their getting it ... If we can prove that Irish freedom causes bondage to no man we shall have done much to help our cause.[18]

However, Clery's views were hardly moderate or progressive. He saw partition as a way for the authentic Ireland to free itself from the 'bigoted aliens' whose 'native feasts and cannibal habits' made them 'the most criminal and least moral section of the population'.[19] In this view, partition was less a matter of compromise, but should be embraced as a form of geographical ethnic cleansing in order to allow the 'clan of the Gael' to flourish.

While the nationalist parties focused on a vague catch-all form of basic Irish nationalism, Irish unionism increasingly became dominated by those who campaigned for a more specific kind of Ulster particularism. Much like their nationalist opponents, they reserved some of their strongest criticism for their fellow unionists, attacking those who sought to maintain a unified Ireland with as strong a British connection as possible. While some of these had accepted the reality of imminent Irish self-determination and sought a more co-operative engagement with the inevitable devolutionary settlement, more doctrinaire unionists saw the acceptance of Ulster exclusion as a betrayal of the 'historic destiny of the original plantation plan'.[20] By consciously conflating the imperialist language of western colonial superiority with sectarian prejudice, such commentators saw Protestantism as having delivered a larger degree of 'order, education and hygiene'[21] to Catholic Ireland, factors which they claimed were symptomatic of a more advanced civilisation.

Rather than retreating into their northern heartlands, they should seize the unique opportunity offered by the uncertain political climate to push this 'age-old mission' forward. In this view, it was not merely a set of economic and political customs that had been transferred to Ireland, but British civilisation itself. It was argued that Ulster should be viewed less as an embattled outpost of empire, but play a role more akin to that of Piedmont in post-unification Italy, modernising an underdeveloped south. One southern unionist leader wrote to Carson in 1912 that the Irish Protestant population represented an,

oasis of culture, of uprightness and of fair dealing, in what will otherwise be a desert of dead uniformity where the poor will have no one to appeal to except the Priest or the local shopkeeper ... whence the rich will fly and where lofty ideals,

---

[18] Quoted in P. Maume, 'Nationalism and Partition: The Political Thought of Arthur Clery', *Irish Historical Studies*, vol. 31, no. 122 (November 1998), p. 230.

[19] Ibid, p. 229.   [20] McNeill, *Ulster's Stand for Union*, p. 115.

[21] Brooks, 'The Problem of Ulster', p. 622.

whether of social or Imperial interest, will be smothered in an atmosphere of superstition, greed and chicanery.[22]

Thus, the achievements of Irish Protestantism were more than just an ideal for all Ireland to aspire to, but rather should be used as 'magic', or 'manure', as one Tyrone unionist politician inelegantly described it, to enrich a 'barren, impoverished, badly governed and backward south ... pauperised owing to the incurable laziness of its people'.[23] He went on to add that unionists all over Ireland should unite against Home Rule, even if it meant they themselves would eventually be sacrificed:

Our job will be to convince the brethren that they will gain nothing by surrender: that the course of events in an Irish Parliament would not be one of moderate and practical reform, but of Russian anarchy, and that if they break with Ulster it will only mean in one form or another an utterly hopeless outlook for the "moderates."[24]

For such unionists in the north-east, who had long seized control of the party's agenda, only special treatment of Ulster could avoid the inevitable slide into full separatism. Metaphors of salvation and survival predominated in their arguments. Thomas Moles, unionist MP for Belfast, spelled out to his southern unionist colleagues the harsh choices Ulster Protestants faced: 'In a sinking ship, with life-boats sufficient for only two-thirds of the ship's company, were all to condemn themselves to death because all could not be saved?'[25] Using similarly apocalyptic language, one correspondent with the *Irish Times* took issue with those who fulminated against, 'Ulster's selfish desire to save itself ... You might as well declaim against the "partition" of a family threatened with the plague because a section of them are isolated so as to make sure they shall not get it, even if the remainder do.'[26]

As such, the election had the character of a referendum on the future of Ireland. While mass involvement in political action had been a feature of nineteenth century campaigns, the 1918 election was the first time politics had to appeal for mass electoral support. The vote was far more unpredictable due to the mass participation of so many new voters. With the passing of the Representation of the People Act, these constituencies themselves were now over twice the size of any which had preceded

---

[22] James Wilson, 'Reflection', Public Records Office of Northern Ireland (PRONI), D989/A/11.

[23] Pseudonymous, 'Light on Ulsteria', The Irish Review, vol. 2, no. 16 (June 1912), pp. 220–1.

[24] Letter from J. R. Fisher, 2 May 1918, PRONI, D627/433/23.

[25] Thomas Moles quoted in D. Gwynn, *A History of Partition, 1911–1925* (Dublin, 1950), p. 192.

[26] *Irish Times*, 7 December 1918.

them. With the franchise now extended to men over the age of 21, the electorate included a whole new generation of voters. Among those voting for the first time were urban working-class and rural agricultural workers who had had little previous say in shaping Ireland. Perhaps even more significant was the extension of the vote to women over the age of 30, who, despite their increasing participation in the mass political movements of unionism and nationalism, remained a largely unknown quantity. Almost 400,000 of them would now have the vote, while in total the Irish electorate rose from 701,475 in 1910 to an enormous 1,936,673 in 1918. Factoring in war casualties and deaths in the intervening eight years, almost 75 per cent of those voting in the December election were new voters. This was the first election in Irish history to be held on a single day, a development which helped to ratchet up the pressure to exploit the power of nationalist and unionist constituencies. Added to this was the redrawing of constituency boundaries to better reflect the new demographic realities. This led to more seats in urban areas – Belfast, for example, increased its representation from four to nine – and the scrapping of constituencies in underpopulated rural regions. With practical and ideological changes on this scale, there is little doubt that the election of 1918, the last ever all-Ireland election, was a singular moment in Irish history, when, for good or ill, the country came together to collectively decide over the nature of the inevitable new Ireland.

In such a new large-scale mass election and with momentous change around the corner, unrealistic simple utopian messages held sway. Russell equated Irish freedom with the 'meaning of the universe' and a future independent state as a way for men 'to illuminate earth with light or wisdom ... or mould external circumstance into the image of the Heaven they conceive in their hearts'.[27] At base, all Irish people were offered the same equivocal, but powerfully attractive, thing – a future in which they could control their own destiny. These appeals involved rhetorical one-upmanship and dire predictions of the consequences for people of failing to show their support. In Lisburn, far to the north, the local unionist club announced that 'without our most sterling efforts the Covenant of 1912 means nothing. This election is a simple choice between civilization and barbarism.'[28] Notorious Ulster unionist leaders such as Arthur Meade warned the British government that if they did try and coerce the northeast they 'would have to make Ulster literally an armed camp, not for days or months, but for years ... you would get a second Poland'.[29] Eamon de Valera spoke of Sinn Féin's mission as a

---

[27] Russell, *The Inner and Outer Ireland*, p. 8.   [28] *Belfast Newsletter*, 14 December 1918.
[29] Hansard, HC vol 15, cols 56–144 (11 February 1914).

'holy task' which must be completed so that the 'Irish race ... be permitted to build up the great nation which God intended Ireland to be',[30] something George Russell saw as akin to preparing a 'physical body for the incarnation of the soul of the Irish race'.[31] Certainly, all sides were desperate to be seen as the authentic representatives of the people's will, despite the fact that they themselves had done so much to shape the parameters within which these choices were made. Allegiance to the ideas of 'Ulster' or 'Ireland' were painted less as political preferences and more as ideals for living. Complaints about petty indignities and banal communal slights, most of them unintended, grew alarmingly. Petty snubs, such as that in 1917 when a nationalist member of Tyrone county council refused to stand for the national anthem, were described without irony in the press as 'atrocities'. In such a fevered political atmosphere, to be called a 'true Irishman' or a 'loyal Ulsterman' became the highest of compliments.

Images of confrontation and analogies of battle peppered the language of the participants as these new political forces defined themselves against one another. On the local level, the parties' paramilitaries in the shape of the UVF and Irish Volunteers led the way as shock troops, descending on marginal constituencies, acting as stewards for political speeches and whipping up propaganda, leading to numerous beatings and woundings. Their aim, as one sympathetic Belfast cleric crudely put it, was to 'continue the work begun by the heroes who went to Heaven last Easter'.[32] Certainly, the rhetoric of violence, what one historian has called 'the misdirected bully-boy tactics of threat and coercion', constantly lurked beneath the surface.[33] Arthur Griffith challenged those unionists in Ulster to 'make up their minds to throw in their lot with the Irish nation or stand out as the English garrison. If they did the latter the Irish nation must deal with them.'[34] Lord Clanwilliam added threateningly that in any future conflict between Catholics and Protestants, it,

would probably be a war of extermination. We have the nationalists sandwiched between our forces and they have only a few old guns to rely on. They could not possibly have a chance. Our men are well armed and guns and ammunition are constantly being run into Ulster. We have the province in the hollow of our hands.[35]

---

[30] Eamon de Valera speech in New York, *Gaelic American*, 20 September 1919.

[31] Russell, *The Inner and Outer Ireland*, p. 5.

[32] Rev. Robert Fullerton speech reported in RIC Special Branch Report, Belfast, 1916, the National Archives (NA), Public Records Office (PRO) CO 904/23/3.

[33] D. O'Corrain, '"Ireland in His Heart North and South": The Contribution of Ernest Blythe to the Partition Question,' *Irish Historical Studies*, vol. xxxv, no. 137 (May 2006).

[34] Arthur Griffith, 'Sinn Fein and Ulster', *Notes from Ireland* (Irish Unionist Alliance, 1917), vol. 26, no. 4, p. 74.

[35] Quoted in M. Foy, 'Ulster Unionist Propaganda against Home Rule, 1912–1914', *History Ireland*, vol. 4, no. 1 (Spring 1996), pp. 49–53.

At one political speech in Armagh, a local unionist stated that 'Ulstermen face a decision between liberty and slavery. Vote first and then, if we have to, fight for it.' Their language was confrontational and crude. In a speech in Cavan the previous September, de Valera spoke of Ulster Protestants as 'planters', 'a garrison for the enemy' and threatened if they continued in their obstruction 'we will have to kick you out'.[36] Such language drew largely on older prejudices with unionists painted as an 'alien garrison', and akin to 'a robber coming into another man's house and claiming a room as his own'.[37] Such proclamations led to the spreading of a crude populist message, disguising the lack of debate over what victory for the radicals would lead to in the end.

Many, though, remained sceptical about these crass messages while others reacted with fear about the millenarian future which was being expounded in some of the most extreme messages. This was particularly the case for those who had most to fear from this growing polarisation. Communities which straddled the Ulster border or those who would be minority groups in any potential settlement were badly affected. Ironically, the deep complexities of Irish identity, which had lain at the root of the problem of solving the Irish question over previous decades, were jettisoned in favour of a simplistic monochrome choice. The specific issues affecting such diverse groups as Northern Catholics, Southern Protestants, Catholic unionists, socialists, trade unionists, women's rights activists, town and country dwellers, to mention but a few, were steamrollered in the drive to the extremes. The complexities between and within these groups and their wildly differing political priorities were now seen as an irritation and akin to treachery in the twin drives to 'save Ulster' or 'win Irish freedom'. Home Rulers in Monaghan called for an end to factionalism, with members who had left the party being asked to return in a countywide campaign:

At a time like the present we can afford to forget every minor and local difference of opinion when the future prosperity of Ireland is hanging in the balance. Every Irishman who holds the belief that his country can only prosper under a system of home government is bound to take an active part during the next twelve months in combating the forces of retrogression and bigotry.[38]

A. M. Sullivan, a lifelong constitutional nationalist and a prominent barrister, wrote scathingly of the descent into confrontation blaming it on,

---

[36] De Valera quoted in C. O'Halloran, *Partition and the Limits of Irish Nationalism* (Dublin, 1987), p. 32.

[37] O'Halloran, *Partition and the Limits of Irish Nationalism*, p. 32–4.

[38] *The Dundalk Democrat*, 13 January 1912. See also A. Carville 'The Impact of Partition Proposals on County Monaghan', *Clogher Record*, vol. 14, no. 1 (1991), pp. 37–51.

the natural development of the brutalising and pagan creed that for the past three years has been proclaimed as "patriotism" in Ireland, while those who should have refused it have sat in cowardly silence.[39]

On the day of the election passions were high. Party agitators worked until the last minute to rouse support while party newspapers urged readers not only to vote, but also to be wary of the inevitable underhand chicanery of their opponents. In the new context, participation in the election became for the first time a mass participation event. Party members and voters held processions. Countless pamphlets, posters, bombastic party rallies, street-corner speeches and paramilitary march-pasts filled public space alongside union flags and tricolours.

When the results were finally released on 28 December, after a two week delay to allow for votes from soldiers to be brought back from abroad, they signalled a staggering transformation of Ireland's political destiny. Of the 105 seats up for grabs, Sinn Féin won seventy-three, virtually wiping out the old Home Rule Party who managed a mere six. Bishop MacRory concluded that the Irish people had grown 'thoroughly and intelligibly tired of the [Irish] Party. It was time to put an end to it.'[40] Although winning less than half of the share of the vote, there can be little doubt that with so many seats uncontested in the more radical counties of the west, they definitely had the support of the large majority of the Irish population. Although much historical study has focused on the Sinn Féin result, arguably more notable was the endorsement of the Ulster demand with the creation of a homogeneous block in the north-east. While de Valera could claim that 'no people on earth ever agreed so overwhelmingly on a great issue',[41] the fact was that unionists had achieved an electoral triumph in Ulster just as conclusive as that achieved by Sinn Féin in the south and west. Outside of the university seat at Trinity College and Sir Thomas Dockrell's victory in Rathmines, a major centre for Dublin's 90,000 strong Protestant community, twenty four of the twenty-six unionist seats were in Ulster. This result signalled a final confirmation of Ulster particularism in the minds of many leading politicians.

Just what people had voted for when they chose to support Sinn Féin remained to be seen. The movement's bombastic and romantic nationalist slogans during the election campaign did not translate easily into a set of coherent practical policies. Indeed, the manifesto itself, aside from

---

[39] *Irish Times*, 21 January 1919.
[40] MacRory, 26 December 1918, quoted in A. C. Hepburn, *Catholic Belfast and Nationalist Ireland in the Era of Joe Devlin, 1871–1934* (Oxford, 2008), p. 205.
[41] *Gaelic American*, 8 November 1919.

confrontational rhetoric calling for full independence, contained little in the way of discussing how this was to be achieved. In the wake of the election, an *Irish Times* editorial concluded: 'Sinn Fein has swept the board but we do not know – does Sinn Fein itself know – what it intends to do with the victory?'[42] The most that could be said is that people in 1918 voted for a more advanced form of nationalism. They did not vote for war, which appeared nowhere in Sinn Féin's literature, even if threatened darkly by the looming presence of the Irish Volunteers, and they certainly did not vote for partition. The *Irish Church Quarterly* argued shortly after the election that despite the widely felt confusion in political circles, the result had at least clarified the shared unpopularity of partition:

The locus standi of the two main parties is thus at last clearly defined. They have shown the widespread and vehement feeling against a policy of partition, a feeling universal among Nationalists, almost universal among Southern Unionists, widespread among Ulster Unionists. Even in Ulster partition is looked upon merely as a makeshift.[43]

Ironically though, for all their rhetoric, the victory of Sinn Féin made partition more, rather than less, likely, inflicting, in the words of Father Francis Shaw, one of 'three grave wounds on … the unity of Ireland'.[44] Their attitude to the issue of Ulster remained crude and unrealistic. The old Home Rule MP Jasper Tully, referring to the period of the Ulster Crisis reflected how irrelevant the Sinn Féin revolution had been in terms of the issue of partition: 'In fact, more than was got under the treaty could have been got if "partition" was swallowed then, as it has been swallowed now.'[45]

Certainly, most Irish nationalists appear to have given little thought to how to reconcile their demands with the maintenance of a united Ireland and slipped into denial. The various strands of Gaelic nationalism and separatist republicanism which came to define Irish nationalism after the Easter Rising were a complete anathema to northern unionists. Despite the fact that Sinn Féin used the threat of partition to undermine their nationalist opponents, it soon emerged after their victory that they had no coherent Northern policy to replace it. Many felt that the Home Rule Party's strategy of reluctantly accepting some kind of Ulster 'exclusion' would have led to a far softer partition than that which was now expected.

---

[42] *Irish Times*, 30 December 1918.
[43] Unificus, 'The Quest for an Irish Settlement', p. 254.
[44] The other two 'wounds' were the southern civil war of 1922/1923 and the exclusion of Ireland's veterans of the First World War from national commemoration. Fr. F. Shaw, 'The Canon of Irish History', *Studies*, vol. 61 (1972), p. 151.
[45] *Roscommon Herald*, 19 May 1923.

The exclusion plan did not envision any kind of local Belfast parliament, remaining under direct rule from Westminster. As such, with a Dublin parliament keeping up a constant pressure for reunification and supporting northern minority interests, the Northern counties could not remain excluded for long, having appeal, not to a native parliament, but only to Westminster which would continue to contain dozens of Irish nationalist MPs constantly pushing for its absorption under Dublin control. J. L. Garvin, the Irish editor of the *Observer* later noted:

The Ireland of the new Gaelic extremists was a pure myth. It could not be. Even the dream of it has brought to the country division, turmoil and tyranny. [The Redmonds] believed in Irish self-government and the purposes of our wider commonwealth ... They died serving a bigger, broader and bolder ideal than that of the exclusionist Gaelic anachronism, not shirking Ireland's response to the modern world looking forward and not back to the golden age.[46]

By contrast, Sinn Féin lacked any kind of clear policy for dealing with the north-east. Despite the efforts of subsequent historians to write subtlety and clarity back into their arguments, they were at best contradictory and at worst incoherent and counterproductive. The utterances of leading Sinn Féin members on the issue of Ulster, their speeches and newspaper interviews being the closest the party got to any kind of defined policy, were either glib or inconsistent. It was clear that to some extent Sinn Féin had secured victory in 1918 due to the Home Rule Party's flirtation with, and provisional acceptance of, partition in 1914. However, the radical separatism of the new party made any kind of integrated all-Irish political solution even more unlikely than it had been before the war. Worse was the fact that the party clearly had no coherent alternative policy. Aside from the usual nationalist rhetoric which recounted 'the tale of a nation crucified' by its 'Vampire neighbour', blame was laid squarely on the British government ('the union of the shark with its prey') who at various times were asked, rather paradoxically, to stand aside or, at the other extreme, coerce their 'Unionist lackeys'[47] into a united Ireland; it was clear that opinions within the movement differed wildly. Even individual leaders contradicted themselves at various times swinging between glib pronouncements of confrontation and conciliation. Eamon de Valera, for example, was able to say in April 1917 that he 'would not like to see any man who was loyal as an Irishman, be he Unionist or Separatist coerced', while in a speech a few months later he could state that 'Ulster must be coerced if she stood in the way'.[48]

[46] J. L. Garvin, *Observer*, 18 March 1927.
[47] Bowman, *De Valera and the Ulster Question*, p. 38.   [48] *Sligo Champion*, 28 July 1917.

The party was certainly hamstrung by its own idealistic hubris. They retained so much fanatical faith in the authenticity of their nationalist project that opposition was characterised as 'unnatural', dismissed as 'child's talk'[49] or a conspiracy fostered by self-serving British politicians. As de Valera outlined to the American press,

The so called Ulster difficulty is purely artificial as far as Ireland itself is concerned. It is an accident arising out of the British connection, and will disappear with it. If it arose from a genuine desire of the people of the North-East Corner for autonomy the solution proposed would be the obvious one. But it is not due to such a desire-it has arisen purely as a product of British party manoeuvring.[50]

In such a world view, Irish unionists were painted contradictorily as either 'aliens', 'foreigners' or 'non-Irish', or, on the other hand, courted as potential converts once they realised 'they have been duped'.[51] As John Bowman has written, republicans 'discounted the intransigence of Ulster unionists and repeatedly forecast their imminent conversion to support for Sinn Fein.'[52] The unionists never replaced the British as the main focus for nationalist ire or were cited as the chief cause of division in Ireland. The British, it was argued, through opportunistic and 'clever politics', had cynically transformed the rebellious temper of the Ulster population, a spirit rather paradoxically admired by many participants in the Easter Rising, including Patrick Pearse, into a squalid sectarian feud between Catholics and Protestants. As such, many leaders remained convinced that the Catholic/Protestant divide was little more than a 'nuisance', and both communities would soon realise that they shared equally their experience of exploitation by the Belfast and London elites. Crass, but fairly typical, interwar racial arguments were used to bolster this latter conviction. De Valera claimed that 'racially Ulster was Irish ... after more than 300 years of intermarriage there were few native born Ulsterman or Ulsterwomen today in whom Gaelic blood does not predominate'.[53]

While leading members of Sinn Féin toyed darkly with some form of future coercion against Ulster, Michael O'Flanagan, Catholic priest and vice-president of Sinn Féin argued that such a plan was inconsistent with nationalist dogmas about the oppression of small nations such as Belgium and Ireland. He concluded forcefully, 'The island of Ireland and the national unit of Ireland simply do not coincide.'[54]

---

[49] Bowman, *De Valera and the Ulster Question*, p. 44.   [50] Ibid.
[51] O'Halloran, *Partition and the Limits of the Irish Nationalism*, p. 31.   [52] Ibid, p. 42.
[53] E. de Valera, *Ireland's Claim to the Government of the United States of America for Recognition as a Sovereign Independent State* (Washington, 1920), p. 67.
[54] Bew, 'Moderate Nationalism', p. 734.

Such voices, however, were almost unique. The policy of abstention was to prove disastrous in that it allowed the British government to pass the Government of Ireland Act through Westminster virtually unopposed. Certainly, when the Ulster issue was addressed, republican rhetoric remained uncompromising. Shortly after the truce was agreed in July 1921, de Valera told the South African leader Field-Marshal Smuts: 'An Ireland in fragments nobody cares about. A united Ireland alone can be happy and prosperous.'[55] The Sinn Féin perception of the Ulster issue remained doggedly wedded to the idea that unionist resistance was inauthentic and due largely to the continued British presence in Ireland. In the spring of 1921, de Valera again reinforced the conspiratorial nature of Sinn Féin views of Ulster resistance:

the difficulty of the problem was not the attitude of Ulster but the attitude of England. It is to the interest of no section of Irishmen to keep their differences alive, but it is to the interest of certain English politicians and statesmen who desire these differences as a cloak to screen their own imperial greed.[56]

During their conversation in London, de Valera told Lloyd George that the issue of the north-east was 'for the Irish people themselves to settle. We cannot admit the rights of the British Government to mutilate our country, either in its own interest or at the call of any section of our population. We do not contemplate the use of force. If your Government stands aside, we can effect a complete reconciliation.'[57] Sandy Lindsay, an old friend of Erskine Childers confided: 'Absolutely everything that de Valera has said to the N[orth] E[ast] he has with the best intentions said the thing most calculated to put their backs up. I think that now you are preserving unity of the South and West at the expense or making impossible or delaying for a long time the unity of the whole of Ireland.'[58] Even in the face of unprecedented levels of sectarian violence in Belfast during 1922, Arthur Griffith, the deputy leader of Sinn Féin, claimed:

All this rioting is worked up, organized, paid for, for political reasons. 100 years ago the Protestants of the North of Ireland were the revolutionaries. There are a number of men in the North of Ireland who think that by keeping up the bogey of the Pope and the Boyne they can keep the industrial population quiet.... Catholics and Protestants would live harmoniously if this jockeying stopped.[59]

Amid all the passion of the election, few dwelt on its most key implication. The crude conclusion drawn by policymakers was that the Ulster unionists

---

[55] Quoted in M. Hopkinson, *Green Against Green* (Dublin, 1988), p. 79.
[56] *Freeman's Journal*, 24 March 1921.
[57] De Valera to Lloyd George, 10 August 1921, NA, CAB/24/128.
[58] Lindsay to Childers, 20 January 1922, Childers Papers, NLI, 7849.
[59] Jones, *Whitehall Diary*, p. 128.

and Sinn Féin had become polarised representatives of a more innate ethnic sectarian division; 'more opposed to each other than the Austrian and the Hun'.[60] For many, this religious divide is seen as the most important underlying factor in the decision to divide Ireland. Even during partition, itself, and subsequently, those who viewed this division lamented the state of affairs and sought for answers as to why Irish Catholics and Protestants had diverged to such an extent. One southern unionist wrote in late 1916:

> The attainment of a settlement and peace in Ireland is far more than a mere political question. It means the rooting out of a canker which pervades every portion of our national life. It is a religious question in a larger sense than is usually meant by that expression, for it must be plain that the Home Rule dispute has engendered among us all a spirit of strife and bitterness which is in many ways at variance with Christianity, and which has quite prevented us from obeying the injunction to "Live peaceably with all men."[61]

Certainly, religious division existed, but, as Ireland approached partition, the heterogeneous struggles between and within communities were engulfed within an all-consuming narrative of sectarian division. For decades, for many communities Ireland had become labelled as a place where religious division was endemic and coexistence was impossible. Politics had made this a self-fulfilling prophecy. Winder Good lamented this cheap exploitation of sectarian animosity, arguing that, if politicians,

> did not create it, it cannot be denied that in later years they have fed and fostered it by every means in their power. Instead of helping to obliterate sectarian enmities they increased them a thousandfold in their venom and virulence. So far from being a wilful paradox, it is the sober truth that the perpetuation of Irish differences is due less to the racial and religious antagonisms which our rulers affect to deplore, than to the exploitation of these antagonisms for the purposes of party politics.[62]

Ironically, as Irish politics became more sophisticated, the constituencies on which it was based became more simplified and honed down to a crude for or against. People's real experiences were vastly different. There were a multitude of localised divisions based on class, religion or region. The politics of partition drew these elements into a simple duality and plundered the past for myths to reinforce it.[63] Even in early–twentieth-century Ireland, secular forms of politics or culture were labelled as springing

---

[60] Pseudonymous, *Ulster on Its Own* (Belfast, 1912), p. 3.

[61] Unificus, 'The Quest for an Irish Settlement', p. 258.

[62] Winder Good, *Ulster and Ireland*, p. 221.

[63] For a nationalist perspective see, for example, T. M. Healy, *The Great Fraud of Ulster* (Dublin, 1917). For unionist, see R. Colles, *A History of Ulster* (London, 1919).

from one community or another. In the new context of modern Ireland, such simple labels were a world away from the diversity of the past from which they drew their foundation myths.

There is little doubt that running in parallel with the debate over devolution, Irish people became more mindful of religious difference. As partition approached, expressions of this contrast grew in crudity. Carson characterised the 'Irish question as a war against Protestantism; it is an attempt to create a Roman Catholic ascendancy in Ireland.'[64] Organised sectarian rioting, long a feature of Belfast political life, grew markedly in intensity from the 1880s and was linked strongly with times of well-defined political crises. Similarly, sectarian groups became more organised and appealing to many. Both the Orange Order and the Ancient Order of Hibernians (AOH) saw a significant rise in numbers, the latter growing from 5,000 in 1900 to almost 65,000 by 1909.[65] Strongest in Ulster, where they butted up against equally stringent Protestant organisations, the Hibernians were nakedly sectarian in terms of their goals, rituals and membership. William O'Brien derided the organisation as 'Catholic Orangeism in green paint'.[66] Restricted to practising Catholics, its avowed aim was to 'defend the Catholic national interest' which was achieved through mass political mobilisation during election campaigns in support of Home Rule candidates, and fraternal celebrations organised through church parishes in which the local priest played a prominent, if largely honorary, role.

Orangeism and Gaelicism, and the many assumptions they entailed, were anchored firmly on Protestantism and Catholicism, respectively. Resistance and aspiration to Home Rule had fostered these more crude and homogeneous senses of identity. The power of print and mass communications gave birth to a whole range of polemicists who were only too keen to highlight the incompatibility of 'the two tribes' and dissecting their distinctive characteristics in a crude framework of racial profiling. Independence became not only a matter of practical state building, but 'a biological, racial and spiritual necessity'.[67] One of the most infamous nationalist polemicists, D. P. Moran, crudely concluded: 'Ireland is de facto a Catholic nation.'[68] Douglas Hyde, the founder of the language movement the Gaelic League and future first president of Ireland, fleshed out this growing Gaelic racialism, tinged with Catholic imagery, in 1906:

---

[64] Quoted in A. T. Q. Stewart, *The Ulster Crisis* (Belfast, 1997), p. 43.

[65] T. Garvin, *The Evolution of Irish Nationalist Politics* (Dublin, 2005), p. 108.

[66] W. O'Brien, *The Irish Revolution and How It Came About* (London, 1923), pp. 31–2.

[67] Russell, *The Inner and Outer Ireland*, p. 11.

[68] P. Delaney, 'D.P. Moran and The Leader: Writing an Irish Ireland through Partition', *Eire-Ireland*, vol. 38, no. 3 (Fall/Winter 2003), p. 194.

A pious race is the Gaelic race. The Irish Gael is pious by nature. He sees the hand of God in every place, in every time, and in everything. There is not an Irishman in a hundred in whom is the making of an unbeliever. The spirit and the things of the spirit affect him more powerfully than the body and the things of the body. In the things he does not see, he does not believe the less for not seeing them: and in the things he sees, he will see more than a man of any other race; what is invisible for other people is visible for him.[69]

As partition approached, Irish people were thus grounded in a culture of communal religious division. By taking part in a Gaelic football match or wearing a sash it allowed for a new mass sense of identity to be crudely communicated. The process by which these identities shifted from forms of patriotic expression to real earthly territories was a long and complex journey. The fact that the hundreds of Irelands of the past became distilled down to two simplistic identities with their own distinct 'traditions' in two states was the greatest and most divisive element of partition. Few would have believed these simple identities would have led to long years of bloodshed and a partition unthinkable only a decade before.

In terms of the practical outcome of the election result of 1918, it was obvious that any future Irish settlement would have to accept the inevitability of Ulster exclusion. The election had hardened the ideological battle lines presenting Irish people with a stark black and white choice. Carson said bluntly of the 1918 election result:

[It has] cleared the air. The issue is between an independent republic or government under the parliament of the United Kingdom. Every other alternative has proved to be a sham.[70]

Trying to restart the old British state anew was an impossible idea. An *Irish Times* columnist complained that radical voices on both sides were so shrill and all-pervasive that 'rational thinkers' were 'being squeezed out of Ireland'.[71] Indeed, there was little room for optimism about the future as both Ulster unionists and Sinn Féin engaged in ever more hyperbolic proclamations about an apocalyptic future. Political choices had now become equivalent to final ultimatums. Sinn Féin saw the choice as deciding if Ireland will 'march out into the full sunlight of freedom or is to remain in the shadow of a base imperialism that has brought and ever will bring in its train naught but evil for our race'.[72] Such pessimistic views did much to undermine the potential for preserving Irish unity. One bewildered Home Rule MP who had lost his seat in 1918 reflected sadly that in all parts of Ireland many groups and individuals were profiting

---

[69] D. Hyde, *The Religious Songs of Connacht* (Dublin, 1906), p. 4.
[70] *The Times*, 29 December 1918.   [71] *Irish Times*, 17 January 1919.
[72] Macardle, 'The Manifesto of Sinn Féin'.

personally and politically from attaching themselves to 'the latest radical fashion' and jumping on 'the bandwagons of speculation'.[73]

The atmosphere was one of impending and unstoppable change. Ireland appeared to be at the end of an era. By the end of the war, Ireland was facing and, to a large extent, experiencing revolutionary change of some kind. The election campaign and subsequent result raised expectations sky-high and politicians now had to deliver on the utopian promises they had made during the campaign. That the British were leaving was now inevitable. The huge number of contradictory and divisive expectations of what Ireland would become when that happened, meant that the final nature of the settlement was anybody's guess.

[73] *Freeman's Journal*, 4 January 1919.

3   Answering the Question

It is a little over century since Thomas Agar-Robartes, the Liberal MP for St Austell, stood up in the House of Commons and called for Ireland to be partitioned. His amendment proposed the exclusion of what Stephen Gwynn referred to as 'the four *really* Protestant counties' of Ireland – Antrim, Down, Armagh and Londonderry – from the operation of the Third Home Rule bill.[1] Agar-Robartes couched his arguments in the basic incompatibility of the two sides: 'I think this Bill makes the mistake of treating Ireland not as two nations, but as one nation.'[2]

For Agar-Robartes, the problem with the Irish question wasn't so much the question, that of devolved government, but rather Ireland itself. As such, his novel solution was that Ireland should be dispensed with and replaced by two new entities which better reflected 'self-evident realities'. This chimera that Ireland had at its heart an 'innate', 'natural' division, and that partition was both legitimate and instinctive, underlay the rationale of the partition project. However, none of this was true. There were many potential Irelands in 1914 and the island contained as many nations as could be safely imagined by populations and their policy-makers. It was above all else a combination of circumstance and political expediency that would make this idea of natural division a self-fulfilling prophecy.

The reaction to the amendment demonstrated just how compromised political principles had become amid the hyperbole of the Ulster Crisis. Some reacted to the idea with derision. Augustine Birrell, the chief secretary for Ireland, described the sentiment it was founded on as a 'delusion', before going on to spell out in detail the strong economic links that existed between Ulster and the rest of Ireland.[3] While many unionists, including Bonar Law himself, would vote for the idea, this was only as part of their broader strategy of using the issue of Ulster to bring

---

[1] S. Gwynn, 'Ireland, One and Divisible', *Foreign Affairs*, vol. 3, no. 2 (15 December 1924), pp. 183–98.
[2] Hansard, HC vol 39, cols 744–824 (11 June 1912).   [3] Ibid.

down the entire Home Rule bill. William Hayes-Fisher, the Conservative MP for Fulham, admitted bluntly that passing the amendment would,

do the very best thing to protect the Protestants in Ireland, because it would absolutely shatter any hope of the passage of this Bill. From any point of view you look at the matter, it must have that effect. Financially the whole Bill will have to be recast if the Amendment is carried. The Prime Minister says we ought not to vote for this Amendment. Yes, we shall vote for it. We want to kill the Bill, and we shall kill it most effectually by voting for this Amendment.[4]

Indeed Asquith himself had made the most principled stand against the idea of partition:

This [Agar-Robartes] Amendment proceeds on an assumption which I believe is radically false, namely, that you can split Ireland into parts. You can no more split Ireland into parts than you can split England or Scotland into parts. Without in any way disparaging or expressing anything in the nature of disrespect for the demonstration in Ulster, I say that you have in Ireland a greater fundamental unity of race, temperament, and, although I agree that unhappily dissensions have been rank, partially by religion, and partially, as the right hon. Gentleman said, by the organisation of partisanship. These dissensions have spread, and have had a most noxious influence, both on the social and on the religious life of Ireland; but they are dissensions I believe which do not go down to the foundation of the national life. The more Irishmen are encouraged and empowered to cooperate in the great works of governing their own country, the more convinced am I that these differences will disappear. It will not be by the waving of a magician's wand, but they will be reconciled, and in the course of time completely disappear in that common sense of fundamental and overpowering unity which I believe to be the centre of Irish nationality.[5]

In the end, the amendment was easily defeated by sixty-one votes, although notably both Lloyd George and Winston Churchill, both cabinet ministers, abstained in the vote. Agar-Robartes himself was dead barely two years later, killed on the western front trying to rescue wounded soldiers near Mons. However, his 'fleeting notion' lay at the root of the partition plan which would see two new states arise from the terminal crisis of British Ireland.

*

The generally negative reaction that Agar-Robartes proposal received highlights that there was nothing inevitable about the partition of Ireland. Partition was, and remained oddly throughout the process, a solution that satisfied no one and one that found very few committed advocates. Partition could not, and would not, have happened outside of

---

[4] Ibid.   [5] Hansard, HC vol 39, cols 744–824 (11 June 1912).

the thin sliver of time during the decade which spanned the First World War. The three political groupings who would negotiate partition, Sinn Féin, the Ulster unionists and the British coalition government, all represented in one form or another radical revolutionary projects fired by notions of militarism and a desire for national unity. The two states which accidentally emerged in 1921 remained deeply artificial and compromised. The coalition of Irish nationalists who came together in the wake of the Easter Rising would prove very fragile, lasting barely five years and breaking apart under their first serious test in bitter civil war. Belfast prosperity itself proved to be transitory and declined soon after the new border was put in place. In this sense, partition can be viewed as largely a historical accident, pushed forwards by a weary political establishment desperate to escape the political implosion of the country. Indeed, that it was partition which emerged as the answer to the Irish question was perhaps the most peculiar thing of all. There were many Irish questions in the decade prior to partition – moral, imperial, administrative, economic, religious – and for many different groups how they viewed the question would define their attitude to the eventual partition settlement.

Just why the issue of Irish Home Rule was to prove such a vexed and bitterly resisted policy in 1914 has much to do with the prominent role the Irish question had assumed in British imperial politics by the eve of the First World War. While the willingness of leading political elites on the right of British politics to tread dangerously close to fermenting civil war may be seen largely as reflecting a short-term electoral crisis for the Conservative Party in the Edwardian era, in the longer-term the Irish question had always been viewed in a broader imperial context ever since its first appearance in the 1880s.

Underlying resistance was the profound fear that Irish Home Rule would be the thin end of a devolutionary wedge. If passed, it would set a precedent allowing for creeping and eventually systematic encroachment of home rule throughout the empire. This principle established, such a move would fatally weaken Britain's position as a global power. By 1914, Russia, France, Germany, Italy, Japan and the USA had all emerged as competing imperial powers. Between 1880 and 1914, one quarter of the world's land surface changed hands in this global scramble for colonies, meaning by the time of the Ulster Crisis there was very little land remaining out of the clutches of these global imperial powers. As land disappeared, retrenchment and imperial competition became the order of the day with most of the European imperial powers moving away from free trade in favour of protectionism. Furthermore, events such as the discovery of gold and diamonds in Southern Africa showed how emerging industrial technologies could make previously unproductive imperial possessions vital economic resources on the global geopolitical stage and led to a desire to hold on to territories, even those which were deeply troublesome such as Ireland and the previous self-governing Boer republics which had been seized by Britain in the costly Boer War of 1899–1902, lest they fall into the hands of an imperial competitor. Long gone were the days when Britain had the advantage of being the world's sole industrialised nation. While certainly true that Britain did not face the daunting challenge of expanding their empire like other European powers, the Irish crisis re-emerged at a time when Britain was seeking to consolidate and develop the existing empire on a more sustainable footing.

Thus, the issue of Ireland was far more than a parochial squabble, its fate was of global significance. Without careful handling, Ireland could act as a magnet for other disaffected peoples in the empire. While the British Empire was viewed as the most advanced economically and most liberal politically, the Irish question highlighted the profound ambiguities which lay at its heart. In particular, the fate of Ireland struck a deep resonance among other subject peoples in the so-called white dominions whose loyalty largely rested on this shared pretension of partnership and partially clothed imperialism.

Such sensitivity had long been reflected in British policy towards Ireland which was characterised by a shrewd use of authoritarianism and conciliation. The British never relied solely on repression, but rather compromised and mollified nationalist opposition, restructuring local government and placing it in the hands of the new Catholic elites; conciliating the Catholic Church and most importantly transferring land from the old Anglo-Irish elites to a class of prosperous tenant farmers which it hoped would prove to be the backbone of native support for the union. Partition would thus be largely an improvised reaction to a series of short-term challenges for which the old answers no longer seemed even relevant.

Despite these efforts, however, there remained widespread calls for Irish autonomy on both sides of the Irish Sea. Liberals saw Home Rule as a way of taking the sting out of nationalist demands for full independence and strengthening, rather than weakening, Ireland's ties with Britain. However, Conservatives saw a Dublin parliament as less the beginnings of a new partnership, but rather a bridgehead for a newly emboldened Catholic nationalist elite who, driven by deep historical and cultural resentments about British control, as opposed to pragmatic economic grievance, would use their political power and patronage to further their real unstated aim of complete separation.

The partition idea would therefore be the manifestation of a big loosely formulated anxiety which had lain beneath the surface of British politics for generations. As derided as the idea was in 1912, five years later it had become the centrepiece of British policy and swept all other solutions from the board. There was little room for principles in such calculations. From the start it was driven by hard-headed pragmatism and short-term expediency. Indeed, throughout the convoluted legislative journey to partition, few asked why and on what criterion Ireland was to be partitioned. By comparison with his predecessor Asquith, the new British prime minister David Lloyd George argued that the partition plan reflected some form of natural political and cultural divide. Speaking in the House of Commons, six years after Asquith had rejected partition as in anyway a natural solution, he said plainly:

In the North-East of Ireland we have a population – a fairly solid population, a homogeneous population – alien in race, alien in sympathy, alien in religion, alien in tradition, alien in outlook from the rest of the population of Ireland, and it would be an outrage on the principle of self-government to place them under the rule of the remainder of the population.[6]

Partition was almost wholly without precedent and there were virtually no models to follow. Certainly, prior to 1914, the notion of dividing Ireland barely featured in the debates over a possible solution to the Irish question. If mentioned at all it was used by critics mainly in order to point out the absurdity of Repeal or Home Rule. For example, in the face of Daniel O'Connell's repeal movement in the 1830s, Thomas Macaulay argued in a parliamentary committee meeting, that,

in blood, religion, language, habits, character, the population of some of the northern counties of Ireland has much more in common with the population of England and Scotland than with the population of Munster and Connaught. I defy the honourable and learned Member, therefore, to find a reason for having a parliament at Dublin which will not be just as good a reason for having another parliament at Londonderry.[7]

It was the introduction of the First Home Rule bill which brought the issue of Ulster into sharper focus. On the fringes of the debate discussion began to focus on the possibility of omitting Ulster, or at least parts of it, from the legislation. In response to the 1886 bill, a faction of the Liberal Party led by Lord Hartington broke with Gladstone over his support for the creation of a Dublin government. Styling themselves as 'Liberal unionists' the group opposed any moves to weaken the power of the Westminster parliament, seeing the granting of home rule to Ireland as the first step in the break-up of the empire. While the Liberal unionists

---

[6] Hansard, HC vol 123, cols 1168–233 (22 December 1919).
[7] *The Times*, 19 February 1832.

represented a broad range of opinion, it was Joseph Chamberlain, the president of the board of trade, who would be the first senior political figure to promote, if not partition, a two-nation view of Ireland.

it is the difficulty, one of the great difficulties of this problem that Ireland is not a homogeneous community – that it consists of two nations ... that it is a nation which comprises two races and two religions.[8]

While most of his colleagues settled into outright opposition, Chamberlain arrived at his own unique answer to the Irish question. He argued that the only way to both answer Irish aspirations to devolved power while also maintaining the integrity of the union was for the adoption of a federal constitution with the creation of a number of devolved assemblies in the four 'nations' of the UK all answerable to a central parliament at Westminster. Although Chamberlain backed a vague model which aped that of the US Congress, it was evident right from the start that the federal idea involved the creation not of partner parliaments, but rigidly limited local entities wholly subordinate to Westminster.

In the end, Chamberlain's compromise solution failed to garner enough support from his political colleagues, especially after the defeat of the bill in June 1886. However, his commitment to some form of federalist solution to the Irish question led him to appeal directly to the constituencies within the nations of the union. After touring both Scotland and Wales he made his way to Ulster in October 1887 where the threat of Home Rule had led to intense periods of sectarian rioting, leaving thirty-two dead. In a major, and much reported, speech at the Ulster Hall, Chamberlain planted the partitionist seed with a rudimentary populist appeal tinged with crude racial references. He began with a rhetorical question: 'How is it that Belfast continues to increase while Cork and Waterford decline?' His answer was that the Protestant settlers of the north 'made up almost all the cultivated intelligence of Ireland and ... the greatest part of its enterprise and a large part of its wealth'. In his view, there were two distinct races in Ireland, one possessing all of the 'qualities of a dominant people', while the 'southern race' had 'always failed in the qualities which compel success'.[9]

It is easy to overstate the importance of these early primitive partitionist initiatives and Chamberlain's flirtation with the Irish issue had as much to do with fostering his own personal popularity than setting out a considered programme for the better government of Ireland. Certainly, most commentators outside of Ulster itself ridiculed the idea of regional

---

[8] Chamberlain, 9 April 1886, Hansard, Parl. Deb., series 3, vol. 304, col. 1200.
[9] T. Crosby, *Joseph Chamberlain: A Most Radical Imperialist* (London, 2018), p. 74.

devolved government. The press mocked the potential Ulster domain as the 'Orange Free State', while Lord Randolph Churchill, despite his virulent leadership of the unionist cause, saw the notion of 'Ulsteria' as 'not so much an argument as a disease'.[10] The defeat of Home Rule in both 1886 and 1893 meant there was little need to create alternative schemes for Irish self-government which would meet the aspirations of the majority of the population, north and south. As such, they never developed much beyond the hyperbole of populist tribalism, with any serious consideration of the idea largely delivered as a political tactic in order to parody opponents. Far more time was spent on the financial implications of the Home Rule bills or the threat to the empire than on political initiatives which reflected the complexities of Irish identity. What had become abundantly clear was that approaches to the issue of Ireland shed far more light on the nature of political manoeuvring in London than the reality of the situation in Ireland itself. The lack of commitment to these nebulous partition plans was demonstrated markedly when the idea was quickly sidelined once its tactical usefulness in the power struggles at Westminster was exhausted. It was also clear that Irish unionists were not as yet prepared to give up the ghost and retreat to their Ulster heartlands.

Despite the retreat of the issue of Irish Home Rule into the shadows of British politics after 1893, the brief debate over Ulster's distinctiveness would play an important role in shaping the parameters of the later partition settlement. Broadly speaking, three distinctive conclusions were drawn. The first was the enduring appeal of a crass racial reading of Irish identity and a consistent appeal to popular Orangism and sectarian superiority by leading British and Irish politicians. Second was the more intellectual, although equally crude, assumption that Ireland could be characterised as two nations, made-up of two distinct ethno-religious populations with different cultural traits and two incompatible historical trajectories. This idea would be exploited cynically and dangerously by many unionist politicians during the partition period itself as a way of derailing the Home Rule project. As one senior unionist politician in west Ulster stated in early 1920:

The danger for us lies in any admission that Ireland is a Nation, and as long as we can keep even a couple of counties out, there would be hope of restoring the Union.[11]

---

[10] R. F. Foster, *Lord Randolph Churchill: A Political Life* (Oxford, 1988), p. 134.
[11] Hugh de Fellenberg Montgomery, Fivemiletown, Co. Tyrone, to John E. Walsh, Hon. Sec. of the Irish Unionist Alliance, Fellenberg Papers, 12 January 1920, PRONI, D627/438/8.

The first substantive appearance of the two nations theory can be traced to 1896 with the publication of the unionist newspaper editor and publisher Thomas MacKnight's *Ulster as It Is*, which proclaimed the existence of 'two antagonistic populations, two different nations on Irish soil' which made 'common citizenship between the two sections of Irish people impossible'.[12] While nationalists objected fiercely to the two-nations theory, it would lodge itself strongly in the minds of many Conservative unionists. Reiterated in 1913 in William Moneypenny's *The Two Irish Nations*, it had a strong influence on later Tory leader Andrew Bonar Law and would play a key role in the later desperate search for a solution to the Irish question both during and after the Ulster Crisis. There was little discussion of the glaringly large political and religious minorities who resided in these two apparently homogeneous nations. As one Southern Protestant journalist deftly argued:

> The two-nation theory goes to pieces on the question, "What is a South of Ireland Protestant?" He is certainly not an Ulster man, though he has much in common with Ulster. Equally certainly he does not belong to the majority of the population of the South, though he has much in common with them also. The Southern Protestant is, in fact, the link between the two larger sections of the community. It may perhaps be the task of our Church and her members-the grandest task of all-to be the bond which will bring all together into a truly united Ireland.[13]

Similarly, nationalist journalist James Winder Good found the idea barely matched the reality of Ireland's intermingled demographics:

> The "two nations" theory is merely a revival of the old fallacy of the opposition of Celt and Saxon, which bears no relation to the facts of the Irish situation. During the fight on the Home Rule Bill I had the curiosity to compile a list of the speakers who used this argument on Ulster platforms. The names themselves are the best refutation of the doctrines their bearers preached, for they included Maguires, Murphys, Quinns, MacNeills, Moriartys, McDoneelees and O'Neills. Deplorable as "the blind hysterics of the Celt" may be, the denunciations of the race sound as oddly on the lips of these "Macs" and "O"'s as would attacks on Germanism by Hindenburgs and Tripitzes.[14]

The third conclusion was political and stemmed largely from Joseph Chamberlain's flirtation with the idea of federalism as a way out of the morass of Anglo-Irish relations. The Home Rule debates of the 1880s had certainly raised some fundamental questions about the nature of the British constitution and it was Chamberlain's own son, Austen, who would go on to expand the federal idea into, not only a solution of the Irish question, but a visionary way of running the entire empire itself.

---

[12] T. MacKnight, *Ulster as It Is*, vol. 2 (London, 1896), p. 379.
[13] Unificus, 'The Quest for an Irish Settlement', p. 252.
[14] J. Winder Good, *Ireland and Unionism* (Dublin, 1920), p. 238.

Federalism, characterised as 'Home Rule all round', was an extremely important aspect of the debate surrounding the solution to the Irish question. Isaac Butt, the first leader of the Irish Party at Westminster, Liberal prime minister Lord Russell and even Benjamin Disraeli had all shown support for the idea. It is also often forgotten, for example, that the first draft of the Third Home Rule bill envisaged the creation of a parliament, not only in Ireland, but also in England, Scotland and Wales. During the bill's second reading, there were twelve 'federal amendments' tabled by both Liberals and Unionists, suggesting all kinds of weird and wonderful constitutional schemes. While such ideas were quietly shelved, Asquith was still enough enamoured with the idea of a final constitutional settlement that in his speech to the Commons he could confidently laud the bill as 'the first step, and only the first step in a larger and more comprehensive policy'.[15]

The federal idea was in many ways a visionary view of the future of the UK and one which at a stroke offered the chance to bring both Irish unionists and nationalists together in its support. For nationalists it offered an immediate devolved parliament and with its equitable nature addressed the key stumbling blocks as to how Ireland was to be represented at Westminster and the extent of its financial powers in the form of taxation. Most importantly, however, federalism was seen as a way of reassuring unionists by smothering separatist tendencies within Irish nationalism. As one Liberal MP wrote in April 1914 'if "Home Rule all round" were accepted, Ulster could not complain that she was cut off from her sister parliaments'.[16] If anything, the federal idea bound Ireland even closer to the Britain and gave it equality with every other part of the UK. As one of its chief advocates noted, any attempt at separatism would be stopped as 'the majority of subordinate parliaments will be able to exercise restraint on the recalcitrant parliament that would cut itself adrift or otherwise misbehave'.[17] For unionists, thus, they would no longer be in a minority, but constitutionally backed by the other three parliaments.

On paper, the federal idea seemed to offer a realistic solution to the Irish question, with the previously unthinkable possibility of Irish nationalists and unionists forging an alliance in arguing for its implementation. In April 1914 *The Times* could report that in the Commons 'upwards of one hundred Liberals, and a smaller number of Unionists' were prepared to vote for the idea.[18] Even as late as 1919, Carson was able to say 'I do

---

[15] Hansard, HC, vol 36, cols 1399–1426 (11 April 2012).   [16] *The Times*, 4 April 1914.
[17] Halford MackInder, Hansard, HC, series 5, vol. 116, col. 1930 (3 June 1919).
[18] *The Times*, 6 May 1914.

not believe that devolution is a step towards separation. Indeed, I am not sure that devolution, if properly carried out, may not lead to closer union.'[19]

However, to many in the world of practical politics, such ideas were treated with ridicule and alarm. The speaker of the House of Commons in 1920, Viscount Ullswater, mused a few years later:

The more I considered the proposal of one supreme and four independent legislatures, the less I liked it. The confusions which might arise, the multiplicity of elections, the novelty of five (possible even more) Prime Ministers and Cabinets of probably divergent political views, the enormous expense of building four new sets of Parliamentary buildings and Government offices and providing all the paraphernalia of administration, frightened my economical soul.[20]

There is little doubt that such initiatives failed due to the existence of a powerful strain of conservatism among political elites when it came to altering the British constitution. William Harcourt, the Liberal chancellor of the exchequer, typified this sense of inertia when he stated that although federalism was an 'ideal', it depended too much on 'independent bodies previously existing to be federated'.[21] Others scoffed that the only previously existing bodies for the English regions were the Anglo-Saxon kingdoms of the Dark Ages and that Chamberlain should use the twelfth-century *Historia Anglorum* as his manifesto. As one Conservative backbench MP stated, federal devolution would lead to the inevitable destruction of the British constitution meaning,

the United Kingdom would be involved in a maze of four parliaments, three local and one imperial. But the process of disintegration could not stop there. A local parliament for Scotland would necessarily lead to a local parliament for Wales also. As long as England, Scotland and Wales were content with the existing constitution, Ireland would not be justified in breaking it into pieces for its own purposes.[22]

Perhaps most damaging was the fact that in the other 'nations' of Britain there was little eagerness for devolved government. Leading figures in both Scotland and Wales expressed fears that the economic effects of such moves would prove disastrous. In England, perhaps most fundamentally, there was virtually no appetite for a devolved government and the idea was treated largely with derision. Lord Longford made sarcastic and very public comments, suggesting that the counties of Kent, Surrey, Sussex and Hampshire should secede from the UK and set-up their own parliament at

[19] Sir Edward Carson, Hansard, HC, series 5, vol. 116, col. 1898 (3 June 1919).
[20] Bogdanor, *Devolution in the United Kingdom*, p. 48.   [21] *The Times*, 14 April 1886.
[22] P. J. Smyth, Hansard, HC vol 230, cols 738–822 (30 June 1876).

Winchester.[23] Certainly, the English were being asked to adopt the idea of an English parliament, not through any positive desire for better government, but largely as a way of allowing the Irish to realise their own national aspirations.

Even then, Irish nationalists themselves showed little interest in the idea. After all, the Irish demand was not for federal devolution, but rather for a form of national self-government. The only way for such a solution to be equitable, of course, would be for England itself to be divided into smaller regions equivalent to the other national parliaments. However, aside from there being no demand for such regional parliaments in England, it would reduce that of Ireland to a similar provincial status, even further away from the ideals of national self-determination for which Home Rule itself was already a compromise. Indeed, many of their demands were contrary to the spirit of cooperation inherent in a federal partnership. When Parnell stated during the debates over the First Home Rule bill that the creation of an Irish custom house was more important than the creation of an Irish parliament, he was implicitly threatening the introduction of tariffs on goods from the other parts of the UK. Indeed, the federal idea relied on all parties having a strong commitment to the union as much as that of self-government. As one commentator perceptively noted,

A federal Government is, of all constitutions, the most artificial. If such a government is to be worked with anything like success, there must exist among the citizens of the confederacy a spirit of genuine loyalty to the Union. The 'Unitarian' feeling of the people must distinctly predominate over the sentiment in favour of 'state rights'.[24]

Ironically, while federalism was designed to assuage Irish grievances, if anything, such a solution demanded even more loyalty than the existing centralised system such as that operating from Westminster. There was little expectation that the Irish had any intention of working constructively within a federal arrangement, even if they had accepted the idea as a stepping stone to eventual full Home Rule. The federal parliament at Westminster would have been as dominated by English interests as the current parliament and many feared that the English parliament, also to sit in London, would be a serious rival to the new federal body. Furthermore, Irish MPs would have even more power to disrupt the new assembly, as they had done so assiduously during the nineteenth century. They could easily bring the whole system to a halt. As Albert Dicey, the Oxford academic and authority on constitutional law, observed in 1913, 'A sick

---

[23] *The Times*, 15 December 1885.
[24] Quoted in Bogdanor, *Devolution in the United Kingdom*, p. 47.

man fears to lose a limb; he will not be greatly consoled by the assurance that his arm may be retained at the risk of his suffering a general paralysis.'[25]

Federalism, therefore, was demanded by no one, especially those who it was designed to placate. For Irish nationalists, of course, such debates over the merits of federalism and the future of the empire were little more than further blocking tactics, attempts to confound Irish Home Rule by placing it at the centre of an implausible spider's web of impractical reforms and fundamental rethinks of Britain's place in the world. Irish nationalists demanded a solution which, in the words of one Conservative peer, was 'fundamentally inconsistent with federalism'.[26] This was particularly the case when Chamberlain's ideal of a federal UK were expanded to include the empire itself. The idea of 'Imperial Federation', the brainchild of Lord Milner's influential Round Table movement, would linger around during the decades of debate over Irish Home Rule. Imperial Federation aimed to bind the empire together by devolving power to the colonies and creating a federal super-state ran by the imperial parliament at Westminster. This, it was hoped would, in the words of one of its keenest advocates, 'ensure the continuance of the colonies [in the Empire] for all time'.[27] Although immensely popular in the colonies, much like the debate over devolution within the UK, there was little desire to destroy the current constitution and abandon free trade orthodoxies and, as with the UK, there were so many heterogeneous demands in the empire that any scheme would have almost certainly collapsed. Most significantly, the experience of the distant white dominions bore little resemblance to that of nearby Ireland. While the creation of devolved parliaments in Australia, Canada, South Africa and New Zealand had not led to the much feared slide into separatism, these states were not, and never had been, directly represented at Westminster, and their distance meant that the extent of their independence did not pose a potential strategic threat to Britain in time of war. Due to these political and strategic concerns, the British government could not offer Ireland the same flexibility, and it would prove almost impossible to square Irish demands for self-determination with the need to keep Ireland as closely tied to the UK as possible. This problem was no better demonstrated with the issue of taxation. Giving Ireland full autonomy to set its own taxes and duties was rejected, as its granting would equal virtual full independence. However, continued taxation also implied that Irish representatives had

[25] Ibid, p. 53.   [26] Henry Cecil, *The Times*, 4 April 1919.
[27] Sir Alexander Galt, High Commissioner for Canada, *The Manchester Guardian*, 27 January 1883.

to retain their seats at Westminster, otherwise the British would face the same incendiary protests that it had with the American colonies of taxation without representation. But in what sense would this fit with substantive devolution and how would it be reasonable for Irish members to continue to vote on issues which affected England, Wales and Scotland when they themselves had their own parliamentary firewall back in Dublin? If, as Gladstone appears to have favoured, the option was taken of only allowing Irish MPs to vote on issues directly relevant to them, thence surely their representation, despite their tax contribution, was, at best, substandard and, at worst, subordinate. The problem boiled down to the seemingly unsolvable question of how Westminster could remain the superior parliament, while at the same time meaningfully satisfying Irish national aspirations.

While many criticisms of federalism were uncharitable misrepresentations of what were substantive and visionary trends within Liberal imperialism, there was little doubt that by the time of the Ulster Crisis these debates were being utilised largely in caricature to oppose Home Rule. Certainly, by 1919 when the Conference on Devolution was held, there was little time to develop such elaborate ideas and an ever-dwindling audience in Ireland prepared to countenance them. Its report published on 12 May 1920 was an irrelevance, a paper exercise for indulged constitutionalists, involving the creation of 'Grand Councils' in England, Scotland and Wales and a series of parliamentary sittings of bewildering complexity. The speaker estimated that, if adopted immediately, he still envisaged a 'transitional period' of eight years before it could come into operation. By the time the report was released, Lloyd George had decided to settle the Irish question himself and the Government of Ireland bill was already making its way through the Commons.[28]

Thus, the Ulster problem remained a particularly Irish one. Attempts to place it in a UK context, let alone an imperial one, had failed due to the incompatibility of the partners who were to be involved. One Irish journalist sardonically observed how quickly the imperial ramifications of the Irish settlement, so long a prominent part of anti-Home Rule propaganda, was set aside as soon as the idea of partition started to gain ground:

What exactly this "Imperial necessity" was no one ever explained, though it was understood to have some connexion with international relations with the United States of America. The phrase was always uttered darkly with bated breath, as something not to be inquired into but to be obeyed. One cannot help wondering what has happened to the Imperial necessity . . . At times one is tempted to wonder

---

[28] For the report of the Conference on Devolution see *The Times*, 13 May 1920.

whether it had any tangible existence apart from its use as a weapon to compel agreement.[29]

It was, however, an important debate, as it was from the federal idea that some sense of accommodating Ulster grievances within the UK would emerge, feeding directly into the debates which would lead to partition. In the midst of the debate over the Third Home Rule bill in 1912, T. A. Brassey advised Bonar Law that a federal solution would allow them to 'give North East Ulster a little show of its own if it really desires it'.[30] Even Carson saw that an acceptance of at least some of the principles of federalism could give Ulster its chance to assert its own unique political character, 'as the tendency to federalism was to minute subdivisions, might not Ulster very fairly propose to separate itself from the Roman Catholic provinces of Ireland and establish a parliament of its own?'[31] Indeed, along with devolving power to England, Scotland and Wales, the federal idea had consistently foresaw the division of Ireland between two native assemblies, one for Ulster based in Belfast and one for the other three Southern provinces of Munster, Leinster and Connacht in Dublin.

There is little doubt that all parties sought to avoid partition. The attempts to find some kind of workable solution were bewildering and seemingly never ending. Despite the defeat of Agar-Robartes proposal in 1912, the idea led to a flourishing of all kinds of solutions to the Irish problem. The most lasting idea was that of some form of Ulster 'exclusion' from the Home Rule Act. Various attempts were made to spell out exactly what form this exclusion would take. John Redmond put forward the idea of a plebiscite by county, leading to a temporary period of exclusion, at first three years and then rising to six. Some sought a way to maintain Irish unity by including all manner of safeguards for the province within the Home Rule parliament. Horace Plunkett played for time with the suggestion of a ten-year trial period for Home Rule to see if the new arrangement would work, and, as discussed, many unionists took up the idea of the exclusion of Ulster largely as a way of bringing down the whole bill. In the end, nothing worked. Instead vague ideas of 'freedom', 'Ulster', 'Ireland' and 'Republic' remained the predominant currency, the word partition was virtually non-existent in debates of the time. One Dublin journalist noted that people in Ireland saw 'self-government as a sort of Aladdin's Lamp, capable of any miracle'.[32] Indeed, if no one

---

[29] Unificus, 'The Quest for an Irish Settlement', p. 253.

[30] John Kendle, *Ireland and the Federal Solution: The Debate over the United Kingdom Constitution, 1870–1920* (Montreal, 1989), p. 156.

[31] Carson quoted in T. F. Fraser, *Partition in Ireland, India and Palestine: Theory and Practice* (London, 1984), p. 34.

[32] Kettle, *The Open Secret of Ireland*, p. 147.

could see what exactly partition was, everyone could certainly see what they wanted it to be. Farmers envisioned the extension of their holdings and a life free of government interference; bureaucrats and politicians saw themselves ascending to the role of international power brokers; cultural activists looked forward to a state engineering authenticity into its populations; while the general populace saw it at the very least as giving them renewed prosperity and purpose. What is most peculiar about the partition solution, however, is how it would be made-up of a conglomeration of initiatives to solve the Irish question which had already been long rejected as unworkable. The attempt to bring together all the things that had shaped the Irish question over the past six years would make the eventual solution a rickety construct. Most importantly, the idea for the exclusion of Ulster and the retention of direct rule sat uneasily with Liberal sentiment, running contrary as it did to cherished ideas of self-determination, which after all had been what the debate had been all about in the first place.

The Government of Ireland Act

The political mechanism for partitioning Ireland was the Government of Ireland Act of 1920. This 'Partition Act' has been underplayed in terms of its significance for Ireland. The continuing obsession with the evolution and consequences of the 'treaty', and its repeated historical dramatisation, compares unfavourably with the lack of prominence given to the 1920 Government of Ireland Act which partitioned the island. While the first three Home Rule bills have retained a prominence in the flow of the narrative of Anglo-Irish relations, the forgotten Fourth Home Rule bill – the non-synoptic gospel of Irish history and the only one of the bills ever to be enacted – had no less dramatic impact than the treaty, leading arguably to more far reaching and fundamental consequences.

It was circumstance rather than principle that dictated the decision to partition Ireland. The British government would constantly bat aside attempts to make them spell out in more detail what exactly partition entailed. Michael Curran, the Catholic rector of the Irish College in Rome, ably summed up the peculiar journey the British government would take to the decision after Sinn Féin's election victory in December 1918:

The whole question of partition was for a long time very vague-partition or exclusion? It was vague, firstly, as to whether it was temporary or permanent. It was vague, secondly, as regards the area affected, whether it covered four, five, six or nine counties. It was further confused with the question of separate treatment for Ulster, that is, what was called "Home Rule within Home Rule." Lastly, the proposals were sometimes private and confidential, sometimes public and official or sometimes discussed with a particular Minister with or without the consent or even the knowledge of the Cabinet. Policy shifted according to circumstances, and according as the different parties believed they were winning.[33]

By the end of 1916, Asquith's attempt to run a total war while remaining faithful to traditional Liberal values had begun to unravel. Succumbing to critics on both sides of the House, he was soon replaced by the more energetic Lloyd George at the head of an unlikely coalition government dominated by Conservatives. While the primary focus of this new government was the more efficient conduct of the war, Lloyd George also saw the advantages in solving the Irish crisis once and for all. A new policy of conciliation was initiated with the release of most of the remaining internees from the Easter Rising, who returned home to a hero's welcome. The avowed separatism and growing resistance from the Sinn Féin movement made the need to find a solution of vital importance.

However, despite what many Irish nationalists may have believed, there were far more fundamental reasons why a hurried settlement was agreed by the British government. The most significant was the prominence of the notion of 'self-determination' which was painted as a way primarily of averting future European conflicts by meeting the national aspirations of various ethno-religious groups. The British government had been prominent in framing the Treaty of Versailles, placing the issue of Ulster's distinctiveness in sharper relief. Arthur Balfour, the Tory grandee and foreign secretary in Lloyd George's coalition government, admitted plainly: 'No one can think that Ulster ought to join the South and West who thinks that the Jugo Slavs should be separated from Austria. No one can think that Ulster should be divorced from Britain who believes in self determination.'[34] However, he was also later to admit that, rather than being a genuine attempt to create a new and inclusive Irish settlement, it was largely dictated by the need to appease opinion in the USA and the dominions:

The main thing we hope for from the Home Rule Act is-not that Ireland is going to be better governed but that we've made our Irish policy on all fours with our European policy of self-determination and which no American can say is unfair. It cuts away the argumentative case from the Canadian and Australian supporters of Home Rule ...[35]

The body which was to attempt to draw together the various strands of a comprehensive settlement was a specially created cabinet committee chaired by the old unionist leader Walter Long, currently first lord of the

[33] M. J. Curran, Bureau of Military History (BMH), NAI, WS 687.
[34] A. Balfour, 'The Irish Question', 25 November 1919, NA, CAB 24/93.
[35] Jones, Whitehall Diary, p. 65.

admiralty. The committee set out a number of key parameters to work within, all of which ruled out the idea of trying to impose a Home Rule settlement on Ireland without some form of special treatment for Ulster. As in 1914, the idea which concerned them the most was the notion of exclusion, whereby sections of the population, most probably ascertained with county plebiscites, could vote to remain outside the jurisdiction of the Dublin parliament. While this idea was by far the most familiar to anyone who had followed the tortuous debates during the Ulster Crisis, it was ultimately to be rejected. Perhaps surprisingly, this was largely due to fears that such a move would militate against any chance of eventual Irish unity and leave the British government open to charges of placing selfish colonial interests over those of good government, especially considering the most likely areas to opt out were also Ireland's wealthiest and most industrialised.

A second option was the old idea of 'Home Rule within Home Rule' where Ulster would be provided with constitutional safeguards, but still be ultimately controlled by a single Irish parliament based in Dublin. The over-representation of Ulster in the assembly was one method suggested, while another envisaged the creation of a council or upper house which had to have the backing of Ulster for it to proceed with legislation. However, such an idea was rejected for much the same reasons as the federal idea had been for the wider British Isles; namely that it would give Ulster a veto over Irish government decisions and would ultimately paralyse any attempt to make self-rule a progressive success.

In the end, the committee decided to take what they felt were the best elements of these two ideas and splice them together in their report. The notion that partition would only be a temporary solution was a prominent principle in their discussions. While there was much talk about the solution being aimed at fostering eventual unity, it was notable that the problem of achieving that unity was now thrown wholly onto Irish shoulders.

The Imperial Parliament can compel Irishmen to govern themselves by the simple expedient of withdrawing its own officials. But once it gives Ireland self-government it cannot compel Ireland to unite. Irish unity can then only come from unity in Ireland itself.[36]

It was with this aim in mind that the committee decided on the creation of two equitable parliaments in Ireland, both with identical powers and responsibilities. One was to be based in Dublin and represented the

[36] Report of the Cabinet Committee on the Irish Question, 4 November 1919, NA, CAB 24/92.

three majority Catholic provinces of Connaught, Munster and Leinster, while another situated in Belfast would have responsibility for the entire nine-county province of Ulster. The decision to not limit the territory of the new Belfast government was recommended as a way 'to minimise the division on religious grounds'[37] and, with a sizeable 47 per cent of the population of nationalist sympathies, would provide 'a natural tendency towards unity'[38] at some future unspecified date.

Certainly, the tone of the report was that partition was a wholly provisional arrangement with the focus throughout heavily weighted to the idea of 'eventual unity'. To this end, a mechanism to foster this unity was achieved by the inclusion of a new 'Council of Ireland' made up of twenty representatives from each of the two regional assemblies. Its remit was to handle issues of general Irish interest, such as transport and agriculture, with a straightforward mechanism, allowing for its assumption of more powers from the two parliaments which it was hoped would eventually be abolished in favour of a new united Irish assembly with the council as its surrogate. Many, especially in the Dublin press, saw unity as the natural and expected state of Ireland. One Dublin journalist looked forward to the inevitable harmony which would emerge between the two states at some future unspecified time:

It will be observed that we are getting on. A nation so busy with realities will have no time to waste on such vapours, and an Ireland, occupied in this fashion-with wealth-producing labour, will have no time for civil war or "religious" riots. With this virus removed, the natural balance of the facts of nature will spontaneously establish itself between the two countries.[39]

There were many less optimistic political voices, however, especially considering the declining security situation. When Churchill offered to the Commons a similarly optimistic outlook for Ireland in the years following the partition act, one Ulster unionist MP was heard to respond: 'We in Belfast will all be dead by then!' to which Churchill replied sardonically: 'Well that would greatly simplify our task.'[40]

In many ways it was an ingenious solution to the Irish question, certainly from a British point of view. In particular, it allowed the government to deflect accusations from the USA and the colonies that it was against the principle of self-determination when applied to its own territories. The committee was wary that no matter the extent of the territory involved, significant enough numbers of Irish nationalists would remain

[37] Ibid.
[38] Walter Long quoted in J. Kendle, *Walter Long, Ireland and the Union* (Montreal, 1992), p. 184.
[39] *Irish Times*, 7 December 1919.   [40] *The Guardian*, 9 February 1920.

under direct British rule against their will. Indeed, by applying these recommendations, the government could now argue, if it could keep a straight face, that the long-standing Irish demand for Home Rule had been met and every inhabitant of the island now had the right to elect members to an Irish parliament of some form. Furthermore, the fact that the Ulster parliament was made up of the full nine counties undercut accusations that Ireland was being divided purely with reference to sectarian geography.

As with so many pseudo-partitionist solutions, however, the beauty of its constitutional architecture did not reflect the disjointed aspirations of the more radical forms of nationalism and unionism which now held sway over Ireland's political culture. Once again, as one of the members of the committee was wont to point out, no one had asked Irish people themselves whether the idea appealed to them. Indeed, the idea, while a perfect riposte to those who accused Britain of double standards in its professed commitment to self-determination, apart from when it affected their own territories, 'strengthening of our tactical position before the world'[41] as Lord Birkenhead remarked, it was largely irrelevant to the confrontational condition of Ireland on the ground.

While to the inattentive observer of Irish affairs it may have appeared that the small Ulster Unionist Party had successfully outmanoeuvred both the British and Irish nationalist leadership, among Irish unionist MPs there was little sincere celebration in this achievement. Behind the smoke and mirrors, it was clear that Irish unionism had been severely compromised. For all their bluster and threats of revolt, Ulster unionists had never sought or expected to be forced to run a state of their own and tens of thousands of Irish Protestants faced life under a Home Rule parliament outside of the homogeneous communities in north-east Ulster. In the British cabinet, unionist disillusion was voiced by hardline Tories such as Balfour, who complained bitterly that the proposals forced 'the loyal and Protestant North into the same political mould as the disloyal and Roman Catholic South'.[42] Their focus, it was argued, was on merely a retention of the status quo. Unionists had not demanded or campaigned for a parliament of their own and, while they accepted that some form of defensive partition was now inevitable, they baulked at the potential imposition of devolution, which was being imposed merely to facilitate the smooth running of the Home Rule settlement they had done so much to oppose.

[41] Birkenhead quoted in N. Mansergh, *The Unresolved Question: The Anglo-Irish Settlement and Its Undoing, 1912–1972* (New Haven, CT, 1991), p.125.
[42] Balfour, 'The Irish Question'.

In the end, Ulster unionists would reluctantly accept the partition idea, although with little seeming comprehension of what such a decision would entail. They had remained satisfied largely with their over-riding achievement of 'saving Ulster'. However, while they had their own much rehearsed ideas of what they had saved it from, they had little seeming grasp of what exactly they had saved it for. When the Northern Irish parliament was officially opened in June 1921, the parade route along which dignitaries passed to attend its first meeting was festooned with banners which read, with unintended irony: 'We will not have Home Rule.' One journalist who attended that day, recalled, after noting the amusing incongruity, looking around at the crowds 'but no one else was laughing'.[43]

The British cabinet gathered in a series of meetings to discuss the proposals in November and early December. Due to the undeniable benefits the plan offered for disentangling Britain from the Irish morass, Conservative opposition failed to impede the transformation of the idea into an embryonic parliamentary bill. Instead, unionists began to focus on the nature of the new Ulster that was being propounded. James Craig's brother, Charles, while reluctantly conceding the principle of Ulster Home Rule, pointed out that a nine-county Ulster would be far too politically unstable an entity to function:

No sane man would undertake to carry on a Parliament with such a small majority. A couple of members sick, or two or three Members absent for some accidental reason, might in one evening hand over the entire Ulster parliament and the entire Ulster position . . .[44]

Picking up on abortive initiatives which had emerged during the Buckingham Palace Conference of July 1914, he argued that the area should be reduced in size to the six counties of Antrim, Down, Londonderry, Armagh, Fermanagh and Tyrone. Such a solution, he argued, would ensure stable government by reflecting the wishes of the majority population and, cleverly reflecting the provisional language of the report, could itself be left open to later amendment by means of an independent commission.

There were other voices from the political right which backed up this more limited plan for partition. Many argued, rather paradoxically considering their own resistance, that the inclusion of the three outer Ulster counties with their large Catholic majority was incompatible with the committee's overarching aim of promoting self-determination. The fact

---

[43] *Irish Independent*, 22 July 1921.
[44] P. Buckland, 'Carson, Craig and the Partition of Ireland, 1919–1921', in Peter Collins, ed., *Nationalism and Unionism: Conflict in Ireland, 1885–1921* (Belfast, 1994), p. 85.

that over 300,000 Catholics would be included in the more limited option was largely glossed over, as were the increasingly angry protests from border Protestants who had been very proactive in supporting the Ulster Covenant and strong in the membership of the UVF, believing their communities to be on the front line of any anticipated frontier conflict. Perhaps what swayed the cabinet most in amending the nine-county solution to six counties was their need, both politically and in the eyes of the world, to retain the faith and support of at least one Irish political grouping. While many Ulster unionists were deeply troubled, both by the idea of losing tens of thousands of Ulster Protestants to the South and also the requirement that they now must run their own native administration, others with more foresight saw the new parliament as a potential protection rather than a burden.

The Government of Ireland Act represented a messy attempt to create an overarching scheme within which Home Rule could flourish. The actual level of devolved government offered was very moderate, with the London government retaining control of military and foreign affairs along with customs, agriculture and internal security. Although Ireland would retain its representation in Westminster, the number of its MPs was reduced from over one hundred to forty-two. The act itself, introduced in December 1919 and taking over a year to pass through parliament, proposed the creation of two separate Home Rule parliaments, one based in Dublin and the other in Belfast. The two new states 'Northern Ireland' and 'Southern Ireland' would consist of six and twenty-six counties, respectively. Northern Ireland would be made up of the four majority Protestant counties of Armagh, Down, Antrim and Londonderry and also, most controversially, the two counties of Fermanagh and Tyrone where Catholics formed a slim majority. The exclusion of Fermanagh and Tyrone, it was felt, would have left Northern Ireland looking too small on a map and also given the southern state control of areas right in the heart of the new Ulster state, including the west bank of Lough Neagh –'a gaping mouth with a catholic tongue'.[45] When it came to the new Ulster, size was always important. Those who advocated for the separation of the north-east remained extremely sensitive to criticisms, such as those from one Belfast professor, which saw such a small northern state as 'silly and unlikely to survive'.[46] One pamphleteer made tortured comparisons with other diminutive self-governing territories:

the population of the [majority Protestant counties of Ulster] is more than any one of the nineteen states of the American Union, and more than half that of the kingdom of Norway ... it would have a population more than half as large as the

[45] Ewart, *A Journey in Ireland, 1921*, p. 174.   [46] Ibid. p. 158.

province of Ontario and more than two-thirds that of Quebec. It is only slightly exceeded by New South Wales or Victoria, while it is twice that of South Australia, and not less than 30 per cent in excess of the whole commonwealth of New Zealand. It is even greater than the whole white population of South Africa, which sent no less than four Prime Ministers to the previous Colonial Conference. There it more to Ulster than mere bigness.[47]

Such defensiveness about its limited proportions, would underlay the later refusal of the Northern Irish government to concede 'not an inch' of its territory during the Boundary Commission of 1924–1925. The Protestant populations of the other three Ulster counties of Donegal, Cavan and Monaghan were sacrificed despite their vociferous protests.

In March 1920, after the majority of the Ulster unionist council voted in support of the partition plan by 301 votes to 82, delegates from the three excluded Ulster counties walked out en masse in protest. These included many members of the Southern unionist elite, including Viscount Bangor and the Earl of Roden. The latter wrote to Richard Dawson Bates, soon to be Northern Ireland's first minister of home affairs, in May:

... I feel that I cannot remain a member of the Ulster Unionist Council in any way. I have heard no arguments that convince me that the Covenant has lapsed or that justify the breaking of its solemn pledge, and as to my mind it has been broken and the Unionists of these three counties have been betrayed – I must regretfully refuse to be any longer a member of a party which I consider to have broken a pledge to those who trusted them.[48]

While such protests from border Protestants would persist right up until the final settlement of the boundary issue in 1925, the eruption of sectarian violence in Belfast and other Northern towns, not to mention the opting-out of large numbers of nationalist councils from the jurisdiction of the proposed Ulster parliament in the summer of 1920, would do much to undermine their arguments for inclusion, demonstrating as it did the unionist government's tenuous hegemony in the six counties, let alone a potential nine-county Ulster. The fact that the Protestant populations of Donegal, Cavan and Monaghan were outnumbered five to one by Catholics would prove most damning to their calls for inclusion. Richard Dawson Bates, who as secretary of the Ulster unionist council was forced to deal with the complaints of border Protestants, complained somewhat illogically about the attitude of the 'nine county people', calling

[47] Pseudonymous, *Ulster on Its Own*.
[48] Roden to Bates, 10 May 1920, PRONI, D1327/18/29.

it 'deplorable' and 'having no regard for the interests of our cause'.[49] Certainly, those Ulster Protestants left out of the new Northern Ireland had themselves voiced similar harsh sentiments when rejecting complaints from Protestants in Connacht, Leinster and Munster that they were being abandoned during the Ulster Crisis. One such voiced the underlying denominational tensions which existed between many Presbyterians in Ulster and their assumed co-religionists in the south and west:

> The "Protestant minority" Ulster is being asked in such harrowing tones to sacrifice herself for what is an Episcopalian minority, which for three centuries has been well able to look after itself . . . the junta of Episcopalian lawyers on the make who presume to lead the people of Ulster at this crisis of their fate. We have seen too much of this breed in the past to trust them for long. It is full time that the Presbyterians of Ulster were rid of [those] who have sucked Ireland as dry as the palace gang did China in the past.[50]

The Council of Ireland was also included in the new legislation and continued to be trumpeted as some kind of embryonic all-Ireland government. How this cross-border component would actually operate, though, was left as vague as possible.

*

Lloyd George outlined the government's solution to 'the old family quarrel'[51] three days before Christmas 1919. The speech itself was verbose and long-winded; a heady mixture of imprecision and idealistic bluster. There was much talk of the virtues of 'self-determination', the wisdom of 'temporary exclusion' and the aspiration to eventual unity. In the debate which followed, MPs appeared genuinely bewildered by the details of the new Government of Ireland Act, with its tedious customs arrangements and complex constitutional mechanisms. Few seemed to have any faith in the plan. One referred to it derisively as a 'half-extinguished fire', while another former prime minister, Herbert Asquith, said the bill was 'passed for the purpose of giving to Ulster a Parliament which it did not want, and to the remaining three-quarters of Ireland a Parliament which it would not have'.[52] The Labour MP Josiah Wedgwood struck a more sardonic tone when he noted mockingly: 'If only these Irish were nice sad, sober, sensible and business-like

---

[49] Dawson Bates wrote to Dunbar-Buller, 29 May 1920, PRONI, D1327/18/29.
[50] Pseudonymous pamphlet, *Ulster on Its Own*, p. 6.
[51] Hansard, HC vol 123, cols 1168–233 (22 December 1919).
[52] Earl of Oxford and K. G. Asquith, *Memories and Reflections, 1852–1927*, vol. 2 (1928), chapter 20, pp. 189–92.

Englishmen what a perfect Bill this would be! Unfortunately, they are Irish, therefore we have to consider whether the Irish people themselves will accept this measure.'[53]

Over three quarters of the debate was spent discussing the intricate financial provisions of the Act, as had been the case in earlier Home Rule bills. While on the surface the Government of Ireland bill seemed meticulous to the point of tedium, its apparent thoroughness was largely illusory. Such lack of clarity on the part of its architects highlighted the profound insecurities which lay behind the idea and served the purpose of masking the earth-shattering changes that it implied. The process was marked, right from the time it was first mooted by the ongoing deferment of difficult questions which threatened to undermine the idea, passing them down the line to successive governments until circumstances meant they could no longer be avoided. This was, in short, an attempt to make partition seem less final than it actually was.

These more fundamental and problematic questions, such as how the promised unity was ever to be achieved, or the fate of the newly created minority populations, were answered in a formulaic and unconvincing fashion. In response to the prime minister's glib promise of future provision for the hundreds of thousands of people who would find themselves on the wrong side of the new border, one MP responded prophetically: 'The Prime Minister said there would be ample securities for minorities. I have no confidence in those securities. I do not believe you can contrive securities.'[54]

The vexed issue of the border line itself was left as vague as possible. The shape of the new Ulster state as outlined by Lloyd George –'taking the six counties as a basis' [55]–was, in the context of events in Ireland at the time, deeply ambiguous. The furthest he would go was to say that the act set out to 'produce an area as homogeneous as it is possible to achieve under these circumstances'.[56] As such, there were no detailed maps or representations of this new division. Newspaper editors and propagandists either imagined frontiers in line with their own prejudices or fell back on cartoonish images from the days of the Ulster Crisis where the whole of the north of Ireland was lopped off and separated from the south and west, or, in one instance, crudely joined via a land bridge to the south-west of Scotland. Indeed, back in 1914, the Irish nationalist MP John Dillon had pressed the government to 'say what they meant by "Ulster" since they could not give any practicable definition'.[57] Five years later

---

[53] Hansard, HC vol 123, cols 1168–233 (22 December 1919).   [54] Ibid.   [55] Ibid.
[56] Ibid.   [57] *Irish Times*, 14 May 1914.

they were still not forthcoming with a definitive answer. Plans to actually call the new northern state 'Ulster' were rejected so as to give a sense of equity with the South and due to a vain hope of avoiding the 're-emergence of the old controversies'.[58] In all quarters, confusion reigned. As one contemporary observer noted angrily:

> Ulster was nine counties. Ulster was six counties. Ulster was four counties. Ulster was something statutory, an undefined area . . . Ulster was any damned thing that a Carsonite politician or some semi-literate London journalist wanted to make it.[59]

Indeed, one of the most surreal features of Lloyd George's speech was that the vast majority of its most critical audience, the Irish members themselves, were not even there to hear it. Since their landslide victory in the December 1918 general election, the revolutionary Sinn Féin movement had chosen to abstain from Westminster and issue a declaration of independence through their own Dublin-based legislative body, Dáil Éireann, which claimed political authority over the whole island of Ireland.

The partition solution would thus be a rushed, messy, temporary expedient and based on a series of solutions which had already been rejected as unworkable. In many ways it was far too clever for its own good. As Paul Bew has insightfully observed, 'the eventual resolution of the Anglo-Irish conflict represented not a triumph of the middle ground, but rather its radical displacement'.[60] In the end, the decision itself was taken by small ruling elites based in London, Dublin and Belfast. While the Sinn Féin leadership rejected the idea out of hand, their successors would later come to see partition, despite their public opposition, as a fundamental part of their state-building project. For those who had dreamed of a future Gaelicised Ireland there were vociferous protests. However, in reality, partition would prove to be a practical necessity for the kind of nation building they ironically envisaged which would have been impossible in a heterogeneous, pluralist Ireland.

The pain of partition would not be felt by the elites in the new capital cities, but rather was reserved for the populations themselves living within or on the borders of the new partition states. Details of the convoluted partition proposals were digested by the public over the following days and weeks. Reactions spread from resignation and fear, to perplexity and denial. Few were overjoyed. Back in Ireland itself, people had far more

---

[58] See Cabinet Conclusions, 19 December 1919, Public Record Office, CAB/23/18.
[59] B. Kiely, *Counties of Contention* (Cork, 1945), p. 55.
[60] Bew 'Moderate Nationalism', p. 748.

pressing concerns. The situation had already moved in an ominous direction. While nationalist politicians continued to agitate around the world for recognition of their new republic, armed militias were steadily intensifying their campaign of violence and intimidation aimed at making the British presence unfeasible. Indeed, three days prior to Lloyd George's announcement of the partition plan, there had been an assassination attempt on John French, the Lord Lieutenant of Ireland, in Phoenix Park, and in the new year the growing confrontation would eventually spill over into full-scale guerrilla war. Fast-moving events on the ground would quickly outpace the plodding progress of the partition plan, leading to a series of hasty revisions and short-term modifications. The collapse of the British state in Ireland was no longer a future possibility. By the time the partition plan was announced the process of dividing Ireland, in every sense of the word, was already well under way.

In Ireland, local political aspirations and developing regional peculiarities were subsumed within this dynamic and devastating solution. There was certainly little attempt by the partitioners to address the profound psychological impact that the Act would have on Irish people themselves in terms of their future personal safety or material well-being. One correspondent noted insightfully: 'The scheme put forward was, in fact, entirely a politicians' solution, seeking to satisfy, not the Irish people, but the two Irish Parties represented at Westminster.'[61]

On the surface, partition appeared in some senses an equitable solution, dividing the island and its resources between two new states embodying incompatible ideologies, the reality was that for Irish people themselves the solution would placate only a small minority of the population. In April 1921, as the elaborate electoral and constitutional machinery of the partition settlement began to crank into action, the *Guardian* editorial passed a devastating judgement on the scheme:

The grant of self-government to Ireland should have been an occasion full of rejoicing and of hope, and so with a consenting Ireland it would have been. But Ireland has not consented. The proffered gift is not welcomed: it is rejected, and rejected with anger and with scorn. An act which should have been an act of conciliation and friendship has taken on the guise of simply another exercise of power. It postulates calm and peace; it takes place in presence of the extremes of violence and in an atmosphere of hate. It forebodes not the cessation but the continuance of strife. Such are the fruits of a policy which has substituted force for statesmanship, which plants thorns and bids us gather grapes. It has brought us nothing but suffering, failure and disgrace. Is there not yet some remnant of sense

---

[61] Unificus, 'The Quest for an Irish Settlement', p. 252.

and courage among our governing men which shall suffice to put an end not, at long last, to this travesty of justice, this mockery of the very elements of statesmanship?[62]

Partition was the greatest experiment as yet in the empire's history. While with partition many politicians felt they had reached a lasting answer to the Irish question, why it had happened and how exactly it was going to work appeared to have been barely considered or discussed.

---

[62] *The Guardian*, 19 April 1921.

Part II

The Process of Partition

4   The Death of Ireland

One of the most notable facts about partition was how slow violence was to emerge in the north-east. Despite the rhetoric of siege which had done so much to shape unionist rhetoric during the Ulster Crisis, there was little evidence that the newly forming province faced any direct threat of violent insurrection or invasion.

One of the primary reasons for this initial quietude had to do with the continued influence of moderate nationalism on the political culture of Northern Catholics. By contrast to the south and west, Northern nationalism was notable for its conservatism, reinforced by a powerful regional Catholic Church which provided a strong source of community identity and advocacy before, during and after the partition period. Belfast Catholics had been the least militant section of the nationalist population and shared a genuine sense of enthusiasm with their Protestant neighbours for participation in the First World War. During the conflict, they were the most willing recruits to the British army, especially through the first two years of the conflict. While the city as a whole provided almost a third of all Irish recruits, Catholic volunteers numbered almost 8,000, 25 per cent of all those in the city. This was despite the fact that Catholics made up less than a quarter of the population and the unionist press remaining suspicious of their motivations. While it is true that outside of Belfast recruiting rates for Catholics dropped dramatically, this was also true of Protestant men in provincial Ulster. Much of this had to do with socioeconomic issues, such as urban unemployment and the division between rural and urban areas, rather than representing any kind of identifiable sectarian split.

Politically, Northern Catholics also bucked the trend of increasing nationalist radicalism. Whereas Sinn Féin had swept the board in the 1918 general election, the old Home Rule Party had managed to retain the support of the majority of Northern nationalists with four of its meagre haul of six Westminster MPs coming from the future six counties. Although this can partly be ascribed to the existence of an electoral pact between both nationalist parties in Ulster, the very fact that the uncompromising Sinn Féin movement accepted the complexities of Northern nationalist sympathies was telling. The differences between these two brands of Irish nationalism was largely strategic. While both shared an abhorrence of the idea of partition, many Northern nationalists understood that direct violent confrontation, increasingly the case in the south and west, would prove deeply counterproductive in Ulster and act to embolden and strengthen rather than weaken unionist control of the province. The rejection of Sinn Féin was evident in the spring of 1918 when, despite the involvement of hundreds of Irish Volunteers and the dissemination of vast amounts of republican propaganda, the Home Rule Party in the North had managed to win two significant by-election victories in South Armagh and East Tyrone, bringing an end to the string of Sinn Féin victories in the south and west the previous year. It certainly appeared that in Ulster the new republican Sinn Féin movement had finally met its match.

Indeed, Ulster was the one place where the Home Rule Party had managed to create a grass roots political machine comparable to that of Sinn Féin. Under the energetic leadership of the West Belfast MP, Joe Devlin, the United Irish League (UIL) and its ancillary Catholic fraternal organisation, the AOH matched both Sinn Féin and the Ulster unionists in terms of their membership and militancy.[1] One South Armagh IRA member, John Cosgrave, admitted that 'the Volunteers got more annoyance and opposition from the Hibernian organisation than from the Unionists'.[2] Despite falling prey to the influenza epidemic which swept across Europe in the wake of the First World War, killing 250,000 people in Britain alone, Joe Devlin easily defeated Eamon de Valera for the safe nationalist seat of West Belfast in 1918. By far the most able and energetic leader of the Home Rule Party, his absence from the national campaign, in the words of John Dillon, 'contributed very largely to the debacle'.[3] Certainly, due to Devlin's popularity, Irish republicanism remained of limited appeal in the North, with party membership patchy and the IRA weak and ineffective. By 1920 there were less than 100 Sinn Féin members in Belfast, compared to almost 7,000 in the UIL. The IRA in the whole of Ulster numbered barely 300 and was confined to homogeneous Catholic areas where it found little support. John McCoy, an IRA leader

---

[1] By far the most authoritative study of Northern nationalism and the role of Devlin in the period is Hepburn, *Catholic Belfast and Nationalist Ireland in the Era of Joe Devlin, 1871–1934.*

[2] John Cosgrave witness statement, BMH, NAI, WS 605.

[3] Letter from John Dillon to T. P. O'Connor, 20 December 1918 (Dillon Papers, 6742/582).

from South Armagh, later confided that his attempts to form some kind of armed group was so hapless that 'no particular notice was taken of it by the British authorities or the Unionists'.[4] The post-Rising radicalism of Sinn Féin had split the nationalist population into two divided camps and internecine violence between Northern Catholics would continue for much of the partition period.

Direct confrontation between Catholics and Protestants in Ulster, however, despite the perceptions of political elites, was confined to the sphere of politics and propaganda. While the IRA campaign gained pace in the south and west during the spring of 1920, the future Northern Ireland remained largely quiet and peaceful. The *Times* newspaper reported: 'In the North complete tranquillity prevails and no incidents have occurred to disturb the harmonious feelings existing amongst all classes.'[5] On the ground, this lack of confrontation was very evident. One constable in the RIC, from Maghera, County Tyrone, recalled the tranquil relations between both communities:

the locals were useful, talk a bit. A lot of them, principally the priests, they'd give you information. We were very friendly with them. Relations with local people were good. As long as you treated them decent and didn't go too hard on them. We played football with them. Life was comfortable enough. They would back me or anybody no matter what I'd do, like, they were very good. There was one ambush. They fired alright but [we] gave them the best hammering ever they got, they went on their knees and begged to let them go.[6]

Typical of this calm atmosphere was the town of Lisburn, which lay barely eight miles to the south-west of Belfast. One RIC man stationed there remembered the early months of 1920, 'Relations were good in county Down. I thought I was lucky getting to county Down at all, that I wasn't sent down south.'[7] A centre of the linen trade, which employed some 60 per cent of the population, this small market town of 12,000 people was notable for the sectarian intermingling of its population with a high level of communal intermarriage. During the war, the huge demand for uniforms, kitbags and later aeroplane coverings led to a boom in the linen industry with some workers working 60–70 hours per week. Despite this, other tensions lingered beneath the surface. The postwar recession saw large-scale layoffs and unemployment especially among returning Protestant workers. As in Derry, Belfast and many other small towns, Catholic workers became the subject of growing resentment. Suspicion

---

[4] John McCoy witness statement, BMH, NAI, WS 492.   [5] *The Times*, 2 May 1919.
[6] James Gilmer quoted in J. Brewer, *The Royal Irish Constabulary: An Oral History* (Belfast, 1990), p. 95.
[7] Ibid, p. 99.

about the increase in the nationalist population of the town had already been growing before the war, with a significant increase in the number of Catholic publicans and shopkeepers. Lisburn would be visited by Edward Carson on two occasions. On 19 September 1912 over 20,000 people turned out for a torchlit parade at which Carson read the Ulster Covenant to loud cheers, painting himself, a journalist recalled, as, 'Gideon mustering his little band against the overwhelming hosts of Midian; tears trickling down his cheeks as he described the perils of the forlorn hope which he had pledged himself to defend.'[8] Over 8,000 people in the town would eventually sign the document. The second visit would occur in February 1918 when in pouring rain thousands of people waited in the town square to hear a speech by Carson in which he pledged that 'no man shall lay a hand upon the privileges we possess'.[9]

In early 1920 there was little sign on the surface that towns like Lisburn were powder kegs of sectarian animosity. However, the explosion of violence in Lisburn would demonstrate how deadly the divisions over partition would be when they arrived in Ulster. At 1 p.m. on 22 August 1920 RIC district inspector Oswald Swanzy was shot dead as he left a service at Lisburn Cathedral. His IRA assassins had travelled down from Belfast that morning after their arrival from Cork a few days earlier. Swanzy had been implicated in the murder of Thomas McCurtain, the Sinn Féin mayor of Cork city, and after much investigation had been tracked down to his home town of Lisburn. It was the response to this shooting that was most ominous. Vitriolic loyalist mobs went on a rampage of looting and arson against the minority Catholic population, most of whom fled the town to seek succour in Belfast, Newry or Dundalk. It is estimated that over 200 families, totalling some 1,000 people, left Lisburn in the next forty-eight hours. Those who were lucky enough managed to get a train and would be joined by other refugees fleeing similar reprisals in towns and villages along the route. Others were forced to walk to Belfast, many suffering threats and attacks along the way, forcing them to wade through fields away from main roads or sleep out in the open until daylight. Most made their way to St Mary's Hall where the Expelled Workers' Relief Committee, already dealing with thousands of expelled Catholic workers in the city, were busy providing food and rudimentary assistance. Back in Lisburn, in one day over 300 Catholic homes, religious buildings including the local convent and businesses were destroyed. An RIC report estimated the damage at almost

[8] Winder Good, *Ulster and Ireland*, p. 200.
[9] *Freeman's Journal*, 21 September 1912; 20 February 1918.

£1,000,000. Fred Crawford, the old UVF leader from the days of the Ulster Crisis, arrived the next morning and surveyed the scene:

It reminded me of a French town after it had been bombarded by the Germans as I saw in France in 1916. We visited the ruins of the Priest's house . . . it was burnt or gutted and the furniture all destroyed. When coming down the avenue I found a small pair of manicure scissors that had been through the fire. I kept them as a souvenir of the event . . . [there were] some very hard cases where Unionists had lost practically all they had by the fire of a house of a Catholic spreading to theirs . . . After the brutal cold blooded murder of Inspector Swanzy one does not wonder at the mob loosing its head with fury . . . .it has been stated that there are only four or five Roman Catholic families left in Lisburn. Others say this is wrong, that there are far more. Be that as it may, there certainly are practically no shops or places of business left to the Roman Catholics.[10]

Many Catholics chose not to return, opting to move south or over to northern England or the west of Scotland. For those who did there was little help and for several weeks Catholic families could be observed sleeping on borrowed mattresses in burned out houses open to the elements. Despite the involvement of thousands of local Protestants and elements of the Lisburn UVF in the attacks, only seven men were ever arrested. Of these, only five received custodial sentences of three months, although on appeal they were eventually acquitted.[11]

The change from peace to war in Lisburn was the culmination of six weeks of violence which had swept across previously peaceful Ulster in the summer of 1920. The victory of nationalist candidates in urban and municipal elections in January and June 1920 across the west of the province emboldened resistance to partition. Nationalists won control of Tyrone county council and ten other urban authorities. As in the south and west these local bodies became the focus for opposition to the fragmenting of the British state. Pledging their allegiance to the revolutionary Dáil in Dublin, their work administering local government took a back seat to elaborate propaganda campaigns and the mobilisation of the local population in a variety of overtly nationalist organisations. The most significant victory came in Derry city where for the first time in 300 years a Catholic was elected as lord mayor. Outbreaks of rioting in the city in June saw the mobilisation of all manner of groups, including a remobilised UVF, the AOH and small numbers of Irish Volunteers. After attacks were launched into the Bogside, the resulting death toll included fifteen Catholics and four Protestants. It was only after the British army moved in to separate the mobs, firing live rounds into the

---

[10] P. Buckland, *Irish Unionism* (Belfast, 1973), p. 187.
[11] For an exhaustive account of the violence in Lisburn, see P. Lawlor, *The Burnings, 1920* (Cork, 2009).

crowds, that an uneasy peace was restored. Such outbreaks of violence would blight numerous small towns during the summer of 1920, including Banbridge, Dromore, Newtownards and Balbriggan, setting a pattern to be repeated across Ulster over the next two years.

The growing insecurity and confusion which was surrounding the partition settlement on the ground in the summer of 1920 was shown no more clearly than in Belfast, the soon-to-be new Northern capital. As with Lisburn, a month later, the insecurity and confusion gave way to a spontaneous, if far more devastating, eruption of violence.

Like in Lisburn, the spark that lit the fuse was the death of an RIC divisional commissioner, Gerard Smyth. Smyth had been targeted by the IRA during his time serving in Cork due to his outspoken and vitriolic comments about how to deal with the growing disorder in the county through a policy of informal reprisal killings. His body was brought back home to his native Banbridge with the funeral set for 21 July, a date which coincided with the return of workers after the holiday of the Twelfth. Thousands attended his funeral and once again the heightened atmosphere led to attacks on Catholic property in Banbridge and nearby Dromore. One republican activist, after being stopped at a hastily organised UVF checkpoint on the day of the funeral, drove through the town: 'When we got some little speed up we found that missiles were being thrown at us and we proceeded to run the gauntlet through the town where 10,000 Orangemen lined the streets.'[12]

It was the eruption of violence in Belfast, however, that would prove most significant. When workers returned to work on 21 July, the seeds that had been sown during the Twelfth holiday were ripe. The scene for the first confrontation was the shipyards of East Belfast. Protestant workers held lunchtime meetings, initiated by crude handbills posted up around the works, where various rabble-rousers called for a boycott of their 5,000 Catholic co-workers. While the vast majority of the Protestant workers offered vocal support, others decided to take things further. Waving Union flags and singing loyalist songs, a mob of 600 workers ordered all Catholics to 'clear out', with those who refused being viciously attacked and beaten. Pelted with bolts and struck with spanners, many fled immediately while others jumped in the River Lagan to escape. Suspect loyalists, so-called rotten Prods, consisting mostly of trade union officials, were also expelled. Quickly, violence spread to the ancillary engineering works clustered around the shipyards and then out into the surrounding streets as Catholic workers were chased back into the city centre. Eventually, soldiers were dispatched to the scene to try and

[12] John McCoy statement, WS 492.

separate the rival crowds, but after firing blank rounds proved insufficient, live rounds were used, leading to the death of one of the rioters.
Even so, the soldiers were soon overwhelmed.

Four days of rioting were to follow. Small Catholic enclaves such as the
Short Strand and the Markets area were attacked mercilessly in an orgy of
burning and looting, leading their Catholic populations to flee to more
homogeneous areas in the west of the city. The rioters used guns, knives,
batons and makeshift weapons, including stones and bricks picked up
from the street. Catholic-owned pubs and off-licences were looted, with
drunkenness driving on much of the violence. The harsh sectarian nature
of the violence was demonstrated by attacks on Catholic churches, con-
vents and monasteries, most notably St Matthew's Church in the Short
Strand and Clonard Monastery in West Belfast where one of the monks
was killed by a stray bullet. The subsequent violence was focused largely
on so-called interface areas between Protestant and Catholic neighbour-
hoods with the forced expulsion of Protestants and Catholics from mixed
areas further adding to the burgeoning refugee crisis and hardening the
lines between both communities. Long before the promulgation of the
eventual political settlement, Belfast was busy partitioning itself. It was
only after troop reinforcements arrived and the imposition of a curfew
that the violence finally abated. The death toll was nineteen, eight
Protestants and eleven Catholics, although hundreds had been injured.
There were hundreds of thousands of pounds worth of property damage
with approximately 8,000 workers expelled from their jobs, almost
10 per cent of the Catholic population of the city, and around 3,000
people now homeless refugees. With the Government of Ireland Act now
passing through Westminster, a *Guardian* report painted the lacklustre
response of the government, and its continued support of the partition
plan, as permitting both communities in Ireland 'unqualified self-
determination in their reciprocity of mutual slaughter'.[13]

The expulsions which took place in Belfast during July 1920 were far
from unique in the context of postwar Britain. Similar expulsions
occurred in many port cities across the country caused by the economic
strains of demobilisation and competition for postwar employment, housing and pensions. In Glasgow, for example, in January 1919, black
colonial sailors working in Govan were attacked by militant members of
the National Seaman's Union. As in Belfast, they were expelled from their
workplaces and homes and beaten up on the street. Similar expulsions
were reported throughout 1919 and 1920 in South Shields, Salford,
London, Hull, Liverpool, Newport, Cardiff and Barry where attacks

---

[13] *The Guardian*, 22 July 1920.

were carried out on Asian, Arab, Chinese and other minority ethnic populations, triggered by intense job competition in the merchant navy, the first sector to feel the bite of the postwar economic downturn.[14] In the Belfast shipyards, the postwar slump had bitten particularly hard. The London journalist Wilfrid Ewart on his journey around Ireland in 1921 visited the yards of east of the city:

Walking the length of an endless row of warehouses and sheds, you find half a dozen men shovelling a few hundred weight of condemned grain into sacks. Belfast has not the money to complete what it has begun . . . You see ships rusted, ships apparently forgotten, ships to be sold, ships without a buyer, ships that it does not pay to repair. You see-stagnancy.[15]

What made the expulsions in Belfast unique, however, was the context of imminent political change in the shape of partition. While there had been similar riots and expulsions in Belfast in the past, the latest in 1912, those of July were notable for their sectarian fervour and finality, 'a Twelfth of July riot turned into a civil war', as one nationalist politician called it. Despite various nationalist campaigns, none of the expelled shipyard workers would ever return to work. This would lead to a consistently high level of unemployment and poverty among the Catholic community of the city. In June 1922, the British civil servant Stephen Tallents reported:

Out of an insured Belfast population of about 158,000, between 32,000 and 33,000 persons or 21.75% are now without work. One has only to see the groups of unemployed men and youths hanging round the street corners to realise what fuel they provide for disorder.[16]

Similar expulsions and attacks on economic targets would continue to characterise much of the violence over the following two years. Ironically,

---

[14] See, for example, J. Jenkinson, 'Black Sailors on Red Clydeside: Rioting, Reactionary Trade Unionism and Conflicting Notions of Britishness Following the First World War' *Twentieth Century British History*, vol. 19, no. 1 (January 2008), pp. 29–60; N. Evans, 'Across the Universe; Racial Violence in the Post War Crisis in Imperial Britain 1919–1925' in D. Frost, ed., *Ethnic Labour and British Imperial Trade: A History of Ethnic Seafarers in the United Kingdom* (London, 1995), pp. 59–88; R. May and R. Cohen, 'The Interaction between Race and Colonialism: A Case Study of the Liverpool Race Riots of 1919' *Race and Class*, vol. 16 (1974), pp. 111–26; M. Rowe, 'Sex, Race and Riot in Liverpool, 1919', *Immigrants and Minorities*, 19 (July 2000), pp. 53–70; J. White, 'The Summer Riots of 1919', *New Society*, 57 (13 August 1981), pp. 260–1. During 1919 and 1920, a large number of demonstrations were also held throughout the country by the National Federation of Discharged and Demobilised Sailors, many of which ended in violence. See, for example, *The Times*, 10 March 1919; 17 March 1919; *Glasgow Herald*, 10 July 1919.
[15] Ewart, *A Journey in Ireland, 1921*, p. 158.   [16] Colonial Office memo, NA, CO 906/30.

the IRA's arson campaign of May 1922 would result in the destruction of large numbers of business premises and the collapse of local firms which employed Catholics, leading to complaints from local community leaders and politicians which did much to undercut support for republicanism in the city.

Despite the conflict's revolutionary aspects, its belligerents, and most importantly its leaders, still faced the same inherent uncertainties. Behind the seeming squalid chaos of the riots it was clear that hard-edged political realities drove the violence. The ideas of siege and resistance which underlay the Twelfth of July holiday were dangerously vague, allowing participants to conflate historic wrongs with current political circumstance. One Tyrone unionist politician wrote in January 1920:

No compromise that I conceive is other than a first step towards a Bolshevist Irish Republic. I think undoubtedly our best policy, win or lose, is to remain in opposition to Home Rule to the end no matter how bad that end may be.[17]

Rioters sought sanction from their political elites, comforting them that their actions could be placed within a broader narrative of the popular assertion of political independence and statehood. One London journalist recalled touring working-class districts in East Belfast during September 1920:

There are pastors in Belfast to-day who are talking and acting like so many Mohammedan Mullahs preaching a Holy War. The Protestant pulpits resound with comparisons between the Israelites and the Ulstermen, the first relieved from the bondage of Egypt, the second from slavery to the " Papists "; and the devil's brew of sectarian bigotry is being handed out in the form of barely veiled incitements to the roughs of the city to attempt a massacre of their Catholic fellow-subjects.[18]

Leaders were happy to condone their actions and cynically manipulate them for political gain. It was clear that members of the unofficially revived UVF were actively involved in organising the violence, while the RIC and Ulster Special Constabulary (the 'Specials') were either overwhelmed or turned a blind eye to the attacks, in some cases colluding with them. As one British press correspondent succinctly put it: 'Specials provide the petrol, fire-arms, and the immunity from interruption.'[19] Fred Crawford turned his chemical factory in East Belfast into a virtual armed camp, stockpiling old UVF weapons and arming his twenty workers as paramilitaries, 'so that they remind me of the building of the walls of Jerusalem when the workers were armed while they worked'.[20] It was evident that in the first major test policing had become at best inadequate

---

[17] de Fellenberg Montgomery to Walsh, PRONI, D627/438/8.
[18] *The Times*, 16 July 1920.   [19] *The Guardian*, 31 July 1920.
[20] Crawford Diary, PRONI, D640/11/1.

and at worst partisan. The shipyard expulsions were also notable because of the role of senior political leaders in fermenting the violence. During a Twelfth of July demonstration at Finaghy, on the outskirts of Belfast, which one reporter described memorably as a 'parade of anachronistic intolerance',[21] Carson gave a venomous speech which was little more than a thinly veiled call to arms:

We in Ulster will tolerate no Sinn Féin. But we tell you this – that if, having offered you [i.e., the British government] our help, you are yourselves unable to protect us from the machinations of Sinn Féin, and you won't take our help; well then, we tell you that we will take the matter into our own hands.[22]

The British liberal press was scathing in its reaction.

It is an appalling fact that this ancient feud should be kept alive for more than two centuries and that Sir Edward Carson should come forward to denounce the great majority of his fellow countrymen as "our enemies." In his speech yesterday there was not a single generous word or a single statesmanlike suggestion. It was barren, bitter, hostile, provocative, and if we were to take this as the last word of "Northern Ireland" to the rest of their fellow-countrymen we might well despair for the future.[23,24]

In the days preceding the expulsions, the unionist press played its part in ratcheting up the pressure, printing an acidic collection of dark paranoid editorials, sensationalist news stories and alleged letters from concerned loyal citizens. One correspondent who signed themselves simply 'Protestant' wrote a few days before the expulsions:

It is only a matter of a very short time and Protestantism will be wiped out of this country altogether. The Roman Catholics are pouring into Ulster and increasing rapidly in this province where Protestants are emigrating and disappearing ... the question is whether Protestants can rouse themselves to do anything apart from processions.[25]

Others stuck to the illusion that Ulster was being penetrated by sinister elements from within the nationalist community bent on conquest:

Sinn Feiners are busy invading our province ... They are busy organising while we prate on the deeds of our forefathers and do nothing. To the shame of the Ulster Unionists be it said that Sinn Feiners can obtain situations in both offices and shipyards, in so called loyal Belfast while our Protestant men walk about idle. It is time Unionists roused themselves to action or we shall be left homeless and helpless very shortly.[26]

---

[21] *The Times*, 14 July 1920.   [22] *Belfast Telegraph*, 14 July 1920.
[23] *The Guardian*, 13 July 1920.   [24] *Observer*, 13 July 1920.
[25] *Belfast Newsletter*, 18 July 1920.   [26] *Belfast Telegraph*, 16 July 1920.

Another pushed this argument on further by challenging the courage of 'Ulster manhood' at this time of crisis:

a sleeping sickness seems to have spread over the whole of Ulster Unionism ... [they] are not what they were before the war. Processions and demonstrations are all very good in their own way, but we want something deeper than these. The old spirit which existed in 1914 is still alive in Ulster, it only needs wakening.[27,28]

In the minds of the architects of partition, the summer violence of July and August 1920, far from giving cause for doubt about the feasibility of the plan, confirmed unequivocally their long-held conclusion that Irish Catholics and Protestants were irreconcilable and must be facilitated to live separately. What was clear, however, was that on the ground Irish people themselves had decided to take the partition process in a completely different direction far from that imagined by political elites in London. The glaring contradictions and holes in the partition scheme were filled in with a message of crude communal tribalism and millenarian expectations. The Church of Ireland synod drew up a petition which painted the partition plan as a wholesale caving in to violent separatists which would be followed inevitably by chaos:

To our Church a cruel and injurious wrong; to the British Empire deep degradation and dishonour; to Ireland the fatal signal for renewed disturbance, social and political confusion, commercial disaster, and, not improbably, for a bitter, protracted, and lamentable civil war.[29]

Similarly, one London journalist found in Belfast, to his bewilderment,

hundreds and thousands of men who veritably believe that Home Rule means Rome Rule, and that a Dublin Parliament will not only tax industrial Ulster out of existence, but will deprive Protestants of their farms, close their workshops, take away their schools, force them to attend Mass, dissolve their marriages by Papal decree and force them to become Roman Catholics at the point of a pike.[30]

In both nationalist and unionist imaginings, the other community had become an active fifth column and one to be suppressed or expelled. Stephen Tallents reported that by the middle of 1922,

the social cleavage between the Protestants and Catholics in Belfast is almost absolute-greater, I should say, than the division between Pole and Jew in Warsaw. Bishop MacRory told me that during the seven years he had spent in Belfast he had hardly mixed with Protestants at all, and that during the last twelve months he

---

[27] *Belfast Newsletter*, 15 July 1920.   [28] *Belfast Newsletter*, 16 July 1920.
[29] Hugh de Fellenberg Montgomery to Primate John Baptist Crozier, 10 February 1918, PRONI, D627/433/44.
[30] *The Times*, 19 May 1914.

could not remember conversing with a single one ... The result is that the leaders of each party are known to each other only through their exaggerated public utterances.[31]

Orange Halls and Catholic churches would increasingly be subject to attack by arsonists or labelled as institutions of alien control. In Monaghan in the wake of the expulsions, residents woke to find green and white placards hung on the gates of Protestant churches in a 'wanton display of bigotry and intolerance',[32] leading one clergyman to complain:

This spirit has only recently developed in Monaghan and we know that something must be done to check it, else it will be responsible for a rupture of the good feelings that have hitherto prevailed between all parties here.[33]

The complexities of identity between and within communities would be increasingly honed down to a simple and sinister religious distinction based on Catholic and Protestant. Political party allegiances were jettisoned in favour of a simple religious call to arms. Robert Tregenna, a union leader in the Belfast shipyards, remarked in a speech in Omagh on 18 April 1922:

I am as strong a labour man as any, but I could never find anything strong enough to put forward in Labour to override the religious question. The Protestant who did not come into the fight for Protestantism was not worthy of its name.[34]

While the architects of the Government of Ireland Act saw their solution as a rational response to communal division and incompatible political aspirations, the reality was that partition would have to be fought for and defended. While the legislation made its way sedately through Westminster, the reality on the ground was that partition was already being actualised by violence, long before the states themselves were ever formed.

Across Ireland, crudely armed militias killed or drove out police and government officials, saboteurs burned police barracks, cut telephone wires or blocked and blew up bridges and railway lines to hinder the movements of troops and supplies. The initial violence which broke out early in 1919 was sporadic and spontaneous, only subsequently becoming more organised and bloody from the latter half of 1920 through to the Truce of July of the following year. The British government responded with brutality of its own, detailing its own paramilitary police forces to supress overt displays of nationalism, ransack homes and torture, beat

[31] Colonial Office memo, NA, CO 906/30.
[32] Carville, 'The Impact of the Partition Proposals on County Monaghan', p. 43.
[33] *The Northern Standard*, 5 October 1912.   [34] *Northern Whig*, 20 April 1922.

and murder suspected radicals. In this confused, dirty war of reprisal, provincial paramilitary leaders on all sides paid only lip service to Dublin and London control, with the conflict descending into a morass of tit-for-tat killings and the vicious scapegoating of entire communities.

In fact, even a cursory examination demonstrates that the overwhelming majority of violent incidents in the partition period consisted of mass communal rioting and the expulsion and murder of innocent civilians. Peter Hart has demonstrated that the numbers of non-combatant deaths rose from 40 per cent during the period 1917–1919 to an enormous 82 per cent during the first six months of 1922.

The focal point for this violence was undoubtedly Belfast, which suffered a higher per capita death rate than any other part of Ireland including famously disturbed counties such as Cork and Tipperary, accounting for 40 per cent of all fatalities in Ireland during the revolutionary period as a whole. Figures vary, but it is clear that almost 500 people were to die in the city in almost exactly two years of intermittent violent outbreaks running from July 1920 through to June 1922. Approximately 3,000 people were injured during the same period, almost 1,000 homes and businesses were destroyed and almost 20,000 people were forced to move as refugees or were expelled from their workplaces. Living five miles outside of Belfast, Lady Lilian Spender, the wife of Wilfred Spender, cabinet secretary to the new Northern Ireland government, recalled the often bizarre nature of these expulsions and forced movements in the city during the summer of 1920:

People pour in, begging for protection. Some of their tales are tragic and some are funny. There are endless cases of people being turned out of their houses – Sinn Feiners turning out Unionists and vice versa, sometimes with violence, sometimes more or less peacefully. Sometimes when the Sinn Feiner lives in a Protestant district and the Unionist in an R.C. one, an exchange is effected [sic], and the cart that removes the Sinn Feiner's belongings also fetches away the Unionist's!! It's a crazy business altogether ... Very much like living on top of a very active and lively volcano.[35]

By any measure, Belfast Catholics suffered more than any community in Ireland during the period. Although the 96,000-strong Catholic population made up only 25 per cent of the city's inhabitants, they would experience two-thirds of the casualties and 80 per cent of all property damage. They also bore the brunt of workplace expulsions with around 8,000–10,000 people being thrown out of their factories and workshops. Similarly, Belfast Catholics made up the bulk of the estimated 10,000 refugees who were forced to move due to forced eviction or intimidation.

[35] Diary of Lady Lillian Spender, 25 August 1920, Spender Papers, PRONI, D/1633/2/26.

However, it must be remembered that the violence in Belfast was a two-sided conflict. One-third of murder victims in Belfast were Protestants and around 1,000 Protestants were expelled from their homes in Belfast with some 200 businesses destroyed and over 2,000 people becoming refugees. In barely two years, Belfast experienced violence on an unprecedented scale, with thousands killed and wounded, millions of pounds worth of property damage, a period equivalent, and certainly more concentrated, than the worst years of the Troubles in the early 1970s.

The violence which Belfast endured between 1920 and 1922 has tended to be painted in a generic way, with a focus largely on its inexplicability and apparent arbitrariness. Certainly, Belfast's experience was unique in the Irish revolutionary context in terms of both its scope and dynamics. Victims of violence were overwhelmingly civilians, as opposed to being members of security forces or any kind of identifiable paramilitary force. Unlike in the south and west where paramilitaries and security forces made up a sizeable, if diminishing, share of the casualties, this was not the pattern in Belfast and the north-east. Between 1920 and 1922 less than 15 per cent of those killed would be members of the security forces or organised paramilitary groups such as the IRA.[36] As was the case in Lisburn and Belfast, it was clear that their presence was provocative rather than definitive, inspiring mass communal outbreaks but suffering little of the consequences themselves directly. Overwhelmingly it is clear that Belfast experienced a communal conflict defined by mass ethnic mobilisation, rather than being driven by paramilitary organisation.

The violence itself has a deep sectarian character, with attacks being launched against whole communities and locales. Fred Crawford recalled his paranoia while travelling 'off home ground' in Catholic areas of the city:

When going through *their* district I keep my automatic pistol handy and keep a sharp look out for strangers, and if I see strangers loafing about I immediately push back the safety leaver on the pistol and get my hand on it in my pocket so that I can have it out in a moment. I do not fear being shot in the front but when I pass these gentlemen I expect to be shot in the back. I am not afraid of the local R.C.s shooting me. They would be afraid even if they wanted to do so, as they think if I were not killed I could identify them. But I would not trust one of them.[37]

The use of sectarian language and the targeting of religious buildings was matched by the targeting of homes and businesses and the intimidation and direct expulsion of people from mixed areas. However, while the violence is often painted as wholly random, involving killings regardless of

[36] P. Hart, *The IRA at War, 1916–23* (Oxford, 2003), p. 79.
[37] Crawford Diary, PRONI, D640/11/1.

age and gender, it is clear that far from being the indiscriminate killing of women and children, the vast majority of victims were men between the ages of 18 and 45, suggesting that men were both the chief instigators and victims of the culture of recreational rioting which defined Belfast during the partition period.

The violence then was defined in space, being focused especially in mixed areas of the city or on the informal frontiers between communities, and also in terms of its victims. It was also defined in terms of time, being clearly inspired by political developments with its worst outbreaks coinciding with particular periods of political tension or decision. Following the summer riots and expulsions in 1920, violence began to drop off again. It re-emerged, however, with a vengeance in April, May and June 1921, a period which coincided with the most violent period of the War of Independence and the establishment of the Northern Ireland parliament in Belfast. While the number of incidents dropped somewhat after the truce in early July, violence spiked again in the final two months of the year, coinciding with the treaty negotiations going on in London and the handing over of security powers to the unionist government in the North. As discussed in a later chapter, however, the worst period of violence occurred during the spring and early summer of 1922 when both new partition states faced off against each other and their respective political and religious minorities. It is notable that the most sustained outbreaks tended to happen when events in the South had reached something of a hiatus, such as during the period of truce negotiations and the subsequent divisions of the treaty period in the six months prior to the outbreak of the southern civil war in June 1922, after which the new Northern Ireland finally returned to something resembling normality. The role of southern militants in the North would prove crucial, especially due to the fact that the IRA in the North was a weak minority within the larger minority. Certainly, the worst periods of violence in the north-east coincided with periods when Southern eyes were turned towards Northern Ireland and diplomatic, propaganda and military attacks against it were carried out.

The violence was therefore largely reactive in nature, whether it be a reaction to a specific incident such as the shooting of a policeman, as with Swanzy and Smyth, or to political developments elsewhere and the fear about their potential impact on the safety of the specific community. As with most violence in Ireland during the period, it took the form of reprisals, although in the north-east such tit-for-tat killings are notable in terms of both their scale and crudity. The pattern which developed was of even the smallest of incidents on the new border inspiring massive violent reaction in both Belfast and other northern towns. For example, in February 1922, a skirmish between some members of the Specials and a local IRA unit in Monaghan led to thirty-one deaths in Belfast over the following two days. These included the horrific bombings in Weaver Street in North Belfast, which saw a bomb thrown among a group of Catholic schoolchildren, two of whom were killed on the spot with three others dying of their wounds in hospital after, an incident described by Churchill as 'the worst thing that has happened in Ireland in the last three years'.[38] This pattern of provocation in one place and response in another would continue right throughout the period leading to a culture of sectarian scapegoating. Bishop McCrory, the Catholic bishop of Down and Conor, which covered the Northern capital, captured the character of the violence, observing that the 'people of Belfast are being punished for the sins of their brethren elsewhere'.[39]

For many, the sheer savagery of the violence made it inexplicable. In June 1922, Susan McCormack, a Catholic housekeeper, answered her door to a gang of men who pushed their way into the house and, after beating her senseless, poured petrol on her clothes and hair and set her on fire before leaving without a word. She was only saved when she fled out into the street in flames. A few weeks earlier, James Smyth, a deaf mute who, according to one newspaper, 'could neither speak no evil nor hear no evil', was attacked outside his home by a group of men and almost beaten to death. Nineteen-year-old James Rice was accosted by a similar group of men who, after administering a severe beating, tied him up and then shot him multiple times before proceeding to savagely mutilate his dead body which was barely recognisable when he was found. To many, the brutality of such acts were as incomprehensible and irrational at the time as they are today. In the words of one contemporary Belfast academic, violence 'spread across Ireland like smallpox'.[40] Another observer noted how, 'Irish people today regard the raids, wreckings, burnings, shootings, and imprisonment without trial as part of their normal life.'[41] In April 1922, a Catholic priest, Patrick Gannon, recalled visiting a house where loyalists had taken revenge for the shooting of a policeman a few days earlier:

A family named Walsh lived in the house, of whom the two adult men-brothers-were ex-soldiers who had been through the Great War. As the policemen were beating with a sledge-hammer at the door, the old mother thought it best to open it. They then swept past her and up the narrow stairs to the bedroom where Joseph

---

[38] Winston Churchill, Hansard, HC vol 150, col 806 (14 February 1922).

[39] R. Lynch, 'The People's Protectors? The Irish Republican Army and the "Belfast Pogrom, 1920–1922"' *Journal of British Studies*, vol. 47, no. 2 (April 2008), p. 391.

[40] Interview with Professor John Henry, QUB published in *The Guardian*, 22 May 1921.

[41] *Manchester Guardian*, 8 June 1921.

Walsh lay, with his son Michael aged seven on one side and little Brigid aged two on the other. They fired some shots; for three were found in Michael, who died next morning. Whether they shot the father or not no one seemed to know. But the sledgehammer sufficed. The priest who came to the house within half an hour told me what he saw. The skull was open and empty; while the Whole mass of the brains was on the bolster almost a foot away. On descending they found a young lad, Frank Walsh, aged fourteen, crouching in the kitchen. Him they kicked and shot in the thigh, but not fatally. Thus was Constable Turner avenged. I asked to see the room upstairs. The wife shrank from conducting me. She had not ventured to enter it since that night. But the brother, an ex-soldier, had stronger nerves and showed me all the bolster soaked with blood, and the two straw mattresses deeply stained with it. He even raised them up and pointed out pieces of the skull upon the floor, and fragments of dried brain. How they swung a sledge-hammer in that narrow space I know not. But the blow smashed the skull as it would a coconut. The brother presented me with a few small pieces in paper, and I still retain this gruesome trophy of Belfast civilisation.[42]

Such killings represented deep personal tragedies for the families of the victims, but their complex emotions were soon submerged within the crude narrative of revolutionary violence. In almost all histories of this period in Ireland the funerals of the dead, which in Belfast were increasingly filling public space, are barely referenced. The victims of partition violence numbered far more than the statistics of those killed or injured. In all kinds of unseen ways, the lived experience of survivors was often one of grief, shame, disability, imprisonment, poverty, alcoholism and domestic abuse. This was played out amid an atmosphere of ongoing victimisation and the lingering undercurrents of communal and paramilitary coercion which would last for generations.

Much like the many national histories written in its aftermath, partition violence was justified and sanctified by a combination of machismo and romanticism. George Russell imagined the killers in the shadows as evidently 'ardent and selfless', because 'just as when I see the clouds warm at dawn I know the glow comes from a yet hidden sun'.[43] Attempts to narrate the complex transition to partition in the public sphere were dominated by the formidable publicity machines of the major protagonists. They pumped out crude propaganda based on reams of caustic testimony and vitriolic denunciation, continuously raising the stakes. The *Irish Bulletin*, the major Sinn Féin publication, deftly played on these fears, carrying lurid descriptions of violence and atrocities, including emotive pictures of dead children and penniless refugees. One Dublin journalist described the escalating violence in Belfast as a 'White Terror' and 'Jihad' carried out by 'Orange

[42] Patrick J. Gannon, 'Studies', *An Irish Quarterly Review*, vol. 11, no. 42 (June 1922), pp. 279–95.
[43] Russell, *The Inner and Outer Ireland*, p. 10.

dupes, glutted with loot and blood'.[44] Bizarrely intermingled with these graphic stories of murder and expulsion were nationalistic poetry, short stories and tales from Gaelic folklore 'to populate the desert depths of national consciousness', painting 'today's political rebels as the highest type of Irishmen',[45] a crass attempt to link together the struggles of the present with those of the past. Nationalist propaganda painted its own struggle as organic, idealistic and real. This was juxtaposed with that of Ulster which was viewed as 'ludicrous', 'artificial', 'commercial', 'modern' and deeply inauthentic. Much like its counterpart, the unionist press did everything it could to maximise the perfidious nature of its opponents, printing reams of unsubstantiated rumour about the plans of the IRA or the suspect loyalties of the Catholic Church. Ulster, one pamphleteer argued, had been 'slowly surrounded over previous decades, nay centuries, by pernicious and devious forces whose vile plots were finally coming to fruition'.[46] Isolated shootings along the border became attempted invasions by the time they reached the Belfast press and this misplaced perception of a state under siege fed the paranoia and tribalism of the Protestant population, becoming one of the state's most enduring foundation myths.[47]

Through a whole range of newspapers, posters, leaflets and public pronouncements, the crude meanings of partition, which one unionist dismissed as 'little more than a claptrap catchword', were transmitted to a bewildered population trying to make sense of complex changes.[48] Much of the Irish press dispensed with any pretence to objectivity or moderation. All kinds of knick-knacks and souvenirs were produced, including postcards, lapel badges and commemorative mugs, which sought to domesticate the conflict and render it in easily digestible forms. Propaganda imagery, heavily gendered in terms of its appeal, symbolised the home state through female representations of Ireland and Ulster or as allegorical symbols of the principles of freedom or justice on which for many the struggle hinged. Such images assumed great significance for the participants. The First World War and earlier Ulster Crisis had created established styles and social processes by which propaganda was internalised and communicated. The multiplicity of meanings inherent in terms such as 'self-determination', 'revolution' and 'freedom' saw the formation of ideologies which sought to mobilise belief and convince people that this was the way the conflict was to be best

---

[44] James Winder Good, 'British Labour and Irish Needs', *Irish Quarterly Review*, vol. 9, no. 36 (December 1920), p. 557.
[45] Russell, *The Inner and Outer Ireland*, p. 16.
[46] Pseudonymous, 'Light on Ulsteria', p. 120.
[47] See, for example, Follis, *A State under Siege*.   [48] *Irish Times*, 7 December 1918.

understood. However, this process was not simply the top–down manipulation of an innocent population at large. Propaganda did not try and create beliefs which hadn't existed before, but rather played on well-rehearsed prejudices, myths and common stereotypes of the enemy. As one nationalist polemicist spelled out on the eve of the Ulster Crisis:

The average Ulsterman is at base a bigot and as such knows as little of the rest of Ireland as the average American knows, say, of Mexico. He does not read anything except the Belfast newspapers; he does not travel through the south and west; if you were to tell him that it is not the factory but the farm that produces most of the wealth of Ireland, he would be simply and unflatteringly incredulous. He is a man whose picture of Heaven is a pocketful of iron nuts, the shelter of a side street, and a 'Papist' procession passing by. The rebellion he launches will last as long as the supply of nuts, bolts, kidneys, and whiskey. He lives in a little world of hatred and hallucinations.[49]

The process was thus both horizontal as well as vertical. Older social and cultural assumptions were enlisted into the struggle and to a large extent Irish society propagandised itself during the partition period.

Dawson Gordon, the unionist president of the Irish Textile Federation reflected on the period as a time when all he heard were '. . . stories that were so much fuel on the prejudice pile'.[50] He recalled a story told to him by his mother in his youth:

When I was small, I believed anything I was told about the Catholics. I remember this tale that my mother repeated to me as she said her Grandmother had told it to her: 'A neighbour of Grandmother's was alone in her cabin one night. There was a knock at the door. A Catholic woman begged for shelter. The neighbour could not bear to turn her back into the night. Then as there was only one bed, the two women shared it. Next morning grandmother heard a moaning in the cabin. On entering, she saw the neighbour lying alone on the bed, stabbed in the back. The neighbour's last words were: "Never trust a Catholic!"' As I grew a little older I found two other Protestant friends whose Grandmothers had had the same experience. And since I have been a labour organizer, I have run across Catholics who told the same story turned about. So I began to think that there was a hell of a lot of Great-Grandmothers with stabbed friends – almost too many for belief.[51]

Fatally. it proved hard to tell what was real and what was hyperbole, with rumour leading to exaggeration and a climate of fear. On 1 June 1922, for example, it was rumoured that every one of the 3,000 full-time policemen in Northern Ireland was to be assassinated in his home that morning, leading hundreds to refuse to sleep at home or attend work the next day.[52]

---

[49] Brook, 'The Problem of Ulster', p. 623.
[50] R. Russell, *What's the Matter with Ireland?* (Ulan, 1920), p. 56.   [51] Ibid.
[52] Colonial Office memo, NA, CO 906/30.

In 1921, a member of an isolated border Protestant community in west Ulster reflected:

[Nationalists] to my mind were a dark, subtle, and dangerous race, outwardly genial and friendly, but inwardly mediating fearful things. I knew that when the signal was given, and one could never tell the moment, they were ready to rise, murder my uncle, possess themselves of his farm, and drive my aunt and myself to perish on the mountains.[53]

Even sympathetic British and foreign journalists reinforced simplistic perceptions of communities at war, providing legitimacy to those who held members of the other religious community responsible for acts of violence hundreds of miles away, whether that be the Catholics of Banbridge or the Protestants of West Cork.

Violence was carried out to a large extent by young men on both sides. The complex causes of conflict were distilled down via crude political messages to become a simplistic justification of 'fighting for Ireland' or 'defending Ulster'. Belfast IRA leader Roger McCorley, himself only 15 years old in 1916, recalled each of the city's paramilitary companies receiving 'instruction and lectures' in Irish history and the broader context for their struggle by what he called 'political commissioners'.[54] An RIC report of November 1917 noted that the radicals of Sinn Féin 'seem to have got hold of the younger members of the nationalist community'.[55] On such a small island, with a population of barely four million, hundreds of thousands of young men associated themselves with a bewildering range of paramilitary organisations. To one London journalist it appeared that,

Ireland's peers, parsons, plutocrats and clerks recently graduated from back offices, boldly dropped their bibles and ledgers for drill-books and beat their ploughshares into swords.[56]

The IRA received almost 200,000 new recruits in the summer of 1921 while the unionist's government introduction of the Specials in September 1920 effectively mobilised every Protestant man of fighting age in the Northern state. Although much of this membership may have been nominal, it did demonstrate that paramilitarism was the conduit through which aspirations to statehood were to be articulated. During the conflict, the Orange Order acted as a recruiting sergeant for the Specials,

---

[53] Doyle, *An Ulster Childhood*, p. 48.
[54] Roger McCorley witness statement, BMH, NAI, WS389.
[55] RIC County Inspectors' Report, Belfast, November 1917, NA, PRO, CO 904/103.
[56] *Observer*, 19 October 1920.

funnelling in recruits from the many paramilitary and vigilante defence groups which had sprung up in the summer of 1920.[57]

Behind the statistics lies a hidden story of the complicity of thousands of individuals actively supporting or condoning acts of brutality. While not being prepared to engage directly in violence, many offered tacit support for the actions of their co-religionists. Many people gave succour to the militias, offering safe houses or moral support. On the more mundane level, hanging out a flag, subscribing to a radical newspaper, joining a chanting crowd, ignoring a fire or making excuses for the violence as 'regrettable but understandable' were all ways of offering positive reinforcement to the crude tribalism which fired the extremists. The sheer exuberance of political change led to a kind of euphoric blood-lust as communities lost their moral bearings. Reflecting on the period in 1924, P. S. O'Hegarty candidly admitted:

We adopted political assassination as a principle, we turned the whole thoughts and passions of a generation upon blood and revenge and death ... We derided the moral law and said there was no law but the law of force.[58]

Many chose to keep their heads down and not to get involved. Speaking out led to individuals being exposed and labelled as suspicious in terms of their communal loyalties. Offering direct opposition to the violence brought with it fatal dangers. The IRA and British crown forces, for example, killed numerous civilians who spoke out, condemning them as spies or informers. Reflecting back on the violence in Belfast, one Catholic cleric, James Kenny, articulated succinctly the pressures of speaking out:

the wild fanatics and the hoodlums of Belfast reverted to their type and their teaching. Only a very small minority were actively concerned in the pogroms, but the vicious system of sectarianism, like the vicious system of nationalism, blocked respectable citizens from taking any action that might be interpreted as sympathy for the enemy.[59]

The daily round of shootings, beatings and expulsions created an atmosphere of fear across Ulster which spread even to areas which had experienced no violence at all, making partition a traumatic experience even for those who were lucky enough to avoid its brutal methodology. One Dublin visitor to Belfast in the spring of 1922 noted the air of tension:

[57] D. Fitzpatrick, 'The Orange Order and the Border', *Irish Historical Studies*, vol. 33, no. 129 (May 2002), pp. 52–67.
[58] P. S. O'Hegarty, *The Victory of Sinn Fein* (Dublin, 1924), p. 91.
[59] James Kenny, 'The Catholic Church in Contemporary Ireland', *The Catholic Historical Review*, vol. 18, no. 2 (July 1932), p. 166.

As I made my way through its streets in the rain of Easter Saturday, it did assuredly look like a city with an uneasy conscience and a sick soul. Grimy, smoke oppressed, and inexpressibly dreary, its very external aspect was depressing. But helmeted soldiers at corners or behind sandbags, policemen in motley uniforms swinging rifles or carrying Webleys in their belts, armoured cars and "cages" careering at breakneck pace along the streets, spies lying perdus in quiet angles all these made the moral aspect of life infinitely more sinister.[60]

In such a context, communities and individuals lost their moral compass. Violence and brutality became normalised, and basic notions of welfare, empathy and respect were set aside. Even self-proclaimed pacifists such as the nationalist poet George Russell were able to say of the murderous months of early 1921 that it was 'well worth some bloodshed to save the world'.[61] One unionist newspaper editorial claimed that after the summer of 1920, Belfast suffered from an 'inexplicable epidemic brain storm'. However, it went on to warn that whereas 'brain-storms pass, whether after a day or two years, the atavistic politico-religious principles remain'.[62] Old systems of guilt and justice became confused and were judged largely by how well they acted to suppress or empower the rival communities. Like many, Fred Crawford, later to be a commandant of the largest contingent of Specials in Belfast, constructed his own apologetic for the suspect response of the authorities in dealing with,

cold blooded butchery . . . which has been going on all over Ireland for two years. Is it any wonder that the patience of the police has been exhausted and that reprisals have taken place? I consider they are justifiable and right in the eyes of God and man.[63]

The grey area between the breakdown of the British state in Ireland and its replacement with provisional forms of revolutionary justice severely crippled the legal power of the state. One commentator stated plainly 'the old system of impartial justice has for a time disappeared in this country'.[64] Old familiar systems of establishing guilt and innocence became confused, with little confidence expressed in traditional systems of justice. Countless trials collapsed as witnesses refused to testify and legal redress became synonymous with a reliance on the innate justice of your community's political cause. One judge in west Cork was 'struck with the statement in nearly every case: "The police have been unable to procure sufficient evidence to bring the perpetrators to justice"'.[65] In 1920, a system of Dáil arbitration courts were established across the south and west of Ireland largely in reaction to the collapse of law and

---

[60] Gannon, 'Studies', p. 280.   [61] Russell, *The Inner and Outer Ireland*, p. 16.
[62] *Belfast Newsletter*, 28 May 1922.   [63] Crawford Diary, PRONI, D640/11/1.
[64] *Irish Times*, 8 June 1921.   [65] Hart, *The IRA at War*, p. 52.

order in the provinces and local radicals taking matters into their own hands. While so often treated as a great success by historians, in that they offered local people some recourse to justice, such initiatives implicitly backed the violent pretensions of the militias and a reliance on the inherent decency of one's own community. Within the embryonic partition, states justice became increasingly arbitrary and biased against the other community. The police were overstretched and demoralised, with the IRA enforcing a boycott of the RIC very early in its campaign.

In Ulster, the violence of the summer of 1920 provided impetus for new security arrangements. In some areas especially along the proposed border, the UVF had started to revive and many had been complicit in the attacks against Catholics in Lisburn and Belfast. Many in government circles voiced their fears about the political reliability of the RIC in the north, expressing fears that more 'loyal' Protestant officers, often younger and more eager, had been sent for service in more troubled areas in Munster, leading to the transfer of older Catholic officers to quieter areas including Ulster many of whom were dismissed on little evidence as suspect. Richard Dawson Bates, the hard-line minister of home affairs, later wrote that,

the better type of men were drafted to the South, and men who could not be trusted or who were inefficient were sent to Belfast. Over 50% of the force in the city of Belfast are Catholic, mainly from the South and many of them are known to be related to Sinn Fein.[66]

Such perceptions, however, were largely illusory. Protestant RIC man Ernest Brookes said of his Catholic fellow officers 'they were all very good. I got on well with them all ... No trouble, all loyal, fight to the last'.[67] Similarly, William Britton recalled that 'there was no hostility, they were all good friends'.[68] Another Protestant RIC constable James Gilmer, said of his fellow Catholic officers: 'Relations were good, no difference at all ... It was different when the RUC and Specials got together.'[69] Such opinions were dismissed by Ulster's new elites and Craig himself called for some kind of native police force based on the model of the UVF who would, in his words, carry out a 'system of organised reprisals'.[70] The British government, despite criticism from General Neville McCready, the senior British army officer in Ireland, and Sir John Anderson, joint under-secretary, acquiesced in the scheme. Demonstrating the harsh reality that violence was now a defining feature of

---

[66] Dawson Bates memo, 9 January 1922, PRONI, CAB 6/37.
[67] Ernest Brookes quoted in Brewer, *The Royal Irish Constabulary: An Oral History*, p. 67.
[68] William Britton quoted in Brewer, *The Royal Irish Constabulary: An Oral History*, p. 56.
[69] James Gilmer quoted in Brewer, *The Royal Irish Constabulary: An Oral History*, p. 95.
[70] Craig quoted in T. P. Coogan, *Michael Collins* (London, 1991), p. 336.

the partition settlement, Northern Ireland would receive its own auxiliary police force even before the foundations of the state were laid.

In both parts of Ireland, paramilitary policing was the order of the day, with attempts at the creation of an impartial police force doomed from the start and attempts to enforce such ideas collapsing due to mutual suspicion from both communities. As early as October 1917, the inspector-general for Cork reported that in Munster and Connaught 'the defiant attitude of the people towards law and authority has made the duties of the police extremely difficult'.[71] Despite the rhetoric, the primary focus for both new partition governments was on bolstering its security apparatus. Much like its counterpart in the North, one of the first acts of the Dublin provisional government was to create its own armed police force in February 1922, to replace the moribund RIC. The Civic Guard, composed almost wholly out of veteran IRA paramilitaries, proved to be a volatile force and after a near-mutiny in mid-May over concerns of lingering RIC influence in its headquarters staff, was disarmed and reorganised. Even so, the provisional government drew on other more shady and unsavoury security forces in the shape of the Criminal Investigation Division, the Protective Officer's Crops and the Citizen's Defence Force, who along with the new National Army would be responsible for ensuring the survival of the Southern state. As in the north-east, this was to be achieved through an increasing focus on authoritarianism and the subjugation of political opponents. As with the Specials in Northern Ireland, the National Army, which grew to number over 45,000 men by April 1923, was an overblown expression of the new state's power, bleeding it dry of its scarce financial resources and ensuring that the new patriotism was to be expressed through organised violence and repression. Like with so many other aspects of partition, there was no middle ground, even within the two new states. Basic principles like justice became profoundly politicised as ordinary crime was lost in a sea of lawlessness and the forces of law and order were intermingled with residual paramilitarism. 'A great deal of ordinary highway violence', one British civil servant concluded after visiting Belfast, 'hides in the shadow of the political outrages'.[72] In such a dysfunctional atmosphere, appealing to the righteousness and impartiality of one's own community was thus, by definition, a political act.

By the end of 1922, an estimated 5,000 people had lost their lives, with over twice as many injured. In Belfast alone, almost 12,000 workers had been forcibly expelled, with a similar number expelled from their homes. Death, displacement and impoverishment had become the method by which the partition settlement was held together. Violence would continue in the Southern state for four more months as the Southern civil war

---

[71] Ibid, p. 51.   [72] Tallents Report, NA, CO 906/30.

entered its most bitter phase and the new Free State government, much like its Northern counterpart, resorted to internment, torture, executions and extrajudicial killings to hold itself together.

Both new partition states, faced with immediate civil wars, became increasingly centralised and authoritarian in character, employing harsh methods, unimaginable under British rule, to deal with their respective religious and political minorities. The cherished idea of armed localised civilian militias electing their own officers was replaced by a rigid and impersonal centralised state military machine. In the North, the legal mechanism was provided by the Civil Authorities (Special Powers) Act, enacted 7 April 1922, but only introduced fully after the shooting of a unionist MP on 22 May 1922. The Act, which would remain a pivotal part of the Belfast government's security apparatus for the next fifty years, allowed for internment of suspects without trial, executions and corporal punishment in the shape of flogging. When they occurred, the round-ups were swift and effective and targeted almost wholly on radical elements within the Catholic minority community. Three internment camps were established; one in Derry gaol, another in Larne Workhouse and most famously on an adapted prison ship, the *Argenta*, which floated offshore in Belfast Lough. Father John Hassan graphically described the conditions for its hundreds of prisoners:

This floating house of filth and misery is called by the splendid name of the *Argenta*. Probably nothing so vile could be found, even in Turkey, at the present day. The unfortunate prisoners are huddled together in sections of forty like cattle in a pen. The food is execrable, and has to be eaten off the floor. The lavatory accommodations consist of a few buckets placed openly at the end of the apartment.[73]

The men were confined to improvised communal cages below decks, with mail, supplies and visitors arriving on the ship by boat. Initially defiant, launching mass hunger strikes and issuing threats, internment, which for some was to last over two years, broke the spirit of the prisoners, many of them signing undertakings promising lawful behaviour or being expelled from Northern Ireland altogether. On their release, the die-hards, unlike in 1916 and 1921, were greeted with ambivalence by the Northern Catholic community, one of them confiding: 'The internees have been disappointed at the reception they received on release, and generally very little notice is being taken of them.'[74]

---

[73] G. B. Kenna (Father John Hassan), *Facts and Figures of the Belfast Pogrom, 1920–22* (Dublin, 1922), p. 152.
[74] 'Wickham report', 24 November 1924, PRONI, Secret Series Files, HA/32/1/46.

In the South, similar measures were taken with the passing of a Public Safety bill on 27 September 1922. Much like the Special Powers Act, the bill allowed for the creation of military courts, summary execution and internment. The first executions of five republicans occurred on 17 November after they had been captured carrying weapons in Dublin. This would be followed most notoriously with the execution of Erskine Childers, the anti-treaty propagandist, who was caught carrying a revolver, ironically given to him by Michael Collins. It was clear that the executions were political in nature, as Childers, in no sense a military leader, was a biting critic of the new Free State regime. As in Ulster, a further crackdown would occur after the targeting of a member of the Dublin parliament, in this case Sean Hales, who was shot dead on a Dublin street on 7 December. In response, on the day after the shooting, four republicans; Rory O'Connor, Joe McKelvey, Dick Barrett and Liam Mellows, who had been in prison since the first week of the civil war, were summarily executed. There was no pretence at any kind of trial.

The draconian methods of the new provisional government, despite complaints from the Church and Labour representatives, would escalate as the war continued. In all, seventy-seven republicans were executed in this fashion. More widespread, however, was the more informal use of reprisal, torture and massacres by elements within the Free State army and its police force. The shadowy Criminal Investigation Department, acting out of Oriel House in Dublin, Ireland's own secret police, instigated a policy of torture and beating of suspects. On the ground, in strong republican areas in the provinces, the army operated a system of summary military executions, and were implicated in a number of massacres, including that at the village of Ballyseedy, where in March 1923 nine republican prisoners were tied together and sent along a road to 'clear' landmines laid by their comrades. Eight of the prisoners were killed with one surviving to later tell his story. Added to this was the internment of over 13,000 suspect persons in large, open camps, dwarfing the number rounded up in the North.

Ironically, it was exactly this scale of violence that partition had been set-up to avert. Few had predicted that the utopian ideals of freedom and liberty would be realised at such a cost. The American writer Ernest Boyd poignantly reflected in 1922: 'What might have been cherished as a lofty dream is being trailed in the dust of ruined homes and burning cities'.[75]

---

[75] E. Boyd, 'Ireland: Resurgent and Insurgent', *Foreign Affairs*, vol. 1, no. 1 (15 September 1922), p. 90.

5   Unravelling Ireland

If partition was anything, it was an attempt to turn the idea of 'Ulster', what Eamon de Valera referred to derisively as 'a thing of the mind only', into an immutable earthly reality.[1] However, the process of partition was characterised by a similar level of denial on all levels. Behind the practical operation of the plan lurked the dangerous assumption that partition was something provisional: a short-term expedient embraced largely in order to facilitate an acceptable level of devolution and independence. Indeed, the lingering impression that partition was an interim solution meant that Ireland was permanently partitioned almost by stealth. There would be no defining partition moment. The varied timelines of the major protagonists meant any year between 1920 and 1925 could be given as the correct answer to the question as to when partition actually took place. The road to a permanent partition solution was a crooked one and there was thus little seeming concern shown about first laying the foundations for an enduring set of state structures.

Certainly, the superficial impression was that Irish unionists had achieved a great victory. Numerous nationalist commentators and later historians have painted partition as the British government bowing down to the wishes of an influential minority unionist elite. In such retellings the whiff of corruption or lingering colonial spite is ever present. However, the reality was immense confusion and disorientation on all sides. James Winder Good recalled meeting a bewildered group of foreign press correspondents in Belfast:

One met ... Germans insatiable for information about the military training of Ulster's army, Frenchmen floundering hopelessly in the morasses of Ulster theological controversies, Americans revelling in a real old-world "stunt" which appeared to them to be as remote from twentieth century concerns as the Wars of the Roses. The world learned at interminable length what Ulster was doing, but it was by no means so easy to discover why Ulster did it, or what it all meant.[2]

---

[1] *Gaelic American*, 24 January 1920.   [2] Winder Good, *Ulster and Ireland*, p. 198.

The image of cool calculation behind these fundamental constitutional changes from sinister London elites was largely a myth. On the ground the reality was chaotic and bewildering, and partition was only sustained through a series of ad hoc legal, administrative and security bodies backed up by a whole range of improvised and often contradictory laws and pronouncements. The bombastic revolutionary rhetoric on both sides had now to be translated somehow into real functioning states.

Nonetheless, for many there was a great sense of relief and celebration at the creation of Northern Ireland. The unionist press trumpeted the settlement as a 'major achievement' and a 'great victory', while James Craig and Edward Carson became the great spiritual leaders of the new nation. As Patrick Buckland has observed, the combination of these two men was very much a 'dream ticket' with 'both having what the other lacked. Carson's mercurial temperament and powers of oratory complimented Craig's stability and organising genius.'[3] The nature of unionist organisation did not lend itself to the rise of an Ulster dictator, but rather a chairman of the board and a safe pair of hands. In that regard, Craig appeared to be the ideal choice. Craig was certainly far more difficult to adore than Carson. However, his east Ulster roots and ascendency to the leadership of the new state came for many to personify the dogged no-nonsense pragmatism of those tasked with building the new Ulster state. As one contemporary biographer dramatically put it: 'James Craig was, under God, chosen to perform a task that must have baffled, if not defeated any other person ... bone of their bone, and flesh of their flesh, alien to them neither in belief nor in birth ... Against that rock, the gates of the Eirean hell could not prevail.'[4] In June 1921, a resident of Banbridge spoke for many in the unionist population when he told a London reporter:

Craig's a great man. In some ways he's a better man for us at the present moment than Carson. He was born among us, you see, and he's always lived here. He's more in touch perhaps with the practical occupations and aspirations of the people. Carson after all is a Galway man. We absolutely trust Craig.[5]

In reality, Craig was far more decent than dour. Not in any way an original thinker, he was an amiable no-nonsense straight talker who despised the 'political twisters' of Westminster. A London journalist recalled interviewing a number of spectators outside Belfast city hall on the occasion of the opening of the Belfast parliament in June 1921:

[3] Buckland, 'Carson, Craig and the Partition of Ireland, 1919–1921', p. 83.
[4] St. John Ervine, *Craigavon: Ulsterman* (London, 1949), p. 4.
[5] Ewart, *A Journey in Ireland*, 1921, p. 161.

Ulster is safe in James Craig's hands, said an old covenanter ... we trust him absolutely, and an Ulsterman cannot say more ... His is the outstanding personality in the new Government ... he is a tower of strength for Ulstermen and he faces with serene confidence a task which might well stagger any statesman.[6]

Craig, the Belfast-born son of a whisky magnate, had begun life as a moderately successful stockbroker, being one of the founding members of the Belfast stock exchange. After a brief low-key stint in the army, where he served as a captain in the Boer War, he moved into politics as a backbench unionist MP for East Down. His steady advancement led him to junior ministerial office working as financial secretary to the admiralty, a position he only relinquished in June 1921 when he became the first prime minister of Northern Ireland, a position he would hold until his death in 1940. Something of his dutiful character can be gleaned from a letter his wife wrote shortly after his resignation from his five-year stint at the admiralty:

I had never seen him so depressed. He told me "All my political career has been bound up with Ulster and this [government of Ireland] Act is the culmination of all my humble efforts. Was I then to say, Take your Act, I will stay in London, and while you work the Act I will look on. If it was a success I would thank God for it, but if it broke down and was a failure, after all the efforts of my colleagues and myself, I would go to my grave ashamed if I did not go down with the ship too."

By contrast, Carson was represented as the great spiritual leader of Irish unionism; his public image was that of an aloof, Olympian paternal prophet. One Dublin journalist observed: 'he bestrode the province like a Colossus, hailed by his admires as a superman, who by stamping his foot could call armies into being, denounced by his opponents as if here were Machiavelli and Bismarck rolled into one'.[7] It is no coincidence that it was Carson's, rather than Craig's statue which was chosen to sit outside the parliament building in Stormont, despite the fact he had little to do with the practical creation of the state it represented. He, himself, was to later admit that 'it was James Craig who did most of the work, and I got most of the credit'.[8] Even his long lean frame, pale face and sunken eyes seemed to represent his steely defiance. Nationalist politician William O'Brien characterised Carson as having 'the complexion of one fed on vinegar and with the features as inexpressive as a jagged hatchet'.[9] In reality, Carson, while certainly a mercurial idealist, was a vulnerable hypochondriac who espoused liberal values of religious tolerance, women's rights and the abolition of capital punishment. Such subtleties

[6] *Sunday Express*, 19 June 1921.   [7] Winder Good, *Ulster and Ireland*, p. 199.
[8] Buckland, 'Carson, Craig and Partition of Ireland, 1919–1921', p. 83.
[9] C. C. O'Brien, *The Shaping of Modern Ireland* (London, 1970), p. 87.

did not, however, alter the prevailing perception of him as 'King Carson'. 'God in His goodness', declared a female supporter at a rally in Carrickfergus in 1919, 'has spared Sir Edward Carson to us, but the day may come when we will see ourselves without him, and I want to be sure that no one in Ulster will have caused him one moment of pain or sorrow'.[10] At the same meeting, British army veteran Donald M. Wilson struck a similar note of adoration:

It is owing to Sir Edward Carson under Almighty God, that we have been saved from Home Rule, and the man that knows these things would rather that his right arm were paralyzed than be guilty of any act that would tend to weaken the work of Sir Edward Carson.[11]

'I am fully persuaded', added William Coote, the unionist MP, 'that the great country of the gun running will never be false to its great leader'.[12]

For Carson, though, partition represented a profound defeat. Although he came to accept the settlement as the only practical way forward, he remained at heart an all-Ireland unionist. In December 1919, during the debate which followed the announcement of the Government of Ireland Act, he stated: 'Ulster has never asked for a separate Parliament ... I cannot understand why we should ask them to take a Parliament which they have never demanded, and which they do not want.'[13] Two years later in December 1921, when partition was a going concern, Carson made a bitter speech outlining his feelings of betrayal and disillusionment at the implications of the recently signed Anglo-Irish Treaty:

I did not know, as I know now, that I was a mere puppet in a political game. I was in earnest, I was not playing politics. I believed all this. I thought of the last thirty years, during which I was fighting with others, whose friendship and comradeship I hope I will lose from tonight, because I do not value friendship that is not founded upon confidence and trust. I was in earnest. What a fool I was! I was only a puppet, and so was Ireland, in the political game that was to get the Conservative Party into power.[14]

Indeed, the oft-repeated irony that unionists, despite their anti-Home Rule stance, were the first to get devolved government in Ireland, misses the fact that the acceptance of partition represented a profound compromise for Irish unionists. James Craig's brother summed up the ambiguous feelings of many of his Ulster unionist colleagues 'we prefer to have a parliament yes, but not one of our own'.[15] Even many leading nationalists were

---

[10] *Belfast Telegraph*, 15 May, 1919.   [11] *Northern Whig*, 17 May 1919.   [12] Ibid.
[13] Hansard, HC vol 123, cols 1168–233 (22 December 1919).
[14] Montgomery, H. Hyde, *Carson: The Life of Sir Edward Carson, Lord Carson of Duncairn* (Portsmouth, NH, 1953), p. 38.
[15] P. Buckland, *James Craig* (Dublin, 1980), p. 41.

surprised by the concession. Back in 1912, at the start of the Ulster Crisis, Home Rule MP William Redmond expressed the opinion that excluding the north-east from that 'shared destiny, Home Rule' as the rest of Ireland, was 'a chimera and a bluff' mainly because Unionists would never condone the idea of their 'own beloved Ulster being partitioned'.[16]

The power shift to Craig, who replaced the ageing Carson as Unionist leader in February 1921, signalled the rise of a more practical and parochial unionism in the wake of the Government of Ireland Act. However, this move increasingly reflected less a positive aspiration to statehood than an increasing sense of insecurity. Despite the bombastic propaganda campaigns launched over the past decade, few knew what Ulster meant anymore. As the Government of Ireland Act had amputated three of Ulster's nine historic counties, the iconic use of term 'Ulster' didn't reflect realities. The issue of territory would be constantly fudged and postponed, allowing both unionists and nationalists to place their conflicting interpretations on the geographic shape of the border. As an image, the six-county state would barely appear in unionist propaganda until after partition, and even then would be wholly divorced from the twenty-six counties which bordered it. Nationalists, themselves, continued to present a united island in their propaganda, referring derisively to the 'short-lived Ulster experiment'[17] as 'Ulsteria' or 'Carsonia'. John Bowman has insightfully pointed out how the map image of the Irish island became itself a symbol of the nation, being used in both official state symbols such as postage stamps, schoolrooms and in popular nationalist propaganda. The fact that this image of a united geographical Ireland, minus the partition border line, remained the commonly used symbol both before and *after* partition has meant that for generations the image did not match the state in which they lived. As Bowman has written, 'The Irish case is complicated by the fact that the state is not coterminus with what is popularly, and – since the enactment of the 1937 Constitution – formally, regarded as the national territory.'[18]

The stark reality of this new-fangled 'Ulster' was six counties. Partition came as a profound shock for the Ulster movement, setting it loose from its ideological moorings. An American journalist who met with some leading members of the Ulster unionist council reported that they didn't seem to have the 'faintest clue of what this new Ulster nation would entail', concluding that it was clear their opposition 'was emotional rather

---

[16] *Dundalk Democrat*, 6 July 1912. See also pamphlet entitled 'No Partition of Ulster', PRONI, D627/435/98A.
[17] *Irish Bulletin*, 19 January 1921.
[18] See Bowman, *De Valera and the Ulster Question*, pp. 15–16.

than practical'.[19] Northern Ireland would be from the start a place of contradictions and paradoxes. As partition was being imagined, the notion of a hard border had never been the ultimate aim and, furthermore, on the ground was largely illusory. Outside of the East Ulster heartland, this new imagined Ulster was fraying at the edges. In the fluid political atmosphere, the experience for many inside the proposed new six-county border was little different from those who had been left out, whereas, inside the new six-county area many were living, and would continue to live for a number of years, under oppositional Catholic nationalist local authorities.

Despite Carson's occasional hyperbolic threat of establishing a provisional government in the province in 1914, a separate state had never been the aim of the Ulster leaders. Privately, he assured sceptical supporters that partition was only to be used as a tactic. As such, the clarion call of Ulster had been borne largely as a result of short-term political expediency, a bargaining counter to acquire for Ulster Protestants a political equality with the more numerous, preponderant Catholics in an undivided Ireland. It had articulated itself as an anti-Home Rule philosophy, and its propaganda and assumptions were shot through with a sustained critique of the dangerous social, religious and economic consequences that devolution would bring. By the end of the First World War, 'Ulster' had become a broad catch-all slogan of conservative protest rather than a positive blueprint for devolved self-government. When handed a new state to run, this ideological deficit became even more glaring. Hugh Montgomery, the Tyrone unionist, confided that the new arrangement was 'humiliating' for unionists and that the 'alternatives were between this miserable settlement and chaos'.[20] Drawing on a fairly typical analogy of Ireland as a sinking ship, the best he could say was that the new Northern Ireland represented 'dry land', and its Protestant-dominated counties were its 'water-tight compartments'. This meant, of course, that those Protestants left outside the six counties were now lost in an unforgiving Catholic sea.

The grandiloquent ideas and propaganda of Ulster resistance in 1913 now had to be reined in as people began to rethink the real implications of partition. Even Ronald McNeill, Conservative peer and cheerleader for Carson, admitted that in Ulster partition was 'accepted with acquiescence rather than with enthusiasm'.[21] Those communities which were destined to lay on the southern side of the border, many of which had provided the most militant support prior to the war, were particularly badly affected.

---

[19] *New York Times*, 16 February 1920.

[20] Copy of a letter to 'My Dear Stewart', from Hugh de Fellenberg Montgomery, Fivemiletown, Co. Tyrone, 17 June 1916, Montgomery Papers, PRONI, D627/429/39.

[21] McNeill, *Ulster's Stand for Union*, p. 110.

The rhetoric and symbols of Ulster were now forsaken as unionists had to turn away from their policy of intransigence to accepting what they had. Partition was thus the start of a new process, rather than an ending, throwing up a whole series of complex questions. What should Protestants in Ireland do? Were they to migrate to the new Northern state? What part will Protestantism play in this new state? Were the population British, Irish or Ulstermen? The big problem was that as soon as Northern Ireland became a reality, then the obstinate and idealistic rhetoric of 1912–1914 became a millstone for those attempting to build the new state. James Craig, himself, outlined the difficulty as follows: 'The whole structure and ethos of Ulster Unionism had been based upon a single object – determined opposition to Home Rule – and no constructive philosophy had been developed to govern a state they had neither expected nor wanted.'[22]

Nationalists faced many of the same ideological contradictions. If anything, they proved to be far more inflexible and unable to accept the new reality than unionists. Painting their own as-yet unformed state as that from which Ulster unionists were seceding, their much-rehearsed rhetoric left them with little choice but to stick to an all-Ireland sea-grit irredentism. In reality, the partition settlement was as fundamental to the existence and functioning of the Southern state as it was to unionists in the North. J. J. Walsh, the pro-treaty Sinn Féin TD, would later admit that the organisation had been struggling for a republic for only three quarters of Ireland and that any further moves towards separatism would 'alienate the North-East Ulster corner and divide our unfortunate country into two separate and distinct areas and into two races for all time'.[23] The debate for politicians thus became not a simple case of practical statehood, but a series of pledges and appeals to a romantic mystical image of a purer, imagined Ireland of the past.

However, there was much genuine horror and dismay among Irish nationalists at the prospect of partition. The image of the island of Ireland had been a fundamental symbol of Irish nationalist campaigns for decades, portrayed consistently as an almost organic entity tended and protected by a female figure of angelic purity. By the time of partition, such images had become ingrained in the nationalist consciousness. In 1904, Arthur Griffith wrote that 'the frontier of Ireland has been fixed by nature'.[24] Father Michael O'Flanagan, in a speech in Derry city in May 1921 argued:

[22] *The Factory of Grievances: Devolved Government in Northern Ireland 1921–39*, p. 5.
[23] J. J. Walsh, Dáil Treaty Debates, 188–9, 3 January 1922.
[24] A. Griffith, *The Resurrection of Hungary* (Dublin, 1904), p. 79.

The boundaries of Ireland were marked by the finger of Almighty God when He surrounded it with the circling sea. No country in the world had so clearly marked boundaries as Ireland had, and there could never be any dispute about them.[25]

Even Lady Lillian Spender fell into this sense of the unnatural nature of partition, observing in June 1923, 'it gave me a strange feeling to see a country so unnaturally and ungeographically divided-like seeing a living creature cut in two'.[26] In the nationalist imaginarium, partition remained a lasting source of grievance; something unnatural and illegitimate. Even the usually more moderate *Irish Times* gave voice to this view when the partition plan was announced:

You can no more dissect her into two separate parts than you can divide the living body. Yet this is what ostensibly has been done. It is against reason, against history, against the very nature of things.[27]

Both during and after the partition period, many nationalists refused even to refer to the new state in Ulster as Northern Ireland, preferring instead evasive terms such as the 'North of Ireland' or the 'Six Counties'.

While the middle-class nationalist and unionist leaderships tried to accommodate the idea of partition within their oppositional ideologies, for the vast majority of the population the overwhelming feeling was one of fear and confusion at what partition implied. Some saw the plan as a final answer to the Irish question, while others maintained their resolute denial, painting the solution as a further sign of British perfidy and the last twitching of a moribund colonial Ireland. The newspaper *Nationality*, for example, summed up this approach in 1918:

There is no such political entity as 'Ulster' . . . it is not Sir Edward Carson, but the Government of England which incited and secretly incites a minority in the north-east of Ireland to oppose the Republic. The so-called 'Ulster' question had neither its root nor its origin in Ulster. Its root and origin are English, and with the disappearance of English Government it would also automatically disappear.[28]

As the partition plan took on its own momentum, other more eccentric and innovative schemes were quickly abandoned or forgotten. While the federal idea had long been discredited in British political circles, a whole array of different ideas to avert partition which stemmed from it were resurrected. Few of the ideas were new and none attracted widespread support. Most flirted with some kind of internal exclusion for Ulster within an Irish Home Rule settlement, with Ulster receiving a permanent artificially engineered majority in the Dublin parliament. An elitist solution, it was to be achieved

---

[25] *Irish News*, 17 May 1921.
[26] Diary of Lady Lillian Spender, 25 June 1923, Spender Papers, PRONI, D/1633/2/26.
[27] *Irish Times*, 21 December 1919.   [28] *Nationality*, 9 February 1918.

by the use of a property qualification for new members and sparked derision as a return to the class-based restrictions of nineteenth-century politics, or, even worse, the Anglo-Irish ascendancy.[29] Notions of joint
sovereignty never got off the ground, although the inclusion of the
Council of Ireland in the Government of Ireland Act signalled the lasting
influence of such ideas. However, by 1921, such alternatives were little
more than gestures to the notion of Irish unity intended to soften the edges
of the harsh reality of the partition settlement. The Council of Ireland itself
was destined never to meet. Although it was established as agreed on
3 May 1921, and the Northern Ireland parliament elected its representatives around three weeks later, the refusal of Sinn Féin to engage with any
aspect of the Government of Ireland Act meant the council was doomed.
It would eventually be abolished in 1925 as part of the wider settlement of
the border issue.

Those who would be the most immediate victims of partition were also
the most virulent in keeping these alternative ideas in play. Many held out
the hope that the new frontier would be expanded or contracted at some
future unspecified date to accommodate them in the state of their choosing. This was particularly true of those who lived near the proposed line
itself. Indeed, the border communities had been some of the most strident
in their support or opposition to Ulster exclusion. For example, in the
small Protestant community of north Monaghan, almost a dozen unionist
clubs with 1,400 members were formed by the end of April 1912, less
than three weeks after Asquith first promulgated the Third Home Rule
bill. Such communities were among the first to militarise in their defence
of Ulster and contained some of the most militant units of the later
UVF.[30] Certainly those who had lived for countless generations strad-
dling the new border were most virulent in their resistance to the new
polarisation and most keenly aware of their possible fate of being minorities within a state run by their political and religious rivals. The fact that
the final extent of the border would not be decided until 1925 did much to
feed those fears and inspire defiance.

However, these protests were also a race against time as the partition
settlement quickly reached critical mass. Indeed, one of the most striking
features of partition was the startling speed with which the whole process
moved. While the Government of Ireland Act made tortuous progress
through Westminster, taking over a year to go through all stages (six
months longer than the contemporaneous Government of India Act),

---

[29] Letter from J. St Loe to Carson, 7 October 1916, PRONI, D/1507/A/19/5.

[30] T. Dooley, 'Monaghan Protestants in a Time of Crisis, 1919–1922' in R. V. Comerford,
    Mary Cullen, J. R. Hill and Colm Lennon, eds, *Religion, Conflict and Coexistence in Ireland*
    (Dublin, 1990), p. 241.

once enacted, partition institutions were established with alarming haste. Even prior to this, the situation on the ground had seen the establishment of a whole host of partitionist institutions that would form the basis of the later states which emerged. Both of the new partition governments were built on their previously illegal revolutionary organisations and institutions. Members of the revolutionary Dáil and the IRA would form the political and military elite of the Southern state, while the Belfast business elites and their paramilitary police forces would play a similar role in the North. Thus, the character and institutions of both states were set in stone long before the arrival of the legislation to sanction them.

The Partition Election

Before the new Northern Ireland was arguably one of the most important ballots in modern Irish history but is so often overshadowed by that of December 1918. Enshrined in the Government of Ireland Act, the two polls on both sides of the border were meant to be held in tandem; that for the parliament of Southern Ireland on 19 May and that for the Belfast assembly five days later. However, while the former elections did take place, their machinery was used to elect a new Dáil, and, apart from four independent unionists at Trinity College, all 124 members were returned unopposed for Sinn Féin. As such, both Sinn Féin and the UIL were able to concentrate all their efforts and propaganda in the North. Indeed, after negotiations in February, an electoral pact was signed between both nationalist parties on 17 March. Running on an abstentionist and openly anti-partitionist manifesto, this alliance appeared to present a formidable challenge to unionist hegemony in the new Northern Ireland. Furthermore, as in the South, the 1921 election was the first to be held under proportional representation, with fifty-two seats in total up for grabs, thus having the potential to maximise the nationalist vote.[31]

As the predominant partner in the nationalist alliance, Sinn Féin turned its legendary propaganda machine against the Belfast government. Anti-partition advertisements were placed in almost fifty northern newspapers and 50,000 copies of a newspaper, *The Unionist*, were printed and distributed to Protestants in east Ulster, warning them of the dangers of separation. The tone of the campaign, however, was preachy at best and deeply patronising at worst. It also employed fear and veiled threats, citing, menacingly, the Belfast Boycott as a sign of the economic strength

---

[31] Candidates for the election consisted of forty unionists, nineteen Sinn Féin, eleven UIL and five independent nominees.

of Southern nationalism. The boycott, the one practical policy instigated by the revolutionary Dáil government, was a half-hearted attempt to place an embargo on goods emanating from the future Northern capital by way of reprisal for the shipyard expulsions of the summer of 1920. Although reluctantly accepted and sporadically applied, the idea, itself, did much to reinforce Northern unionist perceptions of the perfidious nature of this new form of advanced Irish nationalism, also inspiring crude retaliatory attacks by Protestant vigilantes on those engaged in cross-community trade, whatever their political or religious affiliation. As for the practical effects of the policy, it did much to help the partition of the Irish economy, reinforcing Ulster's economic links with Britain and lessening its economic links with the south and west. In 1921, Professor James Henry at Queen's University called the boycott 'the first-fruits of partition'.[32] The fact that such trade as there was consisted largely of the distribution of imported English goods, as opposed to Ulster's own manufactures, meant that the boycott had little effect on the north-east's three main industrial sectors – shipbuilding, linen and agricultural produce.

Threats were twinned with a half-baked attempt to try and recruit Protestant agricultural workers in the west of the province, whom it was argued partition would leave at the mercy of east Ulster's urban industrial elites.[33] One Sinn Féin TD arrogantly stated that 'Ulster has really never had the truth preached to her ... and we should concentrate on the problem of her enlightenment.'[34] This 'truth' was to prove deeply condescending and counterproductive. One contributor to *The Unionist* wrote:

The great urban and rural landlords, the captains of industry, and the inevitable army of lawyers and politicians have turned the religious enthusiasm of the masses to their own ends through the inculcation of a medieval sentiment of ignorant bigotry. The landlords, to keep up rents and stave off agrarian agitation, the manufacturers to divert attention from the sweating and the slums that disgrace Belfast, and the lawyers to get into Parliament and annex all the jobs in sight. By using the rawness of the Orange creed as a laughable stepping-stone to place and power and by trading on the passions that have made the "lower classes" the blind and witless dupes of their own prejudices, the "leaders" have so manipulated the course of affairs that a profoundly Radical community is represented in Parliament almost entirely by Tory merchants, lawyers, landlords, and their agents, and the illusion has been created that loyalty to the British Crown and the cause of Protestantism are bound up in voting for an endless array of

---

[32] Ewart, *A Journey in Ireland*, 1921, p. 158.

[33] For an analysis of Sinn Féin's propaganda efforts prior to the election, see Keiko Inoue, 'Sinn Féin Propaganda and the "Partition Election", 1921', *Studia Hibernica*, no. 30 (1998/1999), pp. 47–61.

[34] Louis J. Walsh to Harry Boland, 4 January 1919, Count Plunkett Papers, NLI, 11,405.

reactionary barristers, property-owners, and wealthy manufacturers. Never, I suppose, in the history of politics was a greater confidence trick so easily and successfully played off on an unsuspecting electorate. Yet I am bound to add that in talking to the industrial "magnates" I found not a few of them just as bigoted and myopic as any "corner-boy," and just as much under the sway of a compound of fears, instincts, hatreds, and traditions in which facts had been metamorphosed out of all semblance to reality. There are business men in Belfast whose names are known all over the world with whom you can no more argue Irish questions than you can argue the race question with a Tennessee planter of the old school.[35]

In South Down, an RIC report spoke of 'wholesale terrorism' at the polling booth, while the local nationalist candidate styled himself as the head of the 'smash partition movement out to preach the truth to the cannon-fodder of the anti-democratic forces', before going on to say that anyone who voted for partition should make their way 'to the nearest lunatic asylum'.[36] In reaction, one Newry Sinn Féin leader wearily accepted how counterproductive the campaign had been:

The only effect that all our literature and leaflets etc. will have upon them is to bring them out to vote against us in greater numbers.[37]

Sinn Féin's decision to field Southern candidates for the election in Ulster, including some of the most high-profile separatists such as Eamon de Valera and Michael Collins, further alienated the unionist population and caused notable resentment within Northern nationalist circles. The editor of the Northern nationalist *Irish News* later opined:

Their standpoint was "southern" from the beginning; the blunder made by too many nationalists in the six counties was their persistence in their policy of approaching the question from every standpoint except their own.[38]

When the results of the election came in, they represented a devastating defeat for the nationalist project in the North. All forty unionist candidates who stood were elected, with the remaining twelve shared between the UIL and Sinn Féin. This result not only emboldened and legitimised the new Belfast government, it also further reinforced the partitionist assumptions of policymakers in London. Perhaps of more significance was the fact that those nationalist candidates who had been successful in the North had no intention of taking their seats in the Belfast parliament, whereas the elections in the South had not actually taken place at all.

---

[35] *The Unionist*, 16 May 1921.
[36] 'Report on election campaign in Newry, May 1921', Ministry of Home Affairs files, PRONI, HA 32/1/49. See also Fellenberg papers, PRONI, D921/2/5.
[37] Donnelly to O'Keeffe, 24 May 1921, de Valera Papers, 140.
[38] *Irish News*, 17 December 1925.

As the editor of the *Observer* noted, the two carefully crafted legislative bodies envisioned in the partition act were stillborn:

What is to happen to these unhappy parliaments? In the South the parliament will never meet, for the four members for Dublin University will clearly not constitute a quorum. In the North the parliament will no doubt meet and act, but it will be a forlorn and partisan assembly. All variety such as would have given it a truly representative character will have been purged out of it. How long can the [British] government plunge on from blunder to blunder, from disaster to disaster?[39]

With the complete victory of Ulster unionist candidates in the partition election, the process of turning the two Irelands into functioning political entities could begin in earnest. The great rhetorical ambitions of Irish nationalism and unionism now had to be crammed within the mundane borders of autonomous territories. The Irish economy arguably took the longest to divide. Certainly, the provisional nature of the partition settlement meant that both Irelands continued to share much of their pre-partition character. This was certainly true during its first decade, until de Valera's Fianna Fáil took power in 1932 and began the slow process of disentangling the Free State from its remaining links to Britain. The currency on both sides of the border was to remain the same and as such was linked to wider fluctuations in international currency markets.

The reality would be in the wake of partition, both new Irelands shared many similarities, most of them largely negative. This was particularly the case when it came to their dire post-partition economic performance. It was in the economic sphere that the attempt to meet the rhetorical ambitions of the state's founders was most jarring. Certainly, while judging the economic effects of partition presents a complex picture, there is little doubt that, following separation, both Ireland's suffered prolonged periods of economic stagnation and decline. The postwar economic depression which started in 1920 began almost simultaneously with the practical onset of the partition project and would define both of the two Irelands for the next two decades. By 1925, nearly a quarter of workers in Northern Ireland were unemployed, a state of affairs that would continue virtually unchanged right up to the start of the Second World War.

Partition had, without doubt, a deep impact on the Irish economy, which remained underdeveloped and largely dependent on its previous colonial ruler. Ireland's economy, much like that of other colonies, had been constructed by Britain primarily as a supplier of cheap agricultural products and even cheaper labour. Even after the Act of Union in 1800, when Ireland was fully integrated into the British economy, there was no

---

[39] *The Observer*, 24 May 1921.

mechanism for protecting fledgling Irish industry which faced over-whelming competition from larger and more technologically advanced firms on the mainland. As such, political union did not equal an end to dependency, but rather its further refinement. As Karl Marx wrote in 1860: 'every time Ireland was about to develop industrially, she was crushed and reconverted into a purely agricultural land'.[40] Partition and self-rule would highlight just how embedded this economic subser-vience had become. There was little attempt made by both new Irelands to foster cross-border economic cooperation or trade with barely 5 per cent of their total exports crossing the new frontier. With partition, the Dublin government was handed a threadbare state to run. Shorn of its most prosperous industrial region in the north-east, the Southern economy centred on small-scale farming. The new Free State government, ruled over for a decade by the Cumann na nGaedheal Party which had developed out of the pro-treaty wing of Sinn Féin, was deeply conservative, backing larger farming interests and failing to promote or protect Irish industry. The treaty gave the Dublin government full fiscal independence. However, for the first decade of its existence it remained linked to sterling rather than following an adventurous policy of eco-nomic independence. In its revolution from above, this new state, bur-dened by civil war debts and a backward economy, had little change in the volume, output or structure of its exports. While the Free State government's ability to balance the budget was a major achievement, certainly when compared to other new postwar European states, its parsimonious attitude to public spending, keeping income tax low, while cutting wages of teachers, police and civil servants in 1923 and the old age pension by 10 per cent the following year, added to its unpopularity and declining support. Radical attempts by their oppo-nents in the shape of Fianna Fáil to establish a rural autarky also failed miserably. Like the South, the North-East, despite its evident economic growth, was heavily dependent on Britain for its economic prosperity, especially its imperial and military expenditure. While in its heyday Belfast had supplied ships and military supplies to a confident expansive colonial empire, by the end of the Second World War it found itself economically shackled to a second-rate world power and the lack of breadth in its own industrial revolution showed up markedly. In both states, unemployment, poverty and declining standards of living were persistent problems. While in the South, mass emigration continued unabated after partition, averaging 33,000 per year, in the North the

---

[40] R. Fox, *Marx, Engels and Lenin on Ireland* (New York, 1940), p. 31.

Catholic minority bore the brunt of the persistent economic failure of Northern Ireland.[41]

On the ground, particularly along the new frontier, the economic damage caused by partition was far earlier to manifest and far more destructive. Previously prosperous areas such as North Monaghan, whose trade with east Ulster had grown sharply after the completion of a rail link to Belfast in 1882, became virtual 'economic cul-de-sacs' with partition. What had been prosperous market towns such as Clones, home to one of the most important rail junctions in Ireland, became economic dead ends with partition. Notably, of the several hundred Protestants to leave Monaghan during the partition period, almost three quarters of them came from the Clones area. The situation was similar in many border areas. In a letter to his local MP, Henry Sloan, manager of the Clogher Valley Railway Company, complained,

Poor Tyrone! The shopkeepers stand to lose about £5,000 a year by the reduction in staff wages, and this on top of the border and bad times will mean closing business for the half of them and the financial endpoint for the nearby villages.[42]

Partition infected every aspect of people's lives, from the sublime aspirations of identity to the mundane realities of everyday life. There was little central direction to these readjustments. Lots of key decisions were taken in haste or not at all. The fact that both states demonstrated a strong desire to ignore each other meant that cross-border institutions and services were allowed simply to decline, rather than be actively targeted for change. The illogical nature of the border as it meandered through villages, farms, fields and even individual shops and houses meant that most people tried to continue their pre-partition practices. It was only over time when this decay in services became seriously debilitating, or both states moved to impose their authority over these grey areas that problems began to arise. For example, postal services were a constant problem. The tedious border meant for many the nearest rural post office was located on other side of the border, leading to all kinds of concern about potentially sensitive security information arriving at a post office in the other state.[43]

---

[41] For an interesting discussion of the impact of partition on Irish economic development see M. Sheehan, D. Hamilton and R. Munck, 'Political Conflict, Partition, and the Underdevelopment of the Irish Economy', *Review of Radical Political Economics*, vol. 30, no. 1 (1998), pp. 1–31.

[42] 'Customs barrier: Irish Free State and Northern Ireland', January 1923–June 1951, NAI, TSCH/3/S1955A.

[43] For the effects of partition on the postal service, see 'Correspondence on reorganising postal services in border areas', PRONI, COM/21/8.

While the negative economic effects of partition were detrimental to many, others found in the new arrangement an opportunity for personal advancement and economic survival, relocating to fill vacancies which sprang up in the two new partition states. Thousands of civil servants, soldiers, lawyers and policemen were thus drawn by opportunities in the new polities north and south to serve in their ministries, police forces and armies. It is ironic that the partition conflicts of 1919–1923 proved to be the one major employment growth area in Ireland. In desperate search of employment, almost 3,000 Northern Catholics – 'out of workers' – headed south to join the provisional government army between April and December 1922, one republican opponent stating that 'their motivation seemed to be twenty-four shillings a week and dyed Khaki uniform'.[44] Similarly, hundreds of RIC men, both Catholic and Protestant, heading in the opposite direction to take up posts in the police services of the new Northern Ireland. By June 1922, Northern Ireland alone had a police force numbering almost 30,000 men furnished with a yearly budget of over £1,800,000.[45] The sheer cost of setting up two new states on such a small island would prove prohibitive. New police forces, civil services, judiciaries, transport infrastructures, postal services, educational facilities, not to mention the new symbols and regalia of the new states, meant the logistics of partition would prove prohibitive.

By the end of 1922, the new Northern Ireland faced imminent bankruptcy. The Government of Ireland Act had initially envisaged two devolved and equitable Irish administrations, both of whom would pay an 'Imperial Contribution' which would go towards the cost of defence, foreign and diplomatic affairs, all functions still being performed by the London government. The notion of an imperial contribution had been at the heart of the financial arrangements in all of the previous Home Rule bills. While the British had wanted it to be the primary financial obligation of the devolved parliament, the Irish saw it as largely a voluntary donation from what was left of Irish domestic expenditure. As such, if ever enacted, it offered a recipe for constant discord between London and any future Irish parliaments. Furthermore, with the shift towards two separate bespoke solutions for the new states, this plan soon began to unravel. Even so, the fact that the fund-raising powers of the unionist government were so restricted anyway meant that they had little room for financial innovation. Initially, Northern Ireland was to contribute £8 million

---

[44] Patrick Maguire statement, BMH, NAI, WS 693.
[45] See Farrell, *Arming the Protestants*, pp. 36–9. For northern recruits to the Free State Army see 'Reports on Recruits Leaving Northern Ireland to Join Irish Free State Army', 'Secret Series' files, PRONI, HA/32/1/168.

per year to the British exchequer. However, it was clear that, in the context of the brief postwar economic boom of 1919, when the Act was presented, the exchequer had grossly exaggerated the future level of this contribution. By 1921, economic recession had already started to bite and it had become clear that the much vaunted Ulster prosperity had its limits. Adding to the inflated imperial contribution were the vast financial demands of the unionist government's growing security apparatus which included tens of thousands of full and part-time police officers and auxiliary police, border installations, new prisons and a vast army of civil servants working within the ministry of home affairs, by far the largest department of the new Northern state. These costs had been supplemented by a series of sporadic one-off payments from the British government, usually made in reaction to desperate pleas from Craig about the impending collapse of his besieged government. Unionist paranoia and a need to sharpen the threat the new state faced in order to maintain the flow of funding did little to calm confrontation on the ground. The twin pressures of the inflated imperial contribution and the overblown security budget led to a squeeze on public expenditure and already it was clear that without amendment the new state would fall behind the rest of the UK in terms of education and essential public services. After desperate appeals and impending bankruptcy, a new committee chaired by Lord Colwyn agreed to reduce Northern Ireland's imperial contribution from £8 million to £6 million per year. The reality was that the payment was largely symbolic. Indeed, by the mid-1930s it reached the token amount of barely £30,000. While making the new state at least nominally financially viable, the eventual report released in December 1924 had serious flaws. The issue of who was responsible for unemployment expenditure was fudged and the focus on only 'necessary expenditure' and the refusal to omit new social improvements and initiatives from its assessments of Ulster's liability to London, meant that it was in the interest of the Belfast government not to peruse progressive and well-funded initiatives in the realm of housing and education. With this further amendment of its terms, impoverishment and scarcity was thus hardwired into the partition settlement and, for the rest of its existence, the Northern Irish government would depend on a series of short-term and ad hoc loans and grants from London to keep it afloat. In the 1930s, Sir Richard Hopkins, later permanent secretary to the treasury, wrote:

Northern Ireland has been a depressed area. So far from receiving any large Imperial Contribution [from them] we have invented a series of dodges and devices to give them gifts and subventions within the ambit of the Government of Ireland Act so as to save Northern Ireland from coming openly on the dole . . .[46]

In such a situation, the Northern Catholic minority became not only an unwanted political burden, but also a financial one, drawing into sharper relief the issue of which members of its population deserved a fair share of the new state's scarce resources.[47]

Some poured scorn on the reality of the changes wrought by partition when compared with the hyperbole of revolution. Ernest Boyd, a Dublin-born American journalist wrote in the summer of 1922:

Government departments associated from time immemorial with an alien bureaucracy continued to function at the hands of an imperturbable staff of permanent officials who, with surprising docility, acquired for official use-a copy of the standard Irish English dictionary, altered their letter heads to a strange modernization of the ancient tongue of the Gael, and substituted Irish phrases for the time-honoured formulae of British official correspondence. Two learned bodies were called into existence to translate the decrees of the new government into Irish, khaki was displaced by olive green worn by the national troops on sentry duty and in other services of the Free State, the red mail boxes, once the symbol and sign of the Sassenach, turned a soft refreshing green, and bore the superscription "An Post." Those who remembered the time, but a few months ago, when such heresies were the price of martyrdom duly marvelled at the signs and wonders which were vouchsafed to the citizens of the Irish Free State.[48]

Despite such cynicism about the meaning of the new states, in local areas the change was much in evidence. In the South, leading members of Sinn Féin and the IRA came out of their hiding places to assume power. Tiny revolutionary elites were left in charge, drawing their legitimacy from either their role in the Easter Rising or their membership of the small commercial classes of East Ulster. Allegations of corruption and nepotism, which were to dog both partition states throughout their existence, were present form the very start. One American commentator noted in 1922:

Economists are bound to be voices crying in the wilderness when the salaries drawn by Ministers in this tiny enclave are equal to those paid for the whole Australian Commonwealth. Placemen are multiplied in Parliament at a rate that would scare even Mr. Lloyd George, with the inevitable result that members who do not figure in the salary list, instead of constituting, as was boasted, a band of brothers, devote all their energies to snarling rancorously at their more fortunate

---

[46] Quoted in P. Bew, P. Gibbon and H. Patterson, *Northern Ireland, 1921–1924: Political Forces and Social Classes* (London, 1995), p. 62.

[47] See Colwyn Committee reports and papers, PRONI, FIN/11.

[48] Boyd, 'Ireland: Resurgent and Insurgent', p. 88.

fellows. There is scarcely a pretence of constructive legislation. After a few academic debates, in which concrete proposals of any kind were barred, education, housing, and schemes of temperance reform have been dropped like so many hot potatoes. The Orange taxpayer in the Six Counties openly gibes at his Parliament as an incubus which drains him of money without making any return.[49]

For good or ill, partition offered freedom for these unionist and nationalist elites to refashion their new domains in their own image. The local press powered out new stories of freedom and nationhood. State building acquired the status of a grand achievement, an enterprise forged by the national will. While the old Ireland was pulled apart by partition, something new had to take its place. New histories, ideas and images had to replace the regalia of imperial pretension which had previously been the norm. Both states lacked the money for grand festivals or celebrations. They were too busy fighting for their lives, too busy buying bullets rather than busts. However, the need for updated foundation myths was desperately pressing. As Estyn Evans observed of Northern Ireland, this process involved,

not only the making of ministries but also the formation of a cultural heartland with cultural centres. In the midst of a civil war and with the state barely functioning, the intention to establish a national Museum and Art Gallery fell by the wayside as every penny was pushed into holding the state together with payment for its massive security apparatus.[50]

Both of the principal ideologies, unionist and nationalist, had been compromised by partition. Something new was needed to quickly repudiate the old order and demonstrate in practical ways the visions of freedom which had been honed and rehearsed over the decades prior to partition.

Lacking the finances for grand gestures, both states opted to advertise their legitimacy in similar ways by focusing on their foundation myths, which were characterised largely as a narrative of resistance, and of democracy surviving against all the odds. Indeed, to demonstrate that they had been right all along, both of the new elites sought to run their states with efficiency and competence in order to validate their revolutionary rhetoric. Many sought to turn the utopian rhetoric of the struggle into reality. William Coote, the unionist MP for South Tyrone, saw the new state as a chance to change Ulster forever. As one observer noted, Coote's speeches were optimistic in the extreme. He promised:

---

[49] Wilson, 'The Irish Free State', p. 324.
[50] E. Evans, 'The Personality of Ulster', *Transactions of the Institute of British Geographers*, no. 51 (November 1970), p. 3.

merely as a beginning, a complete overhaul of the poor law system; development of scientific research in industry, with a college chair and liberal scholarships; root-and-branch reform of the educational system, with better buildings, better equipment, more highly-qualified and highly-paid teachers; improved transport and waterways; and a comprehensive recasting of the licensing laws. All these things were to be done not only without increasing expenditure, but with a sensible reduction in taxation; and Mr. Coote was not alone in prophesying that in happy Ulster the more the Government undertook to do, the fewer the number of officials required to do it.[51]

The reality of the new state institutions was far more humble and prosaic. Ironically, this was most true in Northern Ireland. Despite its professed loyalty to the status quo, unlike Dublin, Belfast had to transform itself into a functioning capital city from scratch. A whole host of civil servants, administrators and officials descended on the city to construct improvised ministries with hardly enough buildings to contain them.[52] Even the state parliament had to make do with makeshift premises. After its initial meeting in Belfast city hall, the new House of Commons of Northern Ireland met in the Gamble Library of the Union Theological College near Queen's University where it would remain for over a decade until the building of Stormont, what Devlin called a 'palace for politicians', in the mid-1930s at the cost of £8,000 per annum.[53] The prime ministerial residence was a school administration building at Cabin Hill in East Belfast, with the billiard room of the house converted to hold meetings of the new cabinet, while outside a motley detachment of Specials and ad hoc militia, assigned to protect the new government, were billeted in the coach house. Craig, himself, as prime minister, managed to gain the services of a barely adequate number of civil servants and was forced to address envelopes himself at home in the evenings while his wife licked and affixed the stamps. The Irish Free State was so impoverished that it resorted to using British stamps with the words 'Saorstát Éireann 1922' crudely embossed on their fronts.

---

[51] Wilson, 'The Irish Free State', p. 326.

[52] The ministries of Northern Ireland were department of the prime minister, ministries of commerce (including agriculture until 1925), education, finance, home affairs and labour.

[53] The move to a permanent home for the new Northern Ireland parliament was made in the Autumn of 1922, although the foundation stone on the new buildings at Stormont was not laid until 1928 and only occupied for the first time in 1931. The parliament project became something of a personal obsession for Craig, who made frequent visits to London to discuss it, even at one point taking out a personal loan of £3,000 to make a deposit on the £20,000 site in East Belfast. For a fascinating discussion of Craig's role in the building of Stormont, see A. Greer, 'Sir James Craig and the Construction of Parliament Buildings at Stormont', *Irish Historical Studies*, vol. 31, no. 123 (May 1999); *The Irish News*, 4 November 1925.

Despite financial restrictions and the ongoing civil unrest threatening the survival of the new states, both managed to spare a day, separated by six months, to mark their foundation. Despite dire warnings and many letters begging them not to go, King George V and Queen Mary came to Belfast to perform the opening ceremony for the new parliament on 22 June 1921. Assembling at its temporary lodging at Belfast city hall, the parliament was officially opened three weeks after its first sitting. Lady Craig later recalled the events in her diary:

The great day. The King and Queen have the most wonderful reception, the decorations everywhere are extremely well done and even the little side streets that they will never be within miles of the ceremony are draped with bunting and flags, and the pavement and lampposts painted red white and blue, really most touching, as a sign of their loyalty. Imagine Radicals in England thinking they would ever succeed in driving people like that out of the British Empire or wanting to![54]

By contrast, one Dublin journalist reported his impressions of the gaudy celebrations:

When Belfast determines to be imposing in an ornamental fashion the effort is woefully like the display of the vulgarian who seeks to dazzle by loading his fat fingers with rings and hanging gold chains across his paunch. The curious thing is that Belfast achieves its worst outrages when it is, as it fondly believes, making concessions to beauty.[55]

After the procession through the streets to the city hall, the ceremony moved to the Ulster Hall where presentations and speeches were made, with Craig seated proudly between the king and queen. The king expressed his wish that the new Belfast parliament would 'prove to be the first step towards an end of strife amongst her people, whatever their race or creed,' and that he 'felt assured they would do their utmost to make it an instrument of happiness and good government for all parts of the community which they represented'.[56] Veteran leaders of the Ulster Crisis, including Crawford and Spender, were awarded CBEs, a number of others made members of the privy council, and Richard Dawson Bates, the new minister of home affairs, was knighted. Notable by his absence was Carson, who remained in London on the pretext of work commitments. Sending his wife in his stead, the reality was he had decided to remain out of the spotlight and give Craig, the new Ulster leader, centre stage. Outside in the streets, Protestant crowds broke into spontaneous cheering and sang the national anthem. One commentator, Ronald McNeill, described the day with his typical fervour:

[54] Diary of Lady Craig, 22 June 1921, PRONI, D 1415/B/38.
[55] Winder Good, *Ulster and Ireland*, p. 255.   [56] *Morning Post*, 23 June 1921.

The enthusiasm of the loyal people of the North rose to fever heat. It was felt in Ulster that the association of this time-honoured ceremonial with the baptism, so to speak, of the latest offspring of the Mother of Parliaments stamped the Royal Seal upon the achievement of Ulster, and gave it a dignity, prestige, and promise of permanence which might otherwise have been lacking. No city in the United Kingdom had witnessed so many extraordinary displays of popular enthusiasm in the last ten years as Belfast, some of which had left on the minds of observers a firm belief that such intensity of emotion in a great concourse of people could not be exceeded.[57]

'On that day', continued another commentator, 'it was difficult not to believe that the entire population of Belfast were loyal citizens of Empire.'[58] This, of course, was far from the case. While all elements of the new unionist power structure were involved, ominously, the ceremony was boycotted by almost the entire Catholic minority community, a third of the new state's population. After the festivities, the royal party were escorted back to the royal yacht by Craig. The whole visit had lasted barely five hours. According to his wife, when Craig returned home he 'breathed the biggest sigh of relief imaginable, after having got them safely on to the Royal Yacht again, after such a marvellous day without any contretemps to either of them'.[59] Indeed, behind the pomp and ceremony of the day had lurked the unstable reality of the new Northern capital. There was enormous security, with armed policemen placed in commandeered houses along the route. Over the following three weeks, long after the king had departed, twenty-five people would be killed in the city with dozens of houses burned to the ground in West Belfast, leaving hundreds of people homeless.

The king's speech in the city hall was designed with politics as well as pomp in mind. Conciliatory in character, it would pave the way for a truce with Southern nationalists and eventual negotiations leading to the signing of the Anglo-Irish Treaty in early December. As such, a similar, if less grand, ceremony would take place in Dublin six months after that in Belfast. The ceremony in Dublin, held on 16 January 1922, was far simpler, but no less symbolic. The Lord Lieutenant, Lord FitzAlan of Derwent, formally handed over Dublin Castle to the provisional government, an event which Michael Collins described unconvincingly as a 'surrender'. *The Times* described the scene as follows:

All Dublin was agog with anticipation. From early morning a dense crowd collected outside the gloomy gates in Dame Street, though from the outside little can be seen of the Castle, and only a few privileged persons were permitted to

---

[57] McNeill, *Ulster's Stand for Union*, p. 112.   [58] *Belfast Newsletter*, 23 June 1921.
[59] Diary of Lady Craig, 22 June 1921, PRONI, D 1415/B/38.

enter its grim gates ... members of the Provisional Government went in a body to the Castle, where they were received by Lord FitzAlan, the Lord Lieutenant. Mr. Michael Collins produced a copy of the Treaty, on which the acceptance of its provisions by himself and his colleagues was endorsed. The existence and authority of the Provisional Government were then formally and officially acknowledged, and they were informed that the British Government would be immediately communicated with in order that the necessary steps might be taken for the transfer to the Provisional Government of the powers and machinery requisite for the discharge of its duties. The Lord Lieutenant ... expressed the earnest hope that under their auspices the ideal of a happy, free, and prosperous Ireland would be attained ... The proceedings were held in private, and lasted for 55 minutes, and at the conclusion the heads of the principal administrative departments were presented to the members of the Provisional Government.[60]

Behind the pomp and pageantry surrounding the birth of these new states, the image of a new beginning was largely an illusion, disguising the reality that power had been placed in the hands of small revolutionary elites whose legitimacy and practical authority was tenuous and vociferously challenged from both within and without. In Belfast, the government was faced with a sharp escalation in sectarian violence and the need to employ increasingly desperate measures to merely stop the state from collapsing. Only days before the handover of Dublin Castle, Eamon de Valera resigned as president and led anti-treaty TDs out of the Dáil: six months later the new state was engulfed in civil war between radical and moderate nationalist factions. For the British, the handover to these new partition governments was the signal for a hurried retreat. Observers noted, even during the muted pageantry of the Dublin Castle ceremony, the chimneys pouring out smoke as British officials hastily burned their files. When the British army left Dublin city hall, they cut down the flagpole and took it with them, while military vehicles, which had previously been used to maintain the crown authority, were advertised in local newspapers with an eye to more prosaic uses, and sold off. Building projects and plans for improvements were scrapped or suspended and money transferred to banks in London, while servants of the old regime in the shape of soldiers and civil servants looked to get out of Ireland as quickly as possible.

Left to their own devices, both of the new Irish governments would face the fight of their lives merely to survive, let alone flourish. This process of survival would be enmeshed with their attempts to impose their respective settlements on their new states. Indeed, the defining nature of both partition states would be a continuation and drastic escalation of the violence which had brought them into existence in the first place.

---

[60] *The Times*, 17 January 1922.

The subtleties of ideology and myth would now be replaced by hard-headed attempts to physically control significant opposition groups. A pragmatic focus on the security of the new states and the armed forces to hold them together, pulled in most of the money and sucked much of the optimistic idealism out.

Thus, the most prominent visible manifestation of the new states' power would be the development of various new security forces. Political elites on both sides of the border now laid aside their previous utopianism and replaced it with a hard-edged policy of physical control and the ruthless persecution of nonconformists. In the grey area between the building of new states and the collapse of the old, all kinds of fanatical paramilitaries, political radicals and armed idealists flourished. Fred Crawford painted the building of the new Ulster state in biblical terms:

It struck me how history repeated itself. Here were our men working with their weapons on them as the Jews did in the time of the prophet Nehemiah at the building of the wall of Jerusalem about 445 B.C. It is stated in chapter IV. 17: "Every one with one of his hands wrought in the work, and with the other hand held a weapon." So with my men.[61]

The IRA in the provinces made provisional government control of Ireland outside of Dublin largely fictive, while the Northern Catholic minority ignored the new Northern Ireland with numerous local elected councils pledging their allegiance to the Southern state.

Across Ireland, the confrontational nature of the partition settlement drew huge numbers of people into membership of these pseudo-militaristic groups. The sheer level and variety of violence Ireland experienced meant that even nominally peaceful groups became drawn into espousing confrontational rhetoric. For example, Joe Devlin, the West Belfast Home Rule MP, spoke to an AOH meeting in the most visceral terms, talking of the organisation as being 'a terror to its enemies and a great source of strength and power to every genuine Irishman and Irishwoman … They stood for toleration in Ireland, they sought to quarrel with no section of their countrymen, but they were there to defend … the twin principles of Faith and Fatherland.'[62]

Other more high-profile groups flouted their paramilitary credentials as defence forces or freedom fighters. These would form the backbone of the later police and military forces who looked to defend the new states, while others, who had resisted partition or offered a different vision of the future would be sidelined, repressed or fade away to nothing. The ideological

---

[61] Crawford Diary, PRONI, D640/11/1.
[62] Quoted in J. Finnan, *John Redmond and Irish Unity, 1912–1918* (Syracuse, 2004), p. 41.

reality of these organisations was their fanatical nationalism and anti-democratic rhetoric. 'The Ulster champion', one Dublin nationalist opined, 'would no more temporise with democracy than an early Christian would deny his faith by burning a pinch of incense before the statue of the emperor'.[63] This culture of paramilitarism would be immensely popular and increasingly so as the partition period progressed, with hundreds of thousands of men and women volunteering for one or other of these heterogeneous groups. The nationalist newspaper, *The Nation*, the creature of the arch-nationalist journalist D. P. Moran, warned that 'Ireland is now given over completely to militarism and reaction.'[64]

These paramilitary groups would form the basis of the security forces, set to defend both partition states. The UVF would transform itself into the Specials, while the pro-treaty IRA would form the backbone of the new security forces of the Southern state. Indeed, in the South, involvement in paramilitary violence would become a key prerequisite for passage into the governing elites of the new state. As the states began to form, there would be an inevitable grey area between these various groups and the new official state forces. The fact that both states were formed by insurrectionary movements left a dangerous ambiguity between the need to create conformity to the new regime and a culture of anti-state activity fired by the unrealistic idealism of the revolutionary leaderships of both states. Violence had become hardwired into the state-building project and membership of a group espousing simple tribalistic messages a key right of passage to the levers of power. This dreadful alchemy would lead to disaster in 1922, and levels of violence, ironically, unthinkable under British control.

[63] Winder Good, *Ulster and Ireland*, p. 202.   [64] *The Nation*, 15 January 1919.

6   Ireland's Other Civil Wars

As Ireland entered the year 1922, it appeared to many that through the device of partition, the Irish question was well on the way to finally being answered. The two new Irish states had been established and were moving tentatively towards consolidating their positions, while a mechanism of sorts had been fashioned for the settlement of any outstanding financial, political and territorial disputes between them. Certainly, few could have predicted the disaster that was to follow.

With hindsight, however, it was clear that the potential for future conflict was an almost inevitable end result of the nature of the agreements and the bad faith and wildly differing expectations of their participants. Both of the Irish states suffered from a crippling lack of legitimacy and both faced aggressive political and religious minorities whose primary goal was to undermine and eventually destroy the states themselves. Both new partition states would be engulfed in damaging civil wars, while a further proxy civil war would be launched between the governments themselves. Hotheads like Crawford even suggested as much:

My plan is a simple one. Take all the soldiers out of Ireland, give Ulster their weapons, rifles, machine guns, etc., and let us fight it out ourselves. We are prepared to take on the job.[1]

While Tallents was to report that 'Ulster is preparing herself to meet graver demands than that of the mere maintenance of internal order behind a shield of British troops.'[2] More generally, the populations of the two states had become highly politicised over the preceding years. They had been fed on a diet of extremist propaganda and irredentist rhetoric, much of which was directly contradicted by the partition plan. Protest and anti-state activity had become normalised by 1922 and large parts of the island had already experienced intense periods of violent upheaval. Murder, rioting, martyrdom and expulsion had all become common currency in Ireland by 1922. Now elements of the very same

[1] Crawford Diary, PRONI, D640/11/1.   [2] Tallents Report, NA, CO 906/30c.

138

armed militias on both sides of the border who had fuelled this confrontation were to be called upon to make the transition to becoming the responsible police and military forces of the new and cripplingly weak partition governments.

Perhaps most concerning for the future stability of the new Ireland was the withdrawal of the British army. During the early months of 1922, 40,000 troops in sixty-eight infantry battalions were evacuated and shipped back to Britain. Despite the very public handover of Beggar's Bush Barracks to the provisional government on 31 May 1922 and the images portrayed on newsreels of British soldiers marching out of Ireland in the full light of day to cheering crowds, the reality was that the bulk of departures took place late in the evening with very little fanfare. However, the British drawdown, while subdued, was prohibitively expensive. Along with the regular army, the 6,000 men of the Auxiliaries and Black and Tans were also withdrawn, and the RIC disbanded in stages and its members pensioned off. Along with over £200,000 of local government arrears to pay, local administration having broken down over the previous two years, the British government faced a bill of almost £1.5 million simply to remove its civil and military presence from the island.[3]

The first British army unit left Dublin port on 20 January 1922. Newspapers reported the inauspicious scene, 'the soldiers cheering and waving their caps as the vessel drew out. Except for the quay labourers in the vicinity, their departure was practically unnoticed and there were no answering cheers.' In the morning 'a row of cold and empty "cookers" [i.e., armoured cars] standing in line ... some handed-over hutments, small flags trampled into the mud and some floating flotsam and jetsam are the sole reminders of the departed British troops.'[4] As part of the first stage of withdrawals, British troops were concentrated in major barracks in Dublin, Cork and the Curragh. When it came to policing, although the formal disbandment of the RIC took place on 31 August 1922, it was demobilised steadily throughout March 1922 at Gormanstown Camp, this process being completed in May.[5]

Throughout the rest of 1922, Britain retained only a limited and non-committal military presence in the south and west of Ireland. The strength of the garrison in Dublin would remain at 5,500, but maintained a very low profile and would play virtually no role in the conflicts to come. The British government had decided, if possible, to implement the partition settlement at arm's length, leaving the two new Irish governments to face each other

---

[3] See *The Times*, 21 February 1921.   [4] *Evening Herald*, 21 January 1922.
[5] A. Kinsella, '"Goodbye Dublin": The British Military Evacuation 1922', *Dublin Historical Record*, vol. 51, no. 1 (Spring 1998), pp. 4–24.

across the fragile new frontier. Violence along the border flared almost immediately with a series of kidnapping raids by IRA units. Shootings along the boundary became commonplace with the inevitable corollary of reprisal attacks in Belfast. Between 13 and 15 February, thirty-one people were killed in Belfast, including six children after a bomb had been thrown into their schoolyard. The following month, the death toll reached unprecedented levels, principally due to the active participation of paramilitaries and new state police forces in the violence. In March, the notorious 'MacMahon murders' witnessed masked policemen shooting six male members of the Catholic MacMahon household in their North Belfast home. The IRA would respond with further sectarian atrocity, throwing bombs onto trams packed with Protestant shipyard workers, and at Altnaveigh in South Armagh, executing Protestant civilians who they had lined up outside their burning houses.[6] James Masterson-Smith, permanent under-secretary at the colonial office, stated in March that 'an explosion on the frontier, leading to open war between large forces, may be expected at any moment'.[7]

In response to the upsurge in violence, the British temporarily halted troop withdrawals and established a grandly titled Border Commission, with Churchill threatening a full reoccupation of the country if the violence continued. However, the commission was little more than a gesture to border security.[8] Made up of a party of well-intentioned, but hopelessly undersupplied, liaison officers from the three governments, the commission proved wholly ineffective in stemming the tide of violence or securing the border. General Neville Macready, would later comment:

To those who knew anything of two of the component parts of the Commission, the IRA and Ulster representatives, the scheme was foredoomed to failure, though no doubt it looked very attractive in Whitehall ... From the first, in spite of the loyal efforts of British officers, the whole affair was a farce.[9]

What was becoming painfully clear during the spring of 1922 was that any lasting solution was unworkable if both sides did not acquiesce in the partition plan.

The British government's rapid evacuation of Ireland during the spring of 1922 was painted as a great victory in the nationalist press. Throughout the long years of violence and struggle, Sinn Féin had stuck rigidly to their opinion that conflict in Ireland was due fundamentally to the British presence. George Gavan Duffy complained directly to the British cabinet:

[6] R. Lynch, 'Explaining the Altnaveigh Massacre, June 1922', *Eire-Ireland*, vol. 38, no. 3 (Fall/Winter 2003), pp. 184–210.
[7] Masterson-Smith memo, NA, CO 906/30.
[8] See, for example, Cabinet Minutes, PRONI, CAB/9/Z/11/2.
[9] Churchill to Cope, 31 March 1922, PRO, CO 739/5.

'The situation has been made by you and demands an act of repentance. You are the obstacle to Ulster. Leave the matter open to us.'[10] Irish nationalists seemed to genuinely believe that unionist opposition was somehow artificial and that if the British left Ireland, nationalists and unionists would revert to a harmonious coexistence. Louis J. Walsh wrote that Ulster unionist opposition was 'an entirely false sentiment produced by artificial causes and stimulants',[11] while the *Irish Bulletin* sounded a conspiratorial note arguing that the 'religious riots have been engineered in the North of Ireland by British agents'.[12] Lying beneath such perceptions, was an unjustified suspicion that partition, rather than being an unwelcome and crude compromise between two incompatible ideologies, was the result of a British plot. During the treaty negotiations, Arthur Griffith gave a neat summary of nationalist orthodoxy:

If the British Government stands aside and does not throw its force behind Ulster we will come to an agreement, but so long as they [i.e., Ulster unionists] feel the British Government behind them there is *non possumus*... They imagine they have special interests contrary to the rest of Ireland. We are prepared to consider these but not to consider separation. Ulster was never eager for partition. If Ulster had not the British Government backing it in any attitude it takes however unreasonable, we could settle the Ulster problem.[13]

Events during 1922 would demonstrate that nothing could have been further from the truth. Such a reading of the situation was to prove profoundly mistaken and goes a long way to explaining why nationalist policy on the issue of Ulster remained so ineffective and ambiguous. Far from facing the reality of partition, nationalists comforted themselves with a tide of anti-British rhetoric and a refusal to accept the legitimacy of unionist opposition. What followed would be disaster. Indeed, by early June 1922 both new states were on the verge of collapse and the failure of the whole partition project appeared to be imminent.

Such attitudes had shaped Southern nationalist assumptions and strategy during the negotiations leading to the Anglo-Irish Treaty. Despite the fact Sinn Féin leaders, aside from flat denial, had done little to prioritise the ongoing division of the country, they were well-aware of the power of the issue as a demonstrable injustice which would garner sympathy from both their own constituencies and wider public opinion in Britain and the USA. However, they failed to capitalise on this advantage and were easily sidetracked and outmanoeuvred by the wily Lloyd George, accepting his

---

[10] Jones, *Whitehall Diary*, p. 130.   [11] *New Ireland*, 15 March 1922.
[12] *Irish Bulletin*, 23 July 1921.
[13] K. Middlemass, ed., *Thomas Jones, Whitehall Diary: Vol. III: Ireland 1918–1925* (Oxford, 1971), p. 127.

vague promise of a future independent boundary commission which would adjust the new border in their favour. The failure to insist on precise details as to when the commission would sit, the criteria it would use and how much territory it would actually transfer, would later have devastating consequences for Ulster's Catholics. Once again, as in 1919, the partition plan, despite the existence of a functioning government in Belfast, was portrayed as provisional and reversible.

Craig was furious about the idea, stating plainly in the Northern Irish parliament:

We will not have any Boundary Commission under any circumstances . . . we will hear no more about a Commission coming to decide whether our boundaries shall be so and so. What we have now hold, and we will hold against all combinations.[14]

He, at least, was ready to accept the reality of partition, and its compromises, and move on. Even so, it was clear that Craig's intransigence on the issue was testing the patience of his previous allies on the right of British politics. While their primary concern was hardly that of creating an equitable border or the welfare of minority communities, the commission idea being fired more by strategic political concerns than lingering liberal principles, they at least had to adhere to the pretence of it, if only to ensure a peace agreement in the south.

Fred Crawford himself noted the change of mood:

Public opinion in England has lost all sense of right, fair play, truth, justice, and liberty of religion, or even political views. One feels dazed at the want of moral sense of the English people at present . . . I would sooner be a decent nigger than an Englishman at the present moment. The Castle in Dublin is trying to irritate Ulster and, being backed by the Cabinet, they will very soon cause the Ulstermen to hate England as much as she is disliked in the South and West of Ireland.[15]

The unqualified support of the British establishment which had been so glaring during the Ulster Crisis a decade earlier had now clearly dissipated. An embittered Carson who increasingly felt abandoned by his once loyal Tory allies, said in the Lords: 'The joy bells of peace have stopped ringing . . . the sequel must be civil war', adding, sarcastically, with 'a voice of terror and tragedy'. 'Do not let us wait for more murders, more kidnappings, more sacrifice. Surrender now. It is far better!'[16]

Lloyd George was pleased with the outcome. Not only had he resisted the unionists, but had also made leading Tories complicit in the settlement. He would later go on to compare himself with Abraham Lincoln in his determination not to negotiate with the Ulster radicals 'of the

---

[14] Craig to Northern Ireland Parliament, 23 May 1922, vol. 2.
[15] Crawford Diary, PRONI, D640/11/1.   [16] *The Guardian*, 9 February 1922.

Confederacy', despite being urged to do so by moderates. While the treaty and the Partition Act may have solved the long-standing crisis in British politics, how it affected Ireland and whether it would work on the ground seemed of secondary importance.

For the rest of 1922 unionist attitudes to the British government would be marked by increasing mistrust and fear. The most insidious impact of the Treaty was in failing to finally settle the partition issue and thus spreading deep uncertainty in the minds of the Ulster population. The promise of a potential amendment to the border, which, by optimistic Free State estimates could involve the transfer of a third of Northern territory to the South, raised the hopes of nationalists in majority Catholic areas and sustained their ongoing resistance and obstruction to the Belfast regime. By contrast, for unionists the threat of an unfavourable boundary adjustment led to deep disillusionment and paranoia, especially after the instigation of the IRA campaign along the border. In May 1922, at the height of the IRA's offensive against the North, Craig left a memorable and perceptive analysis of the impact of the treaty on Ulster:

The Boundary Commission has been at the root of all evil. If you picture Loyalists on the borderland being asked by us to hang on with their teeth for the safety of the Province, you can also picture their unspoken cry to us, "if we sacrifice our lives and our property for the sake of the Province, are you going to assent to a Commission which may subsequently by a stroke of the pen, take away the very area you now ask us to defend?"[17]

Unionist fears over the implications of the treaty and growing mistrust of the British government would lead to a whole new focus on military solutions to the partition question in the first six months of 1922. The disbandment of the RIC during the spring of 1922 reinforced these fears. The ad hoc Special constabulary of 1920 would now be massively reinforced and armed to defend the Northern state against a feared onslaught from nationalist opponents on both sides of the border. By May 1922 there would be over 30,000 men under arms in Northern Ireland, costing, it was estimated, £5 per head for every citizen of the province. The rest of the male unionist population was also effectively mobilised as reservists in case of dire need. Stephen Tallents, the British civil servant sent over to investigate the workings of the Belfast government, noted in his report that these 'C' Specials were made up of 'a high proportion of the remaining adult male population'.[18] Major-General Arthur Solly-Flood, appointed as military adviser to the Northern government in the spring of 1922, would call for the arming of an intermediate force of

[17] Craig to Churchill, 26 May 1922, NA, CO 739/14.
[18] Tallents Report NA/CO/906/30c.

15,000 more 'C1' Specials – a force which Tallents had already described as 'territorial military force in all but name'[19] – and wide-ranging military plans to defend border areas. The total cost of the Specials in the post-treaty period alone would amount to the enormous sum of £2,561,865. Even so, for radical voices such as Solly-Flood and Fred Crawford such preparations were not enough, with both calling for a general mobilisation and the creation of a de facto Ulster volunteer army paid for by the British with arms 'lent without charge'.[20] Solly-Flood's scheme, rubber stamped by the Belfast government, was to cost the enormous sum of £5,000,000, and was to be scathingly dismissed by Tallents as,

the work of a soldier without police experience, whose name carries no weight in the country which seems destined to finance his plans. It has been subjected to no real criticism. A weapon is being forged which in time of crisis might be most dangerously used by other hands than those who now control it.[21]

Indeed, Solly-Flood's paranoia, much like that of his cohort Crawford, knew no bounds, even going so far as to suggest the internment of suspect nationalist children with a system 'on the lines of the Borstal institutions in England',[22] a suggestion which drew indignation even from the reactionary Northern Ireland ministry of home affairs.

In June 1922, James Masterson-Smith wrote to his colleagues in the colonial office about the incongruous situation:

The British government has armed and is paying for forces which it is told by the one who controls them, will in certain eventualities be turned against itself. If Ulster does not accept the award of the boundary Commission the British Government will either have to pour in overwhelming forces and engage on a civil war of the most hateful kind, or else, be accused in the presence of the civilise world of connivance with Ulster. It is difficult to avoid the conclusion that the Government of Northern Ireland has succeeded in assuming the military functions specifically reserved to the British Government, simply by calling their forces "police." Our equivalent force of police in Great Britain would make at least 800,000, or in Germany about 1,300,000 men. What would France say if Great Britain allowed Germany to maintain well over a million "police" armed with rifles?[23]

Even so, the provisional government was hardly in a position to apply more pressure to the Ulster government. Despite the fact that they had now become the acknowledged representatives of the Northern Catholic minority with both the Belfast and London governments, they were in no

---

[19] Ibid.   [20] Tallents Report, NA, CO 906/30.   [21] Ibid.
[22] Solly-Flood to Minister of Home Affairs, 3 August 1922, 'Secret Series' files, PRONI. HA/32/1/252.
[23] Masterson-Smith memo, NA, CO 906/30.

shape to demand the sitting of the Boundary Commission. The Northern Catholic minority deferred to Southern leadership due to a combination of practical political necessity and a positive faith in the assurances of unqualified support they had received. This was to prove a risky strategy, relying as it did on the existence of a united, consistent and stable Dublin regime, hardly characteristics of the weak provisional government facing political meltdown and eventual civil war.

Kevin O'Shiel, the head of the North-Eastern Boundary Bureau, pointed out frankly:

What a ridiculous position we would cut – both nationally and universally – were we to argue our claim at the Commission for population and territory when at our backs in our own jurisdiction is the perpetual racket of war, the flames of our burning railway stations and property and the never-failing daily lists of our murdered citizens.[24]

John Dillon put the situation more succinctly, arguing that starting consultation about the border issue at this time, 'would be perfectly worthless—you might as well consult how to build a skyscraper on a bottomless, shaking bog'.[25]

However, it was also obvious that in the spring of 1922 the new found focus of Southern nationalists on the iniquities of partition was a useful way to unite the moderate and radical wings of the Sinn Féin movement. Certainly, the use of the issue suited the interests of both pro- and anti-treaty groups in the South, offering them a shared crusade and a rare subject on which there was broad substantive agreement.

As such, the spring of 1922 would see for the first time an identifiable anti-partitionist campaign launched by Irish nationalists in the political, diplomatic and military spheres. Covert support was given to IRA guerrillas in Northern Ireland, while the legendary propaganda machine of Sinn Féin was turned towards the perceived brutalities of the unionist government and the sufferings of the Northern Catholic minority. The rationale behind the campaign, however, remains hard to discern. It seems unlikely that it was a concerted effort to bring down the unionist government. Little attempt was made, for example, to occupy border areas containing large Catholic populations which, it was argued, would soon be allotted to the Southern state by the future Boundary Commission. The policy was certainly rather crude in character, with its focus on sporadic border attacks and the shooting of Northern policemen, suggesting it was largely initiated to appease hard-line militarists

---

[24] O'Shiel report, Cosgrave to Mulcahy, 25 January 1923, Mulcahy Papers, University College Dublin Archives Department (UCDAD), P7/B/101.
[25] Dillon to O'Connor, 10 February 1923, DP 6744/916.

who had declared against the treaty settlement. If it's avowed aim was somehow to protect the Catholic minority, it proved to be disastrously counterproductive, with small-scale border incursions by IRA units sparking off prolonged bouts of reprisal rioting in the Northern capital. Indeed, the border became for the first time a functioning front line between the two states. Wilfred Spender on a visit to the frontier in June 1922 compared the border with its customs huts, rows of 'block-houses, sandbags, barbed wire' to the trenches of the Somme where he had fought with 36th Ulster Division in 1916.[26]

One of the key results of the growing violence was increasing tension between the British government and the unionist regime in Belfast. Senior civil servants in London were particularly concerned about the constant demands from Belfast for more resources to shore up its extravagant security apparatus. In March 1922, a cabinet memorandum written by Lionel Curtis expressed disquiet at the over £1,000,000 already paid to subsidise the Northern government, noting that 'When a Government enrols, drills and arms with rifles large numbers of Specials the distinction between military and civil control has broken down.'[27] Winston Churchill himself was irritated by the failure of Craig to demonstrate any engagement with the Boundary Commission plan, with Cosgrave describing the 'Ulster Protestants as the spoilt children of politics'.[28] Lloyd George made the point to Craig that the six-county division was only ever intended as provisional in the first place, and that the lack of a rational examination of the extent of the boundary would

stereotype a frontier based neither upon natural features nor broad geographical considerations giving it the character of an international boundary.[29]

On 8 March, Churchill told the cabinet that 'in view of the heavy obligation in regard to troops and Special Constabulary which we were incurring on their behalf' he was not 'disposed to accept a simple refusal from the Northern government' to engage with the proposed border adjustment.[30] When Craig made his opposition to the Boundary Commission public in May, Churchill responded angrily:

I do not consider your declaration, made without any reference to this Government, that in no circumstances would you accept any rectification of the frontier or any Boundary Commission as provided for in the Treaty is compatible with requests for enormous financial aid and heavy issues of arms. While I was actively engaged in

[26] Diary of Lady Lillian Spender, 25 June 1922, Spender Papers, PRONI, D/1633/2/26.
[27] Curtis Memo, 26 March 1922, NA, CO 739/14.
[28] Cosgrave to Churchill, 20 August 1922, NA, CO 906/21.
[29] Quoted in Ervine, *Craigavon*, p. 444.
[30] British Cabinet Meeting, 8 March 1922, NA, CAB 43/1.

procuring the assent of my colleagues to your requests, you were making a declaration which was in effect in one passage little short of a defiance of the Imperial Government whose aid you seek.[31]

Stephen Tallents made a number of criticisms of the functioning of the unionist government. In particular, he was heavily critical of the partial way the extensive powers of the ministry of home affairs were being used under Richard Dawson Bates, who William Ewart memorably called 'a downright hard-headed zealot, with a clear-cut horizon and no sentiment to spare'.[32] Tallents found Bates to be

the least competent of all the present Ministers to rise to its occasion. His house is, of course, carefully guarded; but the story goes the round in Belfast that this guard is an extravagance, since the Republicans long ago realized what an asset he was to them in his present position.[33]

While calling for Bates to be removed, the major arm of his ministry in the shape of the 'B' Specials was the subject of particular criticism:

This force was, I am told, an invention of Sir James Craig's and he will hear nothing to its detriment. But the Catholics regard it with a bitterness exceeding that which the Black and Tans inspired in the South, and several prominent Unionist public men told me privately that this purely partisan and insufficiently disciplined force was sowing feuds in the countryside which would not be eradicated for generations.[34]

Increasing British concern about the dysfunctional nature of the Northern government was inspired by a wish not to alienate pro-treaty support in the South by its unqualified support for the Belfast regime. Such concerns reveal the profound failure of the partition plan. The idea, inherent in the Government of Ireland Act, of letting the Irish sort out the issue between themselves had failed miserably. While still trying to keep Ireland at arm's length, the British government now tried to paint itself as in 1917, as an honest broker between both parties.

This approach would lead to the instigation of a series of meetings between the two leaders of the new embryonic Irish governments, Michael Collins and James Craig. The need to convene these meetings demonstrated that the partition plan, as originally envisaged, had failed. The fact that, only now, three years after the legislation to divide Ireland had been initiated, was an attempt made for both sides to talk to one another, demonstrated how flawed the original solution was. There had, of course, been one previous meeting between the leaders of the two new

---

[31] Churchill to Craig, 23 May 1922, NA, CO 906/20.
[32] Ewart, *A Journey in Ireland, 1921*, p. 158.   [33] Tallents Report, NA, CO 906/30.
[34] Ibid.

Irelands. Back in May 1921, just prior to the elections to the partition parliaments, de Valera hosted Craig in a suburban house in Dublin. While Hamar Greenwood, chief secretary for Ireland, who had engineered the meeting, referred to it as the 'most hopeful thing to happen in 750 years',[35] the accounts of its two participants highlighted just how far apart they were on the shape of the partition settlement. The resulting 'debate' was almost risible, if the results of its failure had not proved so tragic. According to de Valera's later account:

> Craigavon had been told that I had asked to see him and I was told that Craigavon had asked to see me. So we met rather under false pretences. We sat on opposite sides of a table and I said after the first few moments' silence "Well?" He looked at me and he said "Well?" I then said "I'm too old at this political business to have nonsense of this kind: each waiting on the other to begin" and I started putting our case to him. He spoke of the Union as if it were a sacred thing. "But," said I, "do you not know how the Union came about" and I started telling him about it. After a while he tore a piece of paper from the *Freeman's Journal* which was lying beside him. "I think," he said, after writing for a few minutes, "we ought to issue this statement." He had drafted it to the effect that we had exchanged our respective views on the situation. That ended the talks but I must say I liked him.[36]

Craig's version of the meeting was equally bizarre, being forced to endure a lecture on Irish history from de Valera, who spent most of the time 'harping on the grievances of the last 700 years':

> After half an hour he had reached the era of Brian Boru. After another half hour he had advanced to the period of some king a century or two later. By this time I was getting tired, for de Valera hadn't begun to reach the point at issue. Fortunately, a fine Kerry Blue entered the room and enabled me to change the conversation, and I asked Mr. De Valera what announcement he was going to make to the Press about our meeting. Finally, I tore off a piece of paper and wrote something down.[37]

Churchill, like Greenwood the year earlier, had high hopes for some kind of agreement between Craig and Collins. Collins was evidently more worldly and practical than de Valera, as was the Northern premier, and a concrete arrangement of some kind seemed likely. Much like the Irish Convention five years earlier, the intention was to 'put Irish problems in Irish hands' and allow the British government to remain aloof from the discussions:

> We will do our very best, but it rests with Irishmen who care for Ireland to try and bring about a better state of things. They alone can do it. Great Britain will help,

---

[35] Greenwood quoted in *Gaelic American*, 14 May 1921.
[36] T. P. Coogan, *De Valera: Long Fellow, Long Shadow* (London, 1993), p. 215.
[37] Ervine, *Craigavon*, p. 411.

but the initiative, the controlling administration, has passed out of our hands by our own will, deliberately into the hands of Irish men. Let them meet together, and endeavour to create in a satisfactory manner a decent future for Ireland.[38]

Churchill's optimism was short-lived. Soon after the first meeting in January, he was to confide: 'Everyone in Ireland seems unreasonable. The Irish will not recognise that they, like every other civilised people, must adopt reasonable methods for settling differences.'[39] Indeed, what was being attempted was essentially the renegotiation of the two ailing partition settlements and their amalgamation into one workable solution. These personal meetings between two men would be the nearest that Ireland ever got to fulfilling the grandiose promise of an embryonic all-Ireland body as spelled out in the idea for a Council of Ireland.

While hopes for some kind of agreement were high, in practice the principles and policies they outlined were to prove hopelessly optimistic. The first meeting in January yielded a brief summary of principle. The Boundary Commission was now to be scrapped with any future agreements worked out between the two Irish administrations themselves. How that was to be achieved, considering that at the same meeting the Council of Ireland was also scrapped, was left unresolved. Both leaders also made vague promises to ease the tension between the two states; Craig promising to allow for the return of expelled Catholic shipyard workers from Belfast, while Collins reciprocated with an assurance that he would do all in his power to bring the Belfast Boycott to an end.

However, such promises proved unrealistic, especially considering the upsurge in violence which was to follow in February and March. Fail as it did, there were two aspects of the agreement which would prove of profound significance. The first was that through negotiation the provisional government had moved towards recognition of partition and the legitimacy of the Belfast government. This point, in particular, was much trumpeted by Craig himself after he received huge criticism from his government colleagues who suspected that even agreeing to the meetings involved in some sense a recognition that the Dublin government had some say over what occurred north of the border.

The second and related point was that through their decision to call for a personal conference between the two government leaders, the British government now acknowledged that they were the representatives of their respective minorities within each of the others' states. For Northern unionists, this issue was never of much significance, largely because the

---

[38] M. Gilbert, *Winston S. Churchill: Years of Turmoil* (New York, 2015), p. 773.
[39] I. Chambers, *The Chamberlains, the Churchills and Ireland, 1874–1922* (New York, 2006), p. 243.

vast majority of Ulster Protestants were included in the state and those that weren't had already been rejected with the decision to accept a more truncated territory in Ulster. Southern Protestant opinion had long been divergent from that of its Northern co-religionists and, while there were numerous complaints about their treatment at the hands of the Dublin government, Ulster unionists never consistently moved to advocate on their behalf. As would increasingly be the case with the partitioned Irish nationalist community, those who found themselves in their state of choice, saw their co-religionists on the other side of the border as 'weak' or 'compliant' and pursuing a hopelessly lost cause which they themselves had given up on. One unionist correspondent from Tyrone criticised the seeming compliance of unionists outside Ulster as follows: '... the real difficulty with the Southerns seems to be that they have been bitten with a kind of "Sleeping Sickness" microbe. They think they are hopelessly beaten and that it is of no use for them to wake up and even make an effort.'[40]

When it came to the Northern Catholic minority, however, the situation was different. Northern Catholics were a larger, more vigorous and cohesive group whose leaders were hopeful of their imminent inclusion in the Southern state. Furthermore, Churchill's decision to accept Michael Collins as their spokesman did not reflect the reality of Northern nationalist opinion on the ground. Sinn Féin remained the minority partner in the Ulster nationalist political landscape, with Joe Devlin's UIL still possessing the support of the majority of Catholic opinion. In June 1922, Churchill himself was to admit that his failure to include Devlin in the debates had been a mistake, claiming that

the thrusting aside of Mr. Devlin has been one of the worst disasters in the situation ... He was a better man than the present leaders in Southern Ireland and a tried parliamentarian, who if he had been given a chance would have gone very far.[41]

Despite the abject failure of the first pact, Churchill persisted in his belief that direct negotiations would somehow yield a more substantive agreement between the two Irish governments. The second pact, made public on 31 March 1922, was to offer a far more concrete and detailed set of proposals. For the Southern side, Collins agreed to do all he could to end IRA activity along the border, once again end the Belfast Boycott and return prisoners kidnapped in border raids in the previous two months. Craig again committed himself to the return of the expelled shipyard

---

[40] Letter from J. R. Fisher, 2 May 1918, PRONI, D627/433/23.
[41] Churchill to Lloyd George, 7 June 1922, NA, CAB 21/254.

workers and the release of political prisoners held in Northern gaols. Most significantly, the second pact called for the creation of an arbitration committee and a police advisory group which would ensure the inclusion of Catholic recruits in the security forces of Northern Ireland. A third grouping was to administer a British-funded grant to alleviate hardship for both communities in Belfast.

In many quarters there was an ecstatic welcome to the second pact. Its first clause, insisted on personally by Churchill, pronounced optimistically 'Peace is today declared'. The historian Martin Gilbert, in his biography of Churchill, claimed that the reaction to the pact was 'one of widespread euphoria. It seemed to advance the Irish Treaty from the stage of hopeful declaration to that of positive action.'[42] However, the honeymoon was short-lived. Ironically, the period directly after the signing of the pact witnessed the worst period of violence yet seen in Belfast.

Indeed, if anything, the second pact made things worse rather than better for the two Irish leaders, both of whom were wary of upsetting more hard-line radical elements back home. Craig, on his return to Belfast, was greeted with consternation by some of his ministers. Richard Dawson Bates, for example, was appalled that the agreement meant that the whims of Southern politicians could in effect override that of the British judiciary. As the issues agreed in March related largely to his department of home affairs, his opposition would ensure that the committees never managed to make an impact on the security situation. For Collins, the extent of IRA activity, much of which he was personally sponsoring, was difficult to control and was one of his most important conduits into minority politics. The IRA, in a deliberate attempt to embarrass Collins, re-imposed the Belfast Boycott as the talks were ongoing, leading to much publicised attacks on Northern business interests south of the border. Collins' insistence that his own personal nominees were to comprise the nationalist element on the various committees also further alienated minority opinion. Even without these problems there is little evidence that either side had a true commitment to the pacts as a way of ensuring a positive peace, and, with both states soon facing what appeared to be imminent collapse from internal enemies, the likelihood of prioritising cross-border agreements seemed remote.

Even if the various clauses in the pacts had been followed to the letter, the agreements failed largely because they never attempted to address the fundamental problems of partition. The settling of the border issue, for example, was not even mentioned, nor was any attempt made to normalise relations between the two states through any moves towards formal

---

[42] Gilbert, *Winston S. Churchill*, p. 790.

recognition. Stephen Tallents, in his perceptive report on the reasons for the failure of the second pact, noted:

The Agreement aimed directly at certain symptoms of the unrest that was dividing alike the Southern from the Northern Government, and the Catholic minority in the Six Counties from the Protestant majority. But when it approaches the under-lying causes of these symptoms, it took refuge for the most part-inevitably, no doubt, at the time-in vague pacific gestures ... Both governments started with an honest desire to give effect to the Agreement, ... but they were estranged by causes which were from the start, or were soon found to be, outside of their control.[43]

Understandably, considering the cash-strapped condition of both parti-tion states, the only element of the pacts to receive some degree of unilateral support was the relief committee. The notion of a joint police committee to oversee Catholic recruitment to the Specials and commu-nity sensitive police patrols was totally unworkable. The unionist govern-ment suspected, not without cause, that the committee was merely a front for IRA infiltration into the security services who would use their position to pass information to their compatriots in the South. Certainly, the fact that many of Collins' nominees were senior members of the IRA's Belfast Brigade, some of whom were soon arrested, did not inspire confidence. Similarly, while the 'Conciliation Committee' held some meetings, it never managed to have an effect on Northern security operations and was made wholly redundant with the introduction of the Special Powers Act in May.

With the failure of negotiation, the partition issue entered a crucial endgame. The months of May and June 1922 would see growing confrontation between the North and South, leading to almost open war. The provisional government army leadership's sponsorship of guerrilla attacks both along the border and inside Northern Ireland itself intensified. The context for this renewed offensive was a growing rapprochement in the South between the two sides of the treaty divide. In late May, Collins and de Valera agreed an electoral pact for the forthcoming election whereby both sides would retain their respective numbers in the Dáil through the nomination of candidates, reflecting the balance of the vote on the treaty. The move outraged the British government who now saw Southern divisions over the treaty well on the way to being healed and the half-hearted actions of the provisional government as a reflection of their sympathy with their old comrades. Churchill angrily concluded

---

[43] Tallents Report, NA, CO 739/1.

Had Collins taken strong steps and turned the Irregulars out of their Dublin strongholds the whole situation in Belfast would have improved, but having joined hands with avowed Republicans we could hardly wonder that the North had gone back to its extreme and violent position. I think we have to give them assurances of help.[44]

The South's new-found focus on the Northern issue now became almost obsessive. With at least a temporary political reconciliation being reached, the military side of the movement soon ramped up its efforts at unity. Southern republicans were sent to the North to coordinate a series of border incursions from Donegal, while IRA units inside the six counties were provided with new supplies of weapons and equipment. All this was aimed at launching a full-scale offensive in the North. For the first time since 1914, the partition issue was moved to the centre stage of Anglo-Irish relations. Ironically, it appeared that the pernicious effects of the treaty among Southern nationalists had led also to the crippling of the partition plan itself. Opposition to the Northern government became the only policy on which substantive agreement could be reached among Irish nationalists. Seemingly on every level – administrative, military and political – the north-east became a new nationalist crusade. While military initiatives were left in the hands of the republicans, covertly supported by leading members of the pro-treaty IRA, the provisional government took the lead in applying diplomatic pressure. A memorandum of late May 1922, outlining the approach to be taken by a delegation to meet with the London government to discuss the failure of the second pact, highlighted this new confrontational approach:

... the offensive should be taken by the delegation in regard to the position in North-East Ulster, and that attention should be drawn to the fact that the attitude of the British Government towards North East Ulster was regarded generally as endangering the Treaty ... that not a single Article of the agreement signed by Mr Collins and Sir James Craig in London on the 31st March had been kept by the latter ... that Sir James Craig had publicly stated that he intended to break the Treaty.[45]

The British government realised immediately how dangerous this new Southern coalition could prove in threatening the whole basis of the partition plan. Austen Chamberlain reported to the cabinet on 1 June:

They have seen that they must either quarrel with De Valera or with the British Government. This theory was rather borne out by the way they had used the

---

[44] Coogan, *Michael Collins*, p. 364.
[45] Minutes of North-East Ulster Advisory Committee, May 1922, NAI, SPO, S1011.

interval, namely, to ask for a meeting with the Prime Minister and to raise the question of disturbances in Ulster.[46]

Churchill told Craig he believed that the 'Provisional Government might try to escape from their difficulty by turning the blame on Ulster ...'.[47] Craig, himself, saw the escalating situation as a potential disaster for the partition settlement:

The whole of the Southern organisation which was fully occupied while the British Army was in the South, has now nothing to do and therefore has gone to the North. The North has to cope with that increased force and protect a frontier of 300 miles.[48]

That it would prove unable to do. On 31 May, in the vicinity of the border towns of Belleek and Pettigo on the Donegal border, the British army had to intervene to oust an IRA force which had secured positions inside the Northern Irish border. Even prior to this, nineteen British army battalions had been strung out along the border in the spring to defend the new Northern state, leading the *Guardian* to opine that 'Ulster is on the verge of non-existence.'[49] Of most concern with the Pettigo incident was the fact that this force had consisted of both pro- and anti-treaty units, leading the ever-paranoid Fred Crawford to write to Craig a few days later that such moves were 'only the beginning of a far more devious plot being designed against Ulster':

To my mind this is a serious and unfortunate thing for Ulster . . . What I fear now is that Lloyd George working with Ulster's two arch enemies McCready (General) and Anderson (still secretary, permanent) will occupy the whole boundary by British troops and will then give way to Collins in regard to his claims for Fermanagh and Tyrone. McCready will then order his troops to retire to this new line, pushing back all the police to behind this line, while the troops occupy it till the Free State troops occupy and fortify the evacuated territory. When this is done the British Government will inform the Northern Government that they will use troops against this Government if necessary to prevent any interference to the boundary they have fixed in conjunction with the Free State.[50]

While there was much cynicism in British government circles over the real motives which lay behind the South's sudden interest in the North, the sheer level of disorder and violence led many to question the sustainability of the partition settlement in its current form. The introduction of internment and the arrest of hundreds of IRA members had not stemmed the flow of reprisal atrocities, which now, having previously been largely

[46] Austen Chamberlain, Cabinet Conclusions NA, CAB 23/30, 1 June 1922.
[47] Churchill to Craig, 6 June 1922, PRONI, CAB 6/43.
[48] Craig to Churchill, 31 May 1922, NA, CO 906/20.   [49] *The Guardian*, 28 May 1922.
[50] Crawford Diary, PRONI, D640/11/1.

confined to Belfast, began to occur in large numbers throughout the province. By early June it was clear that the Northern government was not functioning effectively and the British remained acutely aware that they were footing the bill for their vast, and palpably ineffective, security apparatus. Such concerns led Lloyd George to comment bluntly to Churchill:

We have surely done everything that Ulster can possibly expect to ensure its security. Fifty-seven thousand men ought to be equal to the protection of so small a territory. If they require more they can get them. It is our own business as a great Empire to be strictly impartial in our attitude towards all needs.[51]

Lloyd George's frustration yielded immediate results, with a decision to create a judicial enquiry into the workings of the Northern government. However, as a first step, it was decided to send a senior civil servant, Stephen Tallents, to Belfast to investigate both why the Craig–Collins Pacts had failed and whether the full judicial enquiry was necessary. While Tallents laid most of the blame on the disorder on the increased level of IRA activity, he was also heavily critical of the security apparatus of the Northern government and especially the use of part-time Specials.

In the end, Tallents' report would prove to be largely irrelevant. By the time it was presented in July, civil war had broken out in the South. The united policy against the North had proved to be largely unsustainable for the provisional government. Domestically, Collins found it impossible to both placate the radical republicans in the South, while at the same time retaining a public commitment to the treaty. With the start of the civil war, the tense situation in the North was finally ended. The death of Collins in August would further cement this retreat from confrontation with the instigation of a new peace policy by his successors in the provisional government. Roger McCorley, commander of the IRA's Belfast Brigade, later admitted, 'When Collins was killed the Northern element gave up all hope.'[52] Another lamented that 'if [Collins] were alive things would not have gone so far.'[53]

However, even before Collins' death, it was clear that doves within the provisional government had sought to take control of Ulster policy and push it in a more conciliatory direction. The process of Southern disengagement began soon after the start of the Southern civil war. The Northern IRA, which had been hugely rearmed and reinforced

[51] Lloyd George to Churchill, 8 June 1922, quoted in Gilbert, *Winston S. Churchill*, pp. 13–14.
[52] Roger McCorley statement, Mulcahy Papers, UCDAD, P17B/98.
[53] Comments of IRA member 'Watters', 5 December 1923, UCDAD, Twomey Papers P69/35 (120).

under Collins, was now disbanded and those who had escaped internment or imprisonment withdrawn to the South. Sean McConville, an
Armagh IRA man, admitted plainly, 'we looked to the south for help and
assistance. On our own we were faced with overwhelming odds.'[54] Ernest
Blythe, the minister of local government, would be one of the chief
instigators of this 'peace policy', arguing that a continuing policy of
confrontation would lead to the destruction of the Ulster Catholic population. He candidly told his cabinet colleagues:

There is no prospect of bringing about the unification of Ireland within any
reasonable period of time by attacking the North-East ... the belligerent policy
has been shown to be useless for protecting the Catholics or stopping the
pogroms ... There is no urgent desire for unity in the North-East and it would
be stupid obstinacy for us to wait till the Belfast attitude improved.[55]

Blythe would prove to be one of the most clear-sighted and realist commentators on partition. Throughout his long life he would consistently
argue that it was the failure of Irish nationalists to accept the authenticity
of unionist opposition, rather than a perfidious scheme of British politicians, which lay at the root cause of division. 'It is based on the ridicu-
lously false assumption', he would write in the 1950s, 'that if Britain
merely acquiesced, Irish re-union could be quickly and peacefully
achieved'.[56]

   W. T. Cosgrave, the new Southern leader, proudly reported in January
1923:

Since I have assumed office I have striven to bring about a better feeling between
Northern Ireland and ourselves, especially along the inflammable Border regions.
I have gone to great lengths to stop all manner of inciting propaganda. I think I can
claim that my efforts in this direction have been largely successful.[57]

There can be little doubt that the onset of the civil war in the South saved
the partition settlement from collapse. A report in the *Times*
of February 1923 reported on the changed conditions: 'In every part of
Ireland, but Ulster, from the Capital to the wilderness of the western
coast, houses have been reduced to smoking ruins.'[58] During the
Southern civil war, the Northern government were able to consolidate
their hold over their territory. Indeed, it is notable that the unionist
government did not see the new non-threatening Southern government
as a reason to relax its harsh security policy. Round-ups of IRA suspects

[54] Sean McConville, NAI, BMH statement, WS 495.
[55] 'Memo on the North-East Ulster', Blythe papers, UCDAD, P24/70.
[56] O'Corrain, 'Ireland in His Heart North and South', p. 69.
[57] Cosgrave to Lord Devonshire, 10 January 1923, NA, CO 739/17.
[58] *The Times*, 26 February 1923.

continued apace, as did the imprisonment and flogging of those convicted. One prisoner, James McAlorum, an expelled shipyard worker convicted of armed robbery, wrote to his wife about his experience of this cruel punishment:

I had just finished my supper when four warders entered my cell and took me to an underground dungeon where the officials had erected what they call a flogging triangle. Gathered in a cluster around this instrument of torture were the prison doctor, governor, a dozen or so of prison warders and a number of Special Constabulary, all eager to witness the savagery that was to be enacted there, and of which myself and a few other unfortunate prisoners, some of them mere children in their early teens, were to be the victims. I was stripped to the skin and the warders tied me hand and foot to the triangle, and when they had me secured, the Englishman, who was sent over specially to administer torture, commence the barbarity. When I had received the fifteen lashes, and while the officials were bandaging my back, I had a look at the man who had flogged me and the sweat was running down his face. This man, who was almost six feet in height, had exerted all his strength and energy in inflicting this savage operation and left my back in such a state that a whole piece of my skin could not have been touched from my waist to my neck with the point of a needle. One of the victims who was led to the chamber of torture after I had received my flogging was a mere boy of seventeen years of age, named Edward O'Neill, and when they had this boy stripped and tied up, and when the administrator of the torture commenced his foul work the agonising cry of the child prisoner pleading to the prison doctor to intervene and save him from the cruel and unmerciful punishment could be heard all over the prison.[59]

Craig also moved to abolish the safeguard of proportional representation, as enshrined in the Government of Ireland Act, almost as soon as the dust had settled in July 1922. For Northern Ireland, the phantom of an alien force camped on the border waiting ever watchful for the right moment to overrun Ulster was one of the founding mythologies of the state and provided a key rallying cry for what was by any measure a peculiar and dysfunctional state. Despite the almost non-existent security threat, the unionist government remained on a high state of alert. The emergency legislation in the shape of the Special Powers Act was renewed and later made permanent, while the 'B' Specials remained the backbone of the Northern security forces. In many senses, the Northern government never got over the torrid experience of its birth and for the rest of its fifty year existence would remain in a virtual state of emergency. Michael Hopkinson insightfully noted that the Belfast government displayed 'a determination to act in accordance with a siege mentality, even when the siege had been lifted'.[60]

[59] Kenna, *Facts and Figures of the Belfast Pogrom 1920–22*, p. 155.
[60] Hopkinson, *Green Against Green*, p. 251.

By the end of 1922, a type of peace reigned between the two new Irish states. There was no formal ceasefire signed and virtually no attempt at reconciliation. It had become apparent that the partition issue was not simply part of the mechanism of independence, but actually played a key role in informing the sense of injustice which defined Irish political ideologies in its aftermath. One of the founding mythologies of Southern political culture, enshrined in the 1937 constitution, was the notion that partition was an unnatural imposition which would eventually be brought to an end. As the smaller state, Northern Ireland played on its story of heroic survival against the pernicious schemes of Irish nationalists and a commitment to endure at all costs.

Both new states emerged from the upheaval of 1922 broken and traumatised. Their economies and infrastructures, which barely had time to react to the costly challenges of partition, had been targeted mercilessly by their enemies. Both of the new states were thus barely functioning and endemic poverty and economic retardation was to follow. Within one year, both states had supported military forces numbering well over 120,000 men in total, a cost they could ill afford. In total, the partition of Ireland and the conflicts which it engendered cost well in excess of £100,000,000. The psychological damage was harder to measure but of far greater significance than material loss. Few could have predicted the nature of the two new states which emerged to replace pre-partition Ireland. The very process of partition, far from bolstering their ideological foundations, had transformed them into something far more troubled and dangerous.

Part III

The Legacies of Partition

7   Moving Minorities

If there was one fundamental failing of the partition plan it was its inability to address the two key issues which defined it: namely the border and the minorities it enclosed. Without minorities, partition would have remained largely symbolic, a crude reflection of the political aspirations of homogeneous populations. A political and economic tragedy perhaps, rather than a human one.

No matter how much the partition plan appeared to policymakers as a reflection of two homogeneous populations on the island, it couldn't help, no matter what the subjective identities of the participants, alter how they perceived themselves and were perceived by others. The partition plan changed identities. The author Lynn Doyle, reflecting on her youth in Ulster in 1921, wrote: 'In those days it did not enter my head that I belonged to a different race of beings. I am not sure I have learned the lesson yet.'[1] The imagined ethnicities of the two new Irelands now surpassed all else in the crude drive to divide and consolidate. Sir James Stronge, previously a grand master of the Orange Order, candidly told his fellow residents of Armagh, that, 'if we have no friends south of the Newry Mountains, it might be better to draw the boundary line there and be frankly "West Britons" and not Irishmen anymore'.[2]

Partition turned individuals and communities into minorities or majorities just by dint of where they were born, lived or moved to. It divided people from their co-religionists on the 'safe' side of the border and excluded them from the triumphant nation-building projects in the newly created states which were about to commence. For both of the new partition states, minorities became a bad conscience or, at times, an irritating embarrassment. Their existence, and continued significance, signalled the failure of the revolutionary projects of Irish nationalism and unionism and the political limitations of their much-rehearsed

---

[1] Doyle, *An Ulster Childhood*, p. 157.
[2] Letter from Sir James Henry Stronge, Tynan, Armagh, 10 May 1918, PRONI, D627/434/11.

rhetoric. The British government who had midwifed the scheme saw the minorities as less a guarantee of inclusive rights within modern, hetero-geneous, liberal states, but rather as 'a nuisance', both financially and politically, and a potential source of dissent to the workability of the partition plan. The expectation of minorities and their attitudes to the new states of either flight or resistance were therefore just as significant as the perception they engendered among elites as potentially dangerous and seditious groups.

The bald fact was that by 1922 the two new Irish states barely repre-sented even two-thirds of people in them. One-third of the population of Northern Ireland remained virulently wedded to the various brands of Irish nationalism, while in the South, Irish republicans and those who cast their vote against the Anglo-Irish Treaty remained as discontent with the new settlement as its sizeable Protestant population. The fact that the decision on the final extent of the new border was constantly deferred allowed all of the participants to place their own wildly differing inter-pretations on the character of the final shape of the settlement and kept partition provisional until the end of 1925. This uncertainty signalled to many minority populations that partition was reversible and that the struggle, which for some groups became an end in itself, should be continued on an almost indefinite basis. Others, however, viewed parti-tion less as a challenge to be overcome, but rather as a dark and looming threat which would fracture their communities, threaten their economic well-being, supress their religion or even make normal life itself virtually unliveable. Church of Ireland bishop Joseph Peacock reluctantly embraced partition because of what he viewed as an 'impossible future existence' in a Catholic dominated state. He stated plainly: 'I for one most certainly don't want partition, which would leave me with one [leg] on sea and one on shore – but better that than all Ireland given over to the Pope.'[3]

While some accepted their fate and resigned themselves to their new status as a minority, others chose simply to move, whereas more radical elements saw the partition plan as less the end of the struggle than its shift into a new, more deadly phase. Others, including many Southern Protestants, sought to manipulate the settlement to their own advantage or to shape partition in their own image in the hope of eventual compro-mise or assimilation. Overall though, the new minorities reacted with a mixture of fear and bewilderment. For all the talk of freedom and self-determination, partition represented a profound blow to notions of

---

[3] Letter from Joseph Peacock, 18 December 1918, Fellenberg papers, PRONI, D627/436/73.

individual liberty. Partition forced on people a choice. Issues of loyalty and disloyalty suddenly came to the fore and were made mandatory. What did it mean to be Irish now? In December 1921, Major Somerset Saunderson, the son of the unionist leader Colonel Edward Saunderson declared bleakly, 'Now I have no country.'[4] In the transference of rhetorical notions of minority rights through the prism of the foundation myths of the two new partition states, something profound had been lost.

It was of vital importance that the partition plan had at its heart the fate and status of the inevitable minority populations it threw up. After all, the Irish question itself had chiefly been concerned with how best to meet the aspirations of minorities with the UK, be they Irish Catholics or Ulster Protestants, and partition itself was a direct response to these concerns. However, tragically, minority issues were not made a priority of in the partition legislation. At best, they were treated as an insurance policy against future discrimination or guarantors of good behaviour from their host states. Painted in such a way, policymakers failed even to convince the new minorities that the partition states could offer basic protections. The Manchester Labour MP, and later home secretary, John Clynes voiced in devastating fashion the fundamental failure of the agreement to deal with the issue:

And what is to be said of that minority of Catholics who exist in the six counties? Are you, on the assumption of this being a wise and just settlement, to place the minority of Catholics in the six Protestant counties in the keeping of their Protestant fellow-countrymen on conditions that would leave them in a state of permanent minority and helplessness so far as the work of the Northern Parliament was concerned? And if you turn to the Protestants in the South, what is their position? Are we to cancel all the arguments that have ever been used in this House, and in the country at large, as to the pitiable position of the Southern Unionist and Protestant, who is to be left to the mercy of the Dublin Parliament, whose life and property would be in danger, and whose faith and the rights of worship would be undermined by the decrees of a Parliament in Dublin? What becomes of all those arguments? These are the arguments which, in the past, have justified the refusal of the one Parliament in Ireland, and, strangely enough, are now the arguments which justify the imposition of two Parliaments. Neither the Catholic minority in Ulster nor the Protestant minority in the southern parts of Ireland can feel any sense of security from this measure.[5]

Irish minorities were desperately in need of this kind of advocacy but few in elite circles were willing to champion the issue. The fate of minorities, when addressed in the various pieces of legislation, amounted to little more than general statements of principle. While Section 5 of the

---

[4] Saunderson to Hugh de Fellenberg Montgomery, December 1921, PRONI, D627/A/2.
[5] Hansard, HC vol 127, col 951 (29 March 1920).

Government of Ireland Act and Article 16 of the Anglo-Irish Treaty made explicit reference to the protection of religious freedoms, the formulaic inclusion of these clauses was evident as in both cases the wording used was identical.[6] These were largely token efforts to appease liberal opinion and proved deeply ineffective. There was little in the way of practical safeguards.

The one notable protection for minorities was the inclusion of proportional representation (PR) in the 1920 Act. After a hasty trial in the Sligo municipal elections in January 1919 and its further large-scale employment the following year in all of Ireland's 127 municipalities, the single-transferable vote system offered a real, if minimal, political protection for minorities. While the mechanism of the oath would do much to enforce the control of the Free State's ruling elites, in Northern Ireland, PR offered the potential for substantial political representation among minorities in the Belfast parliament. By its very nature it also undermined to some extent the homogeneous voting blocks of nationalists and unionists. For a brief period, a whole host of labour candidates, independent unionists and reform candidates took power at the local and national level. However, PR would prove to be deeply unpopular with the unionist government, being seen in the words of one unionist councillor as 'enabling traitors and disloyal elements to exercise unwarranted power'.[7]

The uncompromising nature of partition had led to the belief that communal diversity opened the door to political subversion, making it a self-fulfilling prophecy. Any further attempts to represent the championing of minority rights as a way of strengthening the new partition states were quickly abandoned when it was obvious they were having the opposite effect. In such a polarising atmosphere, minority rights became, in some people's imaginations, simply vehicles for state destruction.

---

[6] The full sections of the both the Government of Ireland Act and the treaty read: 'In the exercise of their power to make laws under this Act neither the Parliament of Southern Ireland nor the Parliament of Northern Ireland shall make a law so as either directly or indirectly to establish or endow any religion, or prohibit or restrict the free exercise thereof, or give a preference, privilege, or advantage, or impose any disability or disadvantage, on account of religious belief or religious or ecclesiastical status, or make any religious belief or religious ceremony a condition of the validity of any marriage, or affect prejudicially the right of any child to attend a school receiving public money without attending the religious instruction at that school, or alter the constitution of any religious body except where the alteration is approved on behalf of the religious body by the governing body thereof, or divert from any religious denomination the fabric of cathedral churches, or, except for the purpose of roads, railways, lighting, water, or drainage works, or other works of public utility upon payment of compensation, any other property, or take any property without compensation.'
[7] *Belfast Newsletter*, 14 February 1920.

The experiment itself did not survive the realities of confrontational partition politics on the ground. There was little doubt that, spurred on by hawkish elements in the South, many nationalists used the system cynically and as a way of making the new Northern state unworkable. As part of the unionist government's crackdown on dissent, PR was abolished for local elections in 1922 and five years later for elections to the Northern Irish parliament itself. While it achieved the goal of quelling electoral opposition among the minority, it also had the effect of degrading attempts to instil diversity within unionist political culture. The issue of the border and the survival of the six counties trumped everything else. Behind it lay a wish to instil uniformity across the board and reassert a simple duality for or against the new state.[8] The finalising of the partition plan was only the beginning of a far more ambitious project which looked to turn heterogeneous populations into loyal, patriotic citizens of their new states. This was achieved largely by defining these loyalties themselves. A whole range of symbols were employed to enforce conformity and constrain dissent. Revolutionary symbols were transformed into new state brands. Flags became toxic symbols of state power. The flag of the Sinn Féin movement was transformed seamlessly into the Irish national flag, while the Ulster banner, a mixture of the cross of St George and the red hand in a six pointed star representing the six counties of Northern Ireland, would be derived from the coat of arms granted to the Northern Irish government in 1924.[9] Allegiance to the state involved far more than an occasional personal patriotism, but rather brought with it a whole range of expectations and assumptions and the acceptance of a homogeneous pre-packaged product which provided little room for subtlety. By such means, the confrontational politics of the partition period were kept alive and well in Ireland.

In this rapidly polarising atmosphere there was little room for marginalised groups such as new-fangled 'Northern' Catholics and 'Southern' Protestants. Rechristened as minorities in both of these official and popular depictions of the new Ireland, many turned to their respective majority states for support, who proved more than keen to use the minority issue for their own ends. Increasingly it became clear to those who threw in their lot with the majority state that even nominal citizenship in these new diasporas brought with it expectations of conformity. Most government leaders responded to even modest appeals for help from their co-religionists by

[8] Frederic A. Ogg, 'Proportional Representation in Ireland', *The American Political Science Review*, vol. 14, no. 2 (May 1920), pp. 323–4.
[9] For details of the origins of the Ulster coat of arms and its later use as the flag of Northern Ireland see Susan Hood, *Royal Roots, Republican Inheritance – The Survival of the Office of Arms* (Dublin, 2002), pp. 119–20.

unilaterally assuming the role of the minority spokesperson. While this allowed their concerns to be voiced at the highest levels of government, it also meant that they were expected to conform to the crude identities which characterised the majority state. Much time and energy was spent making dramatic accusations against the other state for its treatment of 'their people' and how the long-threatened fears of life under the opposition were now coming true. One Sinn Féin journalist from Dublin, on visiting the Falls Road in May 1922, concluded that without the bravery of the Volunteers and the steadfastness of nationalist populations, 'this could have been us.'[10] The revolutionary campaigns had been so passionate and extreme that fear of belonging to one of the two Irelands was intense. Many felt it meant that they were witnessing the millenarian fears of total ruin, oppression and even death which had been threatened for years in political propaganda. Before the Government of Ireland bill was even written, the West Belfast MP Joe Devlin said in the House of Commons 'I would as soon trust a number of lambs before a jury of butchers as trust Catholic interests to the Belfast Corporation.'[11] Ernest Clark, cabinet secretary to the Northern Irish government, wrote in January 1923 that the new Ulster administration 'should best serve Ireland as a lifeboat than tie ourselves to a sinking ship'.[12]

However, it is clear that many understood the significance and deep contradictions which lay behind the minority problem. In his speech to over forty senior figures of the Ulster Unionist Council announcing his retirement as leader of the Ulster Unionist Party in February 1921, Carson himself called on unionists to be magnanimous to their minority population:

We used to say that we could not trust an Irish parliament in Dublin to do justice to the Protestant minority. Let us take care that that reproach can no longer be made against your parliament, and from the outset let them see that the Catholic minority have nothing to fear from a Protestant majority.[13]

It was clear though by 1922 that any positive competitiveness between the two new Irish states concerning their ability to tolerate and include their respective minorities had given way to state-sponsored coercion. Minorities were treated at best with suspicion by their new hosts or at worst actively suppressed. For hundreds of thousands of people their real experience of partition was exclusion, poverty, imprisonment and torture. The partition plan had evidently gone horribly wrong. The *Guardian* offered the following assessment in June 1922:

[10] *Irish Bulletin*, 22 May 1922.
[11] Joe Devlin, Hansard, HC, vol 115, cols 1269 (9 May 1919).
[12] Hopkinson, *Green Against Green*, p. 81.   [13] Lewis, *Carson*, p. 227.

We cannot now pretend that this partition idea has worked: the whole world would burst into laughter at the suggestion. Both Irish countries are paying for that illusion, and both in much the same fashion, for the spirit of violence and crime is growing more intense in Ireland as we foster it by our tyranny. No arrangement that rests on force can endure or be other than a permanent danger.[14]

Ireland's Partition Refugees

One of the great ironies of partition is that it so often engenders the very thing it is intended to avert. Far from the 'clean cut' highlighted by its supporters, the partitions of the twentieth century have resulted in at best messy compromise and at worst inspired civil war, inter-communal conflict and the oppression of the new minorities it inevitably creates. Perhaps most notably, however, it is the forced displacement of people – those who find themselves on the 'wrong' side of the border – which has been the most identifiable consequence of partition. From India to Palestine, refugees and the minorities from which they spring have become a central part of the historical language of partition. In many cases, most notably India, issues of displacement, migration and refugee rehabilitation have provided seminal approaches to the study of partition itself.[15]

Ireland's experience was little different. Between 1912 and 1925 tens of thousands of Irish people elected or were forced to move due to the polarising effects of partition. However, unlike in the case of these other partitions, Ireland's refugee experience, much like the study of Irish minorities in general, has remained a largely neglected and hidden exodus. It is certainly true that all parties sought to minimise the number, or even deny the existence, of Irish refugees. For both British and Irish governments, taking the step of defining someone as a 'refugee' brought with it both a moral responsibility and an unwanted financial liability. Politicians of all kind impressed on people the need to stay put. William Cosgrave, as minister for local government, stated in 1922: 'It is the desire

---

[14] *The Guardian*, 8 June 1922.

[15] See, for example, M. Rahman and W. Schendel, '"I Am Not a Refugee": Rethinking Partition Migration', *Modern Asian Studies*, vol. 37, no. 3 (2003), pp. 551–84; Joya Chatterji, *Bengal Divided: Hindu Communalism and Partition, 1932–1947* (Cambridge: 1995); Sanjib Baruah, *India Against Itself: Assam and the Politics of Nationality* (New Delhi, 1999); Sarah Ansari, 'The Movement of Indian Muslims to West Pakistan after 1947: Partition-Related Migration and Its Consequences for the Pakistani Province of Sind,' in Judith M. Brown and Rosemary Foot, eds, *Migration: The Asian Experience* (Oxford, 1994), pp. 149–68; Ian Copland, 'The Further Shores of Partition: Ethnic Cleansing in Rajasthan, 1947', *Past and Present*, vol. 160 (1998), pp. 203–39.

of the ministry to discourage by every means in their power anything approaching an exodus of the Catholic population in affected areas.'[16] Similarly in Britain, Austen Chamberlain expressed fears that any relief measures should be minimal as blanket support would only 'encourage a general exodus from Ireland'.[17] Perhaps most importantly, however, the existence of refugees reinforced doubts about the ability of the new states to guarantee the safety of their respective minority populations, a development which could undermine the long-term viability of the partition settlement itself.[18] There is little doubt that the emigration of communities who found themselves on the wrong side of the border or the forced movement of refugees revealed the shallowness of the guarantees which had been put in place to protect minority populations.

Understanding where refugees fit into wider patterns of demographic change in Ireland during the partition period is fraught with difficulty. Such a judgement relies on notoriously subjective contemporary definitions as to who can be defined as a refugee and what exactly constituted a legitimate refugee experience. Certainly, the surviving figures in official records are of little value in clarifying the true extent of the refugee crisis which afflicted Ireland during the partition period. In many cases they recognise only those who were the direct recipients of organised relief. Those who applied and failed or didn't bother to seek help from the state at all are largely absent from the record. So, for example, Free State government figures record only 1,650 'officially recognised' Northern refugees in Southern Ireland between January and August 1922, despite the fact that other evidence suggests the real figure was much larger, by some estimates almost twenty times that number.[19] Similarly, the unionist government recorded 'as a conservative estimate' the cases of over 2,000 Southern Protestants looked after by a variety of voluntary bodies, including the Ulster Unionist Council and Orange Order, who were forced to move permanently over the border into Northern Ireland.[20]

---

[16] *Irish Times*, 17 June 1922.   [17] *Irish Times*, 13 May 1922.

[18] See, for example, the report in the *Morning Post* of 12 June 1922 headlined 'Mythical Irish Refugees'. In a debate on the issue in the House of Commons on 15 June 1922 one Conservative MP, Ronald McNeill, told Churchill that '... in a great number of cases, these so-called refugees are not refugees at all, but men who have been sent out by the Republicans of the North, at the point of the pistol, for propaganda purposes', Hansard, HC, vol 155, cols 526–7 (15 June 1922).

[19] For the official figures see 'Belfast Refugees: general file', Department of Finance files, NAI, FIN 1/924. For other estimates see John McCoy statement, BMH, NAI, WS 492. Ironically, the Southern nationalist propaganda newspaper the *Weekly Irish Bulletin*, funded by the provisional government, claimed that 23,760 Catholics were evicted in Belfast during 1922. See *Weekly Irish Bulletin*, 3 July 1922.

[20] See 'Cabinet Conclusions', 13 January 1925, PRONI, CAB/4/85/4.

British figures, while slightly more revealing, suffer from many of the same shortcomings. They, in particular, do not quantify the substantial refugee communities who relied for subsistence on pre-existing Irish immigrant communities and other local charitable organisations outside of the structure of official relief programmes. These include the several thousand Northern Catholic refugees who fled to large industrial British cities such as Glasgow, Liverpool and Manchester.[21] Certainly, while there were less than 3,500 applications to the newly established Irish Distress Committee during its first six months, following its formation in May 1922, the historian of that body Niamh Brennan has shown that such figures do not reflect the reality of the refugee situation. She estimates that as many as 20,000 people were forced to flee to Britain in this period. Others put the figure at closer to twice that number.[22]

The most reliable figures, those of the censuses of 1911 and 1926, while more consistent than the specific refugee statistics, offer only a rudimentary picture. Both states certainly suffered a decline in their minority populations before, during and after partition. Between 1911 and 1926 over one-third of the estimated 300,000 Southern Protestants left the twenty-six counties which became the Irish Free State. Conversely, the Catholic population of the six counties of Northern Ireland declined only marginally by 10,000, a little over 2 per cent in the same period.[23]

Such figures are misleading, however, and do little to inform our specific understanding of refugee movement. The startling decline in the Southern Protestant population in particular has been the subject of vigorous debate. It has been argued that it must be viewed in the context of a much longer-term pattern of decline which had begun in the aftermath of the Irish Famine in the 1840s and was severely affected by the changes wrought by the First World War. Indeed, within the partition period itself a significant proportion of the decline in Protestant numbers can to a large extent be explained by the post-settlement withdrawal of British personnel and their families, with an estimated 40,000 British soldiers, civil servants, lawyers and other crown servants returning permanently to Britain.[24]

---

[21] File on 'Relief for southern Unionists', S2112, Department of Taoiseach files, NAI.

[22] See N. Brennan, 'A Political Minefield: Southern Loyalists, the Irish Distress Committee and the British Government, 1922–1931', *Irish Historical Studies*, vol. xxx, no. 119 (May 1997).

[23] *Census of population*, 1926: general report. Table 8B: 'Percentage increase or decrease from 1911 to 1926 of persons of each religion in each county borough'.

[24] See, for example, E. Delaney, 'The Churches and Irish Emigration to Britain, 1921–60', *Archivium Hibernicum*, vol. 52 (1998), pp. 102–4.

Such figures also fail to take account of the fact that the decision to move was taken for a number of different reasons. For some the choice was ideological. The creation of two new hostile and ideologically defined states based on the incompatible mythologies of Gaelic Catholic nationalism and Protestant Ulster unionism presented Irish people with a stark, if often unwanted, choice. As such, thousands simply voted with their feet. In 1922, for example, it is estimated that over 800 Northern IRA volunteers headed south[25] to participate in the Southern civil war on the republican side, with many, such as Belfast Brigade commander Joe McKelvey, ending their days as irredentist republican martyrs. For such people it proved a short step from aligning oneself with one or other of these ideologies politically to deciding to locate oneself physically in that space.

At the other end of the scale, the decision to move was a pragmatic reaction to the new economic realities of post-partition Ireland. Partition coincided with a significant economic downturn, with unemployment in cities such as Belfast running at almost 22 per cent.[26] The belief that the refugee problem was informed largely by economic migration was to be a constant refrain from government officials. Thousands moved to take up positions in the new police forces, civil services or armies of the new state, while many left Ireland altogether to seek economic security abroad.

However, while some left in style inspired by deep ideological convictions or the economic realities of partition, others literally fled for their lives. It is these people, drawn almost exclusively from the two new Irish minorities – Southern Protestants and Northern Catholics – who can be defined most clearly as refugees. For them, leaving was a matter of survival. It was a response to violence or the fear of violence, the threat of imprisonment or the real experience of intimidation by extremist members of the other community.

The census figures, while providing little insight into the myriad of motivations behind movement during the partition period, also suffer from their sheer scale, covering as they do a much longer time period than the partition conflicts of 1919–1923 where the overwhelming majority of refugees are situated. Indeed, in the case of Ireland, refugee movement was heavily concentrated into specific periods – the summer of 1920, the autumn of 1921 and most notably the spring and early summer of 1922. This latter period was by far the most significant. Indeed, 1922

---

[25] Lynch, *The Northern IRA*, p. 143.

[26] A. C. Hepburn, *A Past Apart: Studies in the History of Catholic Belfast, 1850–1950* (Belfast, 1996), p. 92.

was in many ways the year of the Irish refugee. Prior to 1922, if people did move, it was still viewed, by themselves and the authorities, as only a temporary inconvenience. The vast majority of those who moved expected to return once the political situation normalised or the immediate threat was removed. As we shall see, it is an analysis of events in those few short months, rather than the fifteen-year inter-census period, which is key to understanding the dynamics of refugee movement.

Perhaps most problematic is the fact that the census figures alone take no account of transitory relocation or short-range movement *within* one or other of the two partition states, both of which are highly indicative of Northern Catholic refugee experience. For example, even a conservative estimate indicates that almost 10,000 people were forced to move within Belfast alone (8,000 Catholics and 2,000 Protestants).[27] Others became refugees for only a matter of weeks or even days, while other families, such as the Malone family of the Short Strand, were refugees on two or more separate occasions, having fled the city for Dublin in the summer of 1920 only to return in the autumn of 1921 and then once again flee the city in the spring of 1922, this time for Glasgow.[28]

However, while a crude measurement, the census figures do hint at deeper truths surrounding the subject of Ireland's partition refugees. Specifically, they reveal the differing nature and experiences of both minorities from which refugees were drawn. Indeed, one of the key ways of uncovering the story of Irish refugees is by comparing the nature and aspirations of these two groups at the height of the crisis in the spring of 1922.

They shared many similarities. During the partition conflicts both suffered from being labelled as a fifth column, and endured prolonged campaigns of violence or intimidation from members of the majority community. Their most concentrated periods of movement were in direct response to outbreaks of intense inter-communal violence. This violence came in many forms, but was starkly similar for both minorities –houses commandeered, arson attacks on business premises, family members murdered and threatening letters warning of dire consequences if they did not leave.

However, while there were many parallels in terms of their experiences, it was their differing reactions to violence and intimidation which is most notable. This is no better shown by a comparison of where they went and

---

[27] See D. Martin, *Migration within the Six Counties of Northern Ireland, with Special Reference to the City of Belfast, 1911–37.* MA thesis, Queen's University of Belfast (1977), pp. 155–63.

[28] File on 'Refugees from Southern Ireland into Northern Ireland and Vice Versa', PRONI, HA/5/967.

where they felt a place of safety existed. For example, Protestants in the three 'Southern' provinces of Leinster, Munster and Connacht were far more likely to leave Ireland all-together than seek refuge in one of the new partition states, be that Northern Ireland or the traditionally more liberal areas of Dublin and East Leinster. Perhaps most notably, they were unlikely to return once they had made the decision to leave, preferring to resettle in Britain, particularly the towns and cities of south-east England.

By contrast, Northern Catholic refugees, although certainly making their presence felt in numerous British cities, such as Glasgow and Liverpool, largely remained within Ireland itself. Travelling to the South, Northern refugees were reported in Cork, Mayo, Sligo, Dundalk, Kilkenny and numerous other small provincial towns. Dublin, however, remained the primary destination for Northern refugees, at least initially. The city's obvious economic attractions were mirrored by the ease of travel on the Dublin to Belfast train line. Organised relief measures that sprang up in 1922 and the city's role as a major recruiting centre for the new Free State army also provided a pull factor for the later waves of refugees from Ireland's other capital city in the North. These were overwhelmingly urban dwellers seeking the familiar. Also, in comparison to Southern Protestants, they were far more likely to return to their homes once the violence had subsided and the political situation had stabilised. This is certainly true of the condition of Ireland by the time of the census of 1926.

There are a number of factors which explain these differing reactions. The first concerns the nature and aspirations of the two minorities during the partition period. Despite the severe blow of partition and experiencing two years of communal violence, Northern Catholics in 1922 remained a highly motivated and resilient minority. They are notable for the level of their political organisation with numerous dynamic and aggressive political group-ings such as the AOH, UIL, Sinn Féin and the Northern IRA. Furthermore, unlike Southern Protestants, many of them retained a reasonable political aspiration to escape minority status by inclusion in the Irish Free State, not only through the mechanism of the Boundary Commission negotiated as part of the Anglo-Irish Treaty in December 1921, but also the strong financial, moral and military support they received from powerful political and religious elites in the South.[29]

Northern Catholics were also a geographically defined minority, grouped together in strong homogeneous communities such as West Belfast, Derry city, South Down, East Tyrone and South Armagh. While we must be wary of hindsight in the sense that this was very

---

[29] See Hart, *The IRA at War*, pp. 254–58.

much a community coming into being in the period, such areas proved crucial in that they gave refugees options in terms of where they felt a place of safety lay. In Belfast, for example, the existence of homogeneous Catholic communities in West and, to some extent, North Belfast meant that, for many, their refugee experience involved a journey of only a few streets to well-established Catholic ghettos within the city. Indeed, a study of a sample of one hundred northern refugees in Dublin shows that they were far more likely to come from areas on the fringes of these homogeneous communities.[30] It is also notable that it was these 'interface areas', and not the heartland majority areas, which became the focus for ethnic rioting in the city. In short, in the early months of 1922, the Northern Catholic minority were far from being the defeated and fragmented minority which they are often portrayed.

By contrast, Southern Protestants outside Ulster shared none of these advantages. There were no nearby homogeneous Protestant areas for them to flee to and they had little hope of avoiding being part of a newly independent or semi-independent Southern state. Even those informal political networks which did exist such as the RIC and Southern loyalist political groups had become demoralised and degraded after suffering two years of political and social ostracism. They also lacked outside support or advocacy. In 1922, there was a far wider ideological, and in some senses religious, gulf between Southern and Northern unionists, than there was between Northern and Southern Catholics, a development which would only come later after the death of Michael Collins and the shambolic failure of the Boundary Commission in 1925. Thus, while Irish nationalism remained at least rhetorically inclusive (albeit temporarily), Irish unionism was exclusive and increasingly defined by the boundaries and foundation myths of the new Northern Irish state.

These differences are to some extent epitomised by the Protestants of the three Ulster counties of Monaghan, Cavan and Donegal which managed to escape inclusion in Northern Ireland. Although relatively small in number, these Ulster Protestant communities shared many of the characteristics of Northern Catholics of the period. While in 1922 they retained only a fading hope of inclusion in the new Northern Irish state, they did retain a homogeneous and geographically defined communal identity, particularly in areas such as North Monaghan and East Donegal. They also retained their political vibrancy and were notable for their high level of political activism, evident in the large numbers who signed the Ulster covenant of 1912 and the high levels of recruiting for both the UVF and the later Ulster Special Constabulary. Over 20 per cent of the

---

[30] See Martin, *Migration within the Six Counties of Northern Ireland*, pp. 155–63.

Protestant population of Cavan joined the UVF between 1912 and 1914, while recruiting in Monaghan was higher than that in Belfast, Down, Antrim, Armagh and Fermanagh. Even Donegal had higher levels of recruitment than any part of East Ulster.[31]

Indeed, in spite of relentless unionist and nationalist propaganda campaigns, movement in border areas was to prove comparatively limited. For example, a mere 2,117 Protestants from the three 'northern' counties of Leitrim, Cavan and Sligo moved across the border and settled permanently in Northern Ireland. Certainly, the census for all its failings shows that Protestants in these three counties declined by around one fifth (22 per cent), the same as their respective Catholic populations, and a lot less than the 42 per cent drop seen in Munster, for example (and the 32 per cent and 36 per cent drops seen in Leinster and Connacht, respectively). In other border areas it was largely pragmatic concerns about the economic effects of partition that motivated movement into Northern Ireland.[32] For example, the Protestant population of Monaghan fell by over 25 per cent in a mere three years. This had much to so with the county's geographical location, jutting into the heart of the six counties, and its use by the IRA as a major launching pad for offensive operations along the border during the spring of 1922. Local economic factors were also important. Areas such as East Cavan and North Monaghan had benefitted hugely from their central location between Belfast and Dublin, especially with the improved rail links completed in the 1880s. To transform such areas into blind economic alleys seemed not only economically damaging but went against geography.

Hundreds of Protestant businessmen, having already suffered two years of intimidation and boycott, were forced to flee. Indeed, of the forty-five Protestant families who left urban border areas of county Monaghan at the height of the violence in the spring of 1922, over three quarters of them were businessmen and their families.[33] For the Protestant community of East Donegal, the retention of Derry city, whose natural hinterland was west to Donegal rather than east into county Londonderry, also reinforced the viability of border Protestant communities.

Similarly, in a broader sense, while the ambiguities of the Boundary Commission clause in the Anglo-Irish Treaty caused huge instability along the new frontier during the first six months of 1922, it also fuelled the expectations and resolve of both communities that the settlement would eventually place them on the 'right' side of the border. Nationalists in South

---

[31] See Fitzpatrick, 'The Orange Order and the Border', p. 53.
[32] *Census of population*, 1926: Table 9: 'Number of persons of each religion in each county and county borough in Saorstat Eireann from 1861–1926', pp. 14–17.
[33] Dooley, 'Monaghan Protestants in a Time of Crisis, 1919–1922', p. 249.

Fermanagh, for example, had hugely different expectations to those in Belfast, as did Protestants in East Donegal and those in west Cork. Whereas it is true that when the commission finally sat in 1925 it failed to transfer any territory, leaving the six-county border intact, this was not the expectation in 1922. Indeed, unlike in the case of other partitions, such as that of the Indian subcontinent, the settling of the extent of the Irish border signalled the end, rather than the beginning, of conflicts over the extent of partition.[34] As such, while short range and temporary movement within border areas was much in evidence, due to the fluid and ill-defined nature of the line itself in 1922, there was little permanence to these early movements. Indeed, a memo from the Ulster Unionist Council concluded that most movement into Northern Ireland occurred only after 1925 when a definitive border had finally been agreed.[35]

Thus, we can identify certain broad dynamics for Irish refugee movement from within the minorities from which they were drawn. Whereas in the case of Southern Protestants, communities were diverse, heterogeneous and socially and politically disorganised, long distance and permanent movement was far more likely. Conversely, wherever minority populations formed a distinct, politically vocal and geographically concentrated community they were least likely to move and those who did more likely to return.

Belfast Refugees

Judged in the light of such arguments, what is perhaps most surprising is that Catholic movement out of Northern Ireland was to prove so significant. Indeed, one of the most hidden implications of such an analysis based on the rudimentary statistics of the census figures is that it minimises the extent of Northern Catholic refugee movement and maximises that of Southern Protestants. The historian Peter Hart, for example, dispenses with the Northern refugees as '1500 people who fled to Dublin'.[36] However, even a cursory examination of the available evidence shows this not to be the case. Newspaper reports reveal almost 10,000

---

[34] The infamous Article XII stated that the border would be settled 'in accordance with the wishes of the inhabitants so far as may be compatible with economic and geographic conditions'.

[35] See 'Memo concerning claim for refugees', 13 January 1925, PRONI, CAB/4/85/4. Also, see minutes of Ulster Unionist Council subcommittee on refugees, Ulster Unionist Council papers, PRONI, D1327/7/4; 'Loyalist refugees: cost of maintenance of refugees from Free State', MIC 523/15; Southern Irish Loyalist Relief Association papers, D 989/B.

[36] Hart, *The IRA at War*, p. 81.

Northern Catholics in Dublin alone during the spring of 1922.[37] This is to say nothing of the many thousands more who were reported in cities and towns right across Southern Ireland nor those several thousand who fled to established Irish communities in Lancashire and Clydeside. Other more anecdotal evidence also suggests an enormous hidden number of Northern Catholic refugees. For example, a correspondent of the *Manchester Guardian* writing in June 1922 reported that border towns like Dundalk and Drogheda were 'packed to overflowing with fugitive Catholics flying from the border disturbances and the horrors of Belfast'.[38] Joe Devlin, the leading Northern nationalist politician, stated in a speech to 1,000 refugees in Govan, Glasgow, in late 1922 that there were '20,000 fewer Catholics in Belfast than five years ago'.[39] Similarly, John McCoy, a South Armagh IRA leader, estimated that in the first six months of 1922 alone, as many as 30,000 Northern Catholic refugees passed through his base at Dundalk on their way to Dublin.[40]

Indeed, the story and complexities of Ireland's partition refugees cannot be understood without reference to the experience of the 'Belfast refugees'. Northern Catholics not only represented the largest majority of partition refugees, but also can be said to have had the most authentic and measurable refugee experience. While Ireland's refugee story is particularly heterogeneous, in many senses the Belfast Catholics *were* Ireland's partition refugees. Not only did they move in far greater numbers than any other community in Ireland, but, unlike others, their refugee experience was a collective one. Wherever Northern refugees went they stuck together, shared their experiences and perhaps most significantly defined themselves and were defined by others as a distinct and alien group. Catholics moved en masse and in haste. In comparison, the refugee experience of Protestant exiles was often a solitary one. Whereas Northern Catholics fell into already pre-existing Irish immigrant communities – in Liverpool and Glasgow, for example – Irish Protestants were far less collective in their experience, with often only single families or individuals being reported in some British cities. Certainly, economically the average Northern Catholic was far worse off than the average Southern Protestant refugee and thus arguably far more likely to seek charity and refuge. Most importantly, however, it was the existence of the

---

[37] Figures based on a survey of daily Dublin newspapers between February and July 1922. The high point of the 'Belfast' refugee crisis occurred in the last week of May and the first week of June 1922.

[38] *Manchester Guardian*, 20 June 1922.

[39] Speech of Joe Devlin reported in *Glasgow Herald*, 7 October 1922. See also the *Irish Times*, 9 October 1922.

[40] John McCoy statement, BMH, NA, Dublin WS 492.

Northern refugees which drove the refugee crisis in Ireland. This is no better demonstrated than by analysing in detail the course and dynamics of the high point of refugee movement in Ireland during the spring of 1922.

The first Northern refugees began to appear in small numbers in Dublin and Dundalk in the early summer of 1920 following the violence and expulsions which had occurred in Derry, Belfast and Lisburn.

The numbers of refugees rose in direct relation to the frequency of such episodes, which would increase dramatically month by month until by the spring of 1922 waves of Northern Catholics were on the move. The hundreds of 1920 would become thousands in 1922. In this period, with the violence in Belfast and along the border rising to unprecedented levels, the number of refugees changed from a steady trickle of economic or political migrants to a tide between March and June 1922. In only two days, 19–20 May 1922, 232 Catholic families were driven out of their homes in West Belfast. One correspondent noted that in the last week of May there were well over 300 refugees arriving in Dublin each day from Belfast and other Northern towns.[41] A further 436 families were evicted during the first week of June.

Northern refugees arrived in Dublin at the most politically sensitive time imaginable. By May 1922, as Northern refugees rolled off trains in Dublin, the South was only a matter of weeks away from the outbreak of civil war. The attempt to avert this conflict had led to the initiation of a unified IRA offensive campaign both in Belfast and along the border from February 1922. The attacks, although sporadic and ill coordinated, were to prove disastrously counterproductive, provoking unprecedented levels of violence in the Northern capital. Between February and June over 200 people were killed in Belfast alone in prolonged sectarian rioting, with over twice as many injured. Expulsions and evictions, long a feature of Belfast riots, increased dramatically with thousands becoming homeless. One particularly damaging aspect of the IRA campaign was a series of arson and bombing campaigns against unionist economic targets, causing over £3 million worth of property damage and resulting in the destruction, not only of potential refuges for displaced people, but also a huge rise in unemployment among the Catholic population of the city. Certainly, by the spring of 1922, civil war in Northern Ireland seemed a distinct possibility. While many thousands of people within Belfast were able to find refuge within their own communities, the sheer scale

---

[41] *The Irish News*, 24 May 1922.

of the spring violence left thousands more destitute. Such people were left with little choice but to seek refuge out of Northern Ireland.[42]

Certainly, wherever Ireland's refugees decided to go, few were prepared for their arrival. Prior to 1922 no one had articulated the fear of the mass movement of people in Ireland in the wake of partition, despite the fact that the displacement of ethno-religious groups was part of the geopolitical language of interwar Europe and such movements were visible right across Europe. The forced displacement of hundreds of thousands of people in the aftermath of the Armenian genocide was a cause for widespread moral outrage in the London press at the time. Refugees were also visible in Ireland when on 14 February 1922 the last 500 Belgian war refugees finally left Dublin for Antwerp.[43] Ironically, these three days coincided with one of the worst periods of violence in Belfast.[44] The idea that partition could be achieved by the relocation or exchange of hundreds of thousands of Irish people between the two partition states was flirted with by Asquith in 1914, although proved unfeasible, not only due to the need to untangle Ulster's notoriously interwoven sectarian patchwork, but also the sheer expense of moving and rehoming almost a quarter of Ireland's population.[45]

Indeed, when the first Northern refugees began to arrive in Dublin, Dundalk and Belfast in the spring of 1920 few had any idea of what to do with them except to send them home. As such, in the initial stages, aid for the refugees was wholly improvised. In Dublin, by far the most significant destination for Irish refugees, a myriad of makeshift relief organisations sprang up supplying direct aid and small sums of cash to applicants. The Society of St Vincent de Paul had been the first to respond to the crisis following the shipyard expulsions in the summer of 1920. From their offices at 23 O'Connell Street they set-up a special relief committee to help expelled shipyard workers and their families. The Central Relief Committee, which only became meaningful and effective by the following spring, reported these early relief efforts as 'anything but nominal'. Even with a lack of publicity and rather stringent application criteria, by February 1921 over seventy-five families were being catered for at a total cost of £515 by the Society of St Vincent de Paul alone. Their volunteers, along with those from the other notable relief organisation,

---

[42] For an overview of the violence in May and June see R. Lynch, *The Northern IRA and the Early Years of Partition, 1920–1922* (Dublin, 2006), pp. 250–80.

[43] For details of the Belgian refugees see the *Irish Times*, 15 May 1922.

[44] *Irish Independent*, 15 February 1922.

[45] Asquith to Venetia Stanley, 15 July 1914 in Michael Brock and Eleanor Brock, eds, *H.H. Asquith: Letters to Venetia Stanley* (Oxford, 1995).

the Irish White Cross, travelled the city visiting Northern refugee families, distributing clothing, food and medicine.[46]

In reality, however, these early efforts offered little but temporary relief. Shortage of funds precluded any long-term planning, and while these aid organisations could keep people fed and clean, they could not furnish them with the two essential requirements: work and accommodation. Indeed, of the seventy-five families on the books of the Society of St Vincent de Paul in February 1921, sufficient funds were only ever raised to house two families, with a mere eight people helped to secure employment and a further eight given paid passage to England for jobs that they had secured.[47] The organisations themselves were severely stretched financially, with dramatic and long-running appeals in the nationalist press for donations failing dismally.[48]

The huge influx of Northern refugees into the South in the spring of 1922 caused these ad hoc relief measures to collapse. In late March, one commentator noted:

It is not difficult in Dublin today to imagine oneself back in London in 1915, in the days of the invasion of the Belgian refugee ... For Dublin now has her invasion and one finds one's tongue stumbling in confusion between "Belfast Refugee" and "Belgian Refugee," and one's brain trying to remember how the Belgians were organised. Our invasion is of course on a smaller scale, but the numbers are growing.[49]

For all governments, much like partition itself, the reality of the refugee problem was met with denial. The confrontational nature of Ireland's partition had led all sides to dismiss the claims of victimhood and suffering put forward by the other side as politically motivated propaganda. The response of the provisional government to the rising numbers of refugees arriving in Dublin and other Southern cities and towns was to ignore it. Government responsibility for the care of refugees fell largely on the shoulders of one man: William Cosgrave. As minister for local government and later chairman of the provisional government, it was he who would, above all else, shape government policy. Throughout, he would remain unsympathetic and suspicious of the reality of the Northern refugee crisis, treating it as a political and financial problem rather than a simple humanitarian one. As early as August 1920 unsympathetic voices on the Dublin Corporation echoed this view. At a meeting on 9 August about the Belfast situation, George Lyons argued that housing could not

[46] *Irish Independent*, 18 September 1920.   [47] *Freeman's Journal*, 14 February 1921.
[48] Between July 1920 and February 1921 a mere £22 was donated to the Society of St Vincent de Paul.
[49] *Manchester Guardian*, 26 March 1922.

be provided in Dublin for Belfast refugees as he 'did not desire to bring down the religious squabbles and bigotry from the North to the South of Ireland'.[50] The chairman argued against any form of accommodation being provided for Belfast refugees, claiming that such moves were 'immoral' considering there was already a list of 6,000–7,000 people in Dublin waiting for houses.[51] Such attitudes would characterise the attitude of the provisional government to the crisis throughout the period. The Northern refugees were to be afforded no special status and, as ever, Cosgrave's prime consideration was minimising the financial burden forced migration entailed, viewing the crisis 'with the safeness that distinguishes a business man examining this problem from the point of view of liability and asset, the liability is against us'.[52] Such views in government circles did not alter throughout the length of the crisis. For example, in 1924 a satisfied Ernest Blythe, ironically, himself an Ulsterman, was pleased to report in reference to the Northern refugees that 'they are nearly all off our hands now'. Although he acknowledged many deserved 'commiseration' he also noted that '... many of these "refugees" were without doubt pretenders and undeserving people'.[53]

The failure of the provisional government to address or recognise the developing crisis in the early months of 1922 left a vacuum which was filled by their opponents in the republican movement. More than any other cause, the anti-treaty IRA would seize on the issue of providing help for the Belfast refugees. Their solution would prove to be extreme and radical. While it provided immediate relief, finding accommodation, food and medicine for thousands of Northern Catholic refugees, it was achieved by the instigation of a violent sectarian campaign against the minority Protestant population in the South, thus inspiring a further exodus among Ireland's other significant minority. It is indeed ironic that the involvement of the IRA would create far more refugees than it ever helped.

For the IRA, the intense violence which had engulfed Belfast since February 1922 had inspired an impetus to action. Although such moves must be viewed in the context of increasingly frantic attempts to unify the IRA south of the border in a crusade against the Northern government, the direct emotional response of the IRA cannot be ignored. With poignant stories of pogrom and murder filling the pages of the nationalist press, the 'northern refugees' became for many walking symbols of unionist oppression – 'the victims of a persecution as ferocious as

---

[50] *Irish Times*, 10 August 1920.   [51] Ibid.

[52] 'File on Belfast Refugee Relief', Department of Taoiseach files, NA Dublin, S1230.

[53] Dáil Éireann 'Debate on Special Relief Fund', 16 November 1922.

that of Nero or Caligula'.[54] Ernie O'Malley, one of the IRA commanders in Dublin, described his first sight of the Ulster refugees:

... they had to depend on charity; officially they had not been cared for. Some had a dazed, hopeless look in their eyes. They carried little bundles; their nerves had been shattered during the period of waiting, always expecting that their houses would be attacked by rifle fire and burned by the mob.[55]

Maude Gonne MacBride, the leading light in the republican refugee effort, recalled many years later: 'I had occasion to help in the care of the Belfast refugees who flocked to Dublin so fast it was impossible to find accommodation for them. It was piteous to see the maimed children and the nerve-shattered mothers.'[56]

Appearing in major Southern towns and cities with their personal tales of suffering and the nightly horrors of Belfast, the image of bedraggled and broken widows and orphans did much to inflame republican opinion.[57] Under the guiding hand of leading Northerners on the IRA executive, most notably Joe McKelvey, former commander of the Belfast Brigade, the executive took the decision in March 1922 to reintroduce the Belfast Boycott. The boycott, despite its evident failure as a weapon of economic warfare, had proved popular with many provincial IRA units as it gave them a distinct and straightforward policy to follow. On the ground, the imposition of the boycott involved acts of coercion against those suspected of trading with Belfast businessmen. Blacklists of proscribed shops appeared in towns across Ireland and IRA Volunteers carried out a nagging campaign of low-level intimidation and violence. Overwhelmingly, it was Protestant traders who were the major targets of the attacks, playing on existing suspicions and sectarian prejudices in local areas against the perceived unionist establishment. Arson attacks on business premises and goods vehicles were reported across Ireland, almost 800 in the first six months of 1921 alone, although they were particularly common along the Ulster border.[58] In Dundalk, huge rolls of cloth from Belfast were removed from shops and burned ceremoniously in the main street.[59] Although not overtly sectarian in its rhetoric, there is little doubt that the practical result of the boycott was the branding and isolation of many people as enemies of the republic. This early

[54] 'The Refugees: Increasing Numbers Arriving in Dublin', *Freeman's Journal*, 1 June 1922.
[55] E. O'Malley, *The Singing Flame* (Dublin, 1978), p. 67.   [56] *Irish Press*, 24 April 1939.
[57] For the effects of the 'Belfast Refugees' on southern opinion see the *Manchester Guardian*, 20 June 1922.
[58] See RIC bimonthly reports January–June 1921, PRONI, HA/5/231.
[59] Ewart, *A Journey in Ireland, 1921*, p. 140.

campaign would prove crucial in dictating which individuals and organisations would become targets in the spring of 1922.[60]

With its reintroduction in the spring of 1922, in the context of the Belfast refugee crisis, the boycott pushed an already volatile situation over the edge. In many cases it became an excuse for a campaign of intimidation, expulsion and murder against Protestant communities across southern and western Ireland. As in Belfast, the crude sectarian logic of reprisal against the minority community was evident. Those who were perceived to be supportive of the violence in Belfast – unionists, Orangemen and Freemasons – were vigorously targeted by members of the republican movement. Bishop McCrory's statement that Belfast Catholics were being 'punished for the sins of their brethren elsewhere'[61] was equally applicable to the Southern Protestant community.

Ominously, suggestions began to appear in the nationalist press that Southern Protestants should do more to make up for the perceived pogromist activities of their co-religionists in the North (ironically some of these letters came from concerned liberal Protestants who compared the lack of help to the funds made available to help Belgian refugees during the First World War).[62] At a meeting held in Cork in June 1922, Mary MacSwiney suggested: 'It was time that each Unionist and Protestant in Cork put his family into two or three rooms and gave the rest of his house up to Belfast refugees.'[63] Others called for a survey of all Protestant homes to see how many rooms they had available to house Northern refugees.[64] Along with such worrying pronouncements, the situation on the ground had already moved in a sinister direction. Reports began to emerge of Protestant homes being visited by armed men, warning them of dire retribution if they did not give up their houses for the use of the Belfast refugees.

Targets varied enormously from small provincial shops and rural farms right through to the vast estates and 'big houses'. In this latter regard the case of Major Pearse of Roxborough, co. Galway, was typical. In early May he was visited at his 12,000-acre estate, one of the largest in the county, by armed men who ordered him and his family to pack up and leave. They fled

---

[60] For the effects of the Belfast Boycott see D. J. Johnson, 'The Belfast Boycott, 1920–22' in J. M. Goldstrom and J. A. Clarkson, eds, *Irish Population, Economy and Society: Essays in Honour of the Late K.H. Connell* (Oxford, 1981). For the role of local IRA units in enforcing the boycott see Lynch *The Northern I.R.A*, pp. 73–6.

[61] R. Lynch, *Revolutionary Ireland, 1912–1925* (London, 2015), p. 99.

[62] Letter to editor from anonymous Protestant woman dated 7 May 1922 stating that Protestants should set-up a fund to help the Belfast refugees very like that which helped Belgians who were housed in Dalkey during the First World War, *Irish Times*, 18 May 1922.

[63] Ibid.   [64] *Irish Times*, 21 June 1922.

the same day. He was instructed that his property was to be used to house Belfast refugees and told blatantly that he was being singled out because he was a unionist and a Freemason. In Cork, James Regan, was woken from his bed at gunpoint at 2 a.m. and told he and his family had to be gone the next morning because 'the Belfast refugees were coming in the next day'.[65] While the deliberate expulsions were erratic and far from an organised campaign of 'ethnic cleansing', there is little doubt that many people left, as in Belfast, due to a growing perception that they and their communities were being targeted. It is impossible to judge just exactly how many Protestants left due to direct intimidation, although there is little doubt that somewhere between 20,000 and 40,000 people made the decision to leave or were forced to migrate.[66]

The crude sectarian undercurrent behind the noble principles of aiding the Belfast refugees was notable by the fact that the campaign had a negligible effect in helping the expelled Northern Catholics. There is little evidence that the hundreds of properties abandoned by Protestants under threat of execution by the IRA in the spring of 1922 ever saw a Belfast refugee. The existence of the Northern refugees in provincial areas was far from illusory, however. Most had moved to Munster on advice of the IRA being promised greater care in the 'Munster Republic', although more often than not when they arrived they were housed in public buildings, abandoned barracks, commandeered hotels or the local workhouse. For the refugees themselves, the grandiose proclamations of sympathy from republicans appeared as little more than convenient rhetoric to embarrass the provisional government over its handling of the Northern issue. One Catholic refugee, Dermot O'Brien, who had arrived in Cork in early June, angrily summarised his experience of arriving in the west in a letter to the *Irish Independent* under the heading 'Refugees Not Wanted'. He reports the poor reception he and his fellow refugees received when they arrived in Cork after a journey which had cost them most of their remaining money. Most ended up in ad hoc accommodation, such as the 300 reported to have taken over the Grand Railway hotel in Bundoran, while others ended up sleeping rough.[67] After desperate and unsuccessful attempts to get local papers to carry an appeal for funds, O'Brien claims he and a number of other refugees approached a local councillor who had been in charge of distributing Irish White Cross aid in Cork, only to be told 'You people had no business coming here [i.e., Cork]. It was creating a bad morale.' O'Brien even tried to get

[65] *Irish Independent*, 3 May 1922.
[66] For the Southern Protestant experience, see Hart, *The IRA at War*, pp. 223–40.
[67] *Irish Times*, 1 July 1922.

a meeting with Eamon de Valera to propose a scheme to organise a new linen business for the refugees. After waiting two weeks for a reply, O'Brien claims he saw de Valera in Cork city and approached him only to be told by de Valera that he couldn't back such a scheme as 'he could not be sure of the bona fides of the refugees'. In the wake of this meeting, O'Brien concluded angrily: 'It is idle for Mr. De Valera to go on with his humbug-like sympathy on public platforms about the six counties. We are sick at heart of this make-believe. One of the refugees whose bona fides is questioned is 70 years old . . . Do some people think it was for fun she left home, got £9 for her furniture, and paid £7 for travelling expenses to Cork?'[68]

While in provincial Ireland the experience of refugees and the unsavoury campaign of expulsion against Southern Protestants which accompanied it remained largely hidden, in Dublin, by far the principal destination for Northern refugees, the sectarian undercurrent behind the IRA's policy of refugee rehabilitation were all too clear. This was symbolised no better than in the Southern capital where during March and April a number of large public buildings were seized to accommodate Catholic refugees from Belfast. The most significant of these were the headquarters of the Orange Order at the Fowler Memorial Hall in Rutland Square, the Masonic headquarters in Molesworth Street, the YMCA in O'Connell Street and the Kildare Street Club, a bastion of the Southern unionist establishment. All were raided on behalf of shadowy organisations under the auspices of the anti-treaty IRA styling themselves under such names as the 'Belfast Refugees Committee', 'Northern Boycott Committee' or 'Belfast Expelled Workers' Committee'. The language of sectarian scapegoating in such moves was all too clear. All of these organisations had been targeted sporadically by the IRA throughout the preceding two years.

As in the west, individual Protestants and their families also became targets. Between April and June around fifty private houses belonging to Protestants were reportedly commandeered by the IRA for the use of refugee families. There was little planning in evidence. A large proportion of these homes were visited in the dead of night by armed men accompanied by a number of newly arrived Northern refugees and simply ordered to take care of them. For example, on 26 April, Protestant judge Mr Justice Wylie was woken from his bed at gunpoint around 2 a.m. and told to provide shelter for seven Belfast refugees (two women and five children).[69] One of the women, Irene McAllister, recalled that, although

---

[68] *Irish Independent*, 15 June 1922.   [69] *Freeman's Journal*, 28 April 1922.

they were surprisingly well-looked after by the family, they never saw any member of the IRA again.

The IRA's aggressive and poorly planned efforts to address the refugee crisis were viewed increasingly by provisional government officials as symptomatic of the growing state of anarchy within Dublin. One complained that the republicans were occupying an average of three buildings per day in the Southern capital, many of them private homes belonging to prominent pro-treatyites and key government and judicial figures. Others complained that the increase in commandeering to feed and clothe the refugees was 'draining the country of its precious resources'.[70] Certainly, such a chaotic situation couldn't last. Indeed, as the IRA's relief efforts began to get out of hand and as signs of unity on the Northern issue on other fronts became more apparent in June 1922, discussions were opened between both sides in an effort to rationalise relief efforts.

Certainly, by mid-June it had become obvious that the IRA's twin strategy of commandeering and intimidation was not a sustainable way of helping the refugees. The buildings they had chosen for occupation were targeted more for a belief that they housed the perceived architects of the 'pogrom' than their suitability for refugee relief. Indeed, conditions in the commandeered buildings were cramped and unsanitary. One reporter recalled his first visit to the Freemason's hall: 'It is a typical refugee centre, vividly recalling Belgian days, with its swarms of children, its crowds of beshawled and anxious looking women . . . and its sprinkling of apathetic looking men'.[71] Within days of being seized, all of the buildings were inundated with Northern refugees, quickly becoming over-crowded. In the Fowler Memorial Hall, seized on 26 March, over 200 people crowded into its small and unsuitable offices and store rooms. The upper floors were reserved for the forty women and fifty children who had been the first to arrive at the hall, with most of the cramped offices providing shelter for two or three families at a time. The larger ground floor rooms were used as ad hoc dormitories for single men and the few husbands and fathers who had managed to travel with their wives and children, although there were only twelve mattresses and no blankets for its 70 inhabitants. It appears that most people were forced to sleep on the floor, with what little comfort there was reserved for children and infants. The hall was also draughty and damp and little money was available for coal. Washing, sanitary and cooking facilities were also rudimentary and the spread of illness was a genuine concern. There were only two functioning lavatories on the premises, a small washroom and an ill-equipped kitchen which had previously been used as a lunchroom for the hall's

[70] *Freeman's Journal*, 23 April 1922.   [71] *Irish Times*, 18 June 1922.

fifteen staff. As such, there was little hot food available and most got by on a diet of dried biscuits, meat and bread. It was a similar, if not worse, story in the other major commandeered buildings. In the Kildare Street Club, occupied since 15 April, there were 240 Belfast refugees, almost 90 per cent of them women and children. They were looked after by only three volunteer members of the Cumann na mBan, none of whom had any medical training. In all the buildings, those looking after the refugees and administering direct care were largely women, with the exception of the YMCA in O'Connell Street, taken over on 21 April the same day as the Freemason's hall, which had a male doctor visiting each day. Most significantly, all buildings contained numbers of permanent armed IRA guards who cordoned off a section of the buildings for their personal use. Their job was largely to maintain order among the refugees, issuing strict instructions that drunkenness, profanity and vandalism would result in their expulsion. Similarly, all single men were ordered to leave the premises each day at 8 a.m. ostensibly to look for work – although few found any – being only allowed to return after 5 p.m. While women and children were permitted to remain in the hall during the day, there was little for them to do except wait for the men to return. No attempt was made at refugee rehabilitation – no education classes were held, no planned exercise for the children and little attempt even to collect basic information on who the refugees were.[72]

The IRA's erratic policy of commandeering goods to aid the refugees was also to prove wholly disorganised. For example, while they had managed to acquire several hundred blankets and boxes of tobacco, there was a shortage of basic foodstuffs and clothing. Commandeering across Ireland was erratic and poorly directed, being largely informed by the incompatible goals of supplying the refugees and continuing the gratuitous destruction of these same goods in the name of the Belfast Boycott. For example, in Offaly five barges of much needed food heading North were seized and destroyed along with £200 worth of clothing made in Belfast. In Killarney, traders were ordered to provide the equivalent 'money value' of confiscated goods, while the IRA expended great energy in collecting and burning Northern 'unionist' newspapers (the *Belfast Telegraph* and *Belfast Newsletter*, in particular). More bizarrely, on 7 April members of a 'Belfast Refugee Committee' visited the committee of the Royal Hibernian Academy and ordered all exhibits and pictures loaned from or originating in Belfast to be removed.[73] Meanwhile, in the

---

[72] For details of conditions in the various buildings see *Irish Times*, 28 April 1922, *Irish Independent*, 2 May 1922 and *Manchester Guardian*, 20 May 1922.
[73] *Irish Independent*, 8 April 1922.

overcrowded buildings the refugees continued to suffer, with some turning to desperate methods. One of these, Thomas Gallagher, an expelled Belfast shipyard worker, was arrested for stealing and pawning three billiard balls from the Fowler Memorial Hall. At his trial he claimed he only resorted to theft so he could buy food for the 'old men practically starving in the hall'.[74]

Republican appeals for donations from other sources had also proved unsuccessful. Maud Gonne MacBride made numerous heartfelt and, at times, desperate appeals in the press for funds, but to little avail. Between February and May private individuals donated a mere £14 and a small supply of blankets, coal, bread and eggs to the various republican committees set-up to care for refugees. The failure of these appeals had much to do with the provisional government's politicisation of the refugee crisis, with officials warning through the pro-treaty press that to give funds to the Belfast refugee committees was equivalent to putting weapons in the hands of IRA gunmen.[75] A similar attitude was displayed by the Catholic Church who were reluctant to become embroiled in what one spokesman called 'the furtherance of anarchy in the national capital'.[76] By mid-May it became obvious that lack of funding and the unpredictable nature of the IRA strategy of commandeering were proving insufficient to cater for the increasing number of refugees arriving in Dublin. With buildings full to overflowing, attacks on Protestant houses rose sharply, as did the number of appeals to the older charitable agencies such as the Irish White Cross. The occupation of the Freemason's hall in Dublin, an experience shared by Masonic lodges right across the country throughout March and April, was particularly self-defeating, as the Masons, along with many other Protestant organisations, had been at the forefront of improvised fundraising and charitable relief for refugees. Such self-defeating policies, driven by a heady mixture of strong emotion and blind prejudice, meant that by the end of May 1922 the republican relief effort was on the verge of collapse and destitute and starving refugees once again became common sights on the streets of Dublin.

The failure of the republican relief effort occurred as the number of refugees began to increase in the aftermath of the IRA's Northern offensive in late-May and early-June which inspired unprecedented levels of violence in Belfast. With stories of this new surge in violence filling the pages of the nationalist press, and the evident failure of the noteworthy clause in the Craig–Collins pacts to ensure the return of all refugees to their homes, public opinion turned once again into sympathy for the

---

[74] *Irish Times*, 4 April 1922.   [75] *Irish Independent*, 10 April 1922.
[76] Hopkinson, *Green Against Green*, p. 121.

plight of the Northern refugees. This letter to the *Freeman's Journal* on 29 May was typical:

The country is horrified by the atrocities on Belfast Catholics, but so far it has not made a concerted effort to relieve distress and afford shelter to the refugees. There are innumerable untenanted mansions in Southern Ireland that could be utilised to shelter these unfortunate people, but without bedding and a systematic scheme of relief it is useless to take them over. During the Great War prominent Irishmen were falling over each other to relive the distress of the Belgian refugees. Why cannot they exhibit similar fervour now? We have resolutions, prayers and threats galore. As the Americans say, these cut no ice. And those most generous in this form of sympathy are generally very frugal when it comes to parting with money. We have had collections for the starving children of Europe, the heathen Chinese, and many others, and it seems remarkable that we are not having collections for our own Catholic brethren.[77]

It was certainly obvious that by the end of May, unless checked, the refugee situation would become a significant humanitarian disaster. The writer's call, echoed by many others, for a 'systematic scheme of relief' was answered when provisional government officials held negotiations with the executive representatives Rory O'Connor and Leo Henderson on the need for a shared approach to the growing refugee problem. The meetings resulted in a typically confused compromise solution whereby the 'Dáil Éireann government', working through the Irish White Cross, would take responsibility for the refugees. However, it soon became apparent that, despite the public show of unity and bipartisanship on the refugee issue, to all intents and purposes the provisional government had taken over. There is little doubt that the pro-treaty government saw taking control of the refugee issue as a way of lessening the number of buildings occupied by the republicans. Indeed, as a prerequisite for their involvement, the provisional government insisted that the IRA must evacuate all public buildings it had commandeered to house refugees. Only after this was achieved would they arrange for the creation of a single central reception centre to be paid for out of Dáil (but in reality provisional government) funds.

The choice of building was the imposing Marlborough Hall in Glasnevin. Taken over by the British army in January 1921, it had previously served as the Irish Counties War Hospital during the First World War and prior to that was a hostel for female students attending nearby Marlborough Street College. Evacuated by the British on 10 February 1922, it was soon occupied by large numbers of new recruits to the provisional government army. Ironically, the anti-treaty IRA had attacked the building in early April.

---

[77] *Freeman's Journal*, 29 May 1922.

In order to accommodate the refugees, all troops were sent to the Curragh. The first evacuations took place on 27 May when the Masonic hall and Fowler Memorial Hall were evacuated by the Four Courts Executive. Other buildings were vacated in subsequent weeks, culminating on 8 June when the last 200 refugees left the Kildare Street Club and were moved en masse, under armed guard supervised by Dublin IRA leader Oscar Traynor, to Marlborough Hall.[78]

The involvement of the provisional government allowed for a rationalisation of previously haphazard relief efforts. Certainly, Marlborough Hall was a far more suitable venue as a refugee centre than any that the IRA had occupied. However, although well-equipped it was far too small. With almost 12,000 Northern Catholic refugees reported in Dublin by the Southern press at the time the hall was handed over, its capacity of less than 700 was to prove wholly inadequate. A report by the Dublin poor law guardians stated that in the two weeks following the opening of the hall in June they had been inundated with refugees, over eighty each day, and had asked that the situation was now so serious that every county in Ireland should take its 'fair share of refugees'.[79] A further problem was the stringent entry criteria employed by those in charge of administering relief. Only the neediest cases were deemed to deserve attention. In practice, this meant women, children and the elderly. Young men were very much shunned. One refugee, Peter Daly, recalled that after queuing for two hours outside of the hall, he and seven other men were turned away by a Free State soldier and told to 'stop making mischief'. Such views were reflected at higher levels of the government, with Cosgrave, never the most sympathetic to the plight of the refugees, claiming in the Dáil that 'these young men had come south with the sole aim of joining the growing bands of irregulars'.[80] When the independent deputy Darrell Figgis stated that many had also come south to join the provisional government Army, Cosgrave responded: 'I think not-not very many. We have never encouraged these young men to flee from their responsibilities in the six counties.'[81] Indeed, it is notable that the largest expenditure of the provisional government's 'special refugee relief fund' was in paying for train fares for young men to return home to Belfast.[82] Such perceptions were certainly not helped

---

[78] For reports of these evacuations see *Irish Times*, 27 May, 29 May and 9 June 1922.

[79] Report from Dublin Poor Law Guardians, *Irish Times*, 22 June 1922, p. 23.

[80] Letter from Peter Daly, 'Belfast Refugees: general file', Department of Finance, FIN 1/924, NAI.

[81] *Irish Times*, 23 September 1922.

[82] For details of provisional government expenditure on refugee relief see 'Belfast Refugees: general file', Department of Finance FIN 1/924, NAI.

by the arrival of a large number of political exiles fleeing internment in the North during May 1922, or those who were steadily released from the Argenta prison ship and the Larne Workhouse over the following twelve months.

The most damaging aspect of this policy was that many families were shorn of their male relatives. The severe psychological impact on women and children of being separated from male relatives at such a time, especially as so many of them had already suffered loss or bereavement back in Belfast, can only be imagined. Few testimonies on their experiences remain, although the surviving photographs, news reports and statements that do exist certainly back up this perception. For example, Patrick Reilly, who had brought his wife, young daughter and several other children belonging to friends and relatives (two of whom were orphans) safely from Belfast, recalled that he was separated from them after their move from the YMCA building and didn't manage to see them again for six weeks when they had been moved to the South Dublin Union. Peter Mitchell, from Lisburn, stated in a letter to his mother that he had been forcibly separated from his sister and her two sons, being told that, as they were not his children he wasn't considered part of the family. While, ironically, the 'family' remained the basic unit of measurement for refugees, these were overwhelmingly artificial or reconstructed families. They are also very large, with an average of ten people in each of them. The general character of these 'families' is one of a few adult female carers (a grandmother, a mother and her sister, for example) and then six to ten children of varying ages. There were very few men, certainly after the move to Marlborough Hall. For example, on 18 June there were 728 Belfast refugees in residence at the hall: of these 194 were women, 196 children from 8 to 16 years, and 265 children under 8 years, but only seventy-three men, most of whom were elderly, infirm or designated as the sole carer. Certainly, in comparison with republican relief efforts, which were well-meaning, but ultimately disorganised and deeply counterproductive, provisional government policy was extremely limited and unsympathetic.[83]

The refugees themselves are the most hidden aspect of the partition exodus. They left no surviving memoirs of their experiences and, due to the chaotic nature of relief efforts, qualitative material is limited. However, a number of common themes do emerge. Certainly, the first thing to note is that the grand nationalist rhetoric of refugee rehabilitation was at odds with the harsh reality for many. They were used largely as

---

[83] For a brief, but excellent, overview of provisional government attitudes to the Northern refugees, see O'Halloran, *Partition and the Limits of Irish Nationalism*, pp. 131–3.

a tool to intimidate or embarrass other communities and political opponents in Ireland, quickly discarded when they became of little use. Despite the pleas for aid and the almost daily tales of 'the horrors of Belfast', there was no groundswell of popular support for the plight of the refugees. Many became exasperated at the dichotomy between the rhetoric of sympathy and the practical help they were actually receiving. One refugee wrote: 'Why not hold up the traffic for an hour some night in O'Connell Street and let some of the Belfast refugees state how matters stand in the North and the barbarism their women and children are subjected to ... Let us show our sympathy in L.s.d [i.e., pounds, shillings and pence] and not in mouth-vapourings.'[84] James Reilly, a Cavan press correspondent noted, as did numerous others, the warm welcome given to Belgian refugees in contrast with those from Belfast.[85]

Indeed, the journey itself was often a further physical cruelty for already shell-shocked and psychologically damaged people. Travelling on a train from Belfast to Dublin in June 1922, British journalist Richard Caldwell, recalled:

I met fugitives of all classes, kinds, and politics, united by only one common bond – that they were Catholics and therefore suffering ... many of the poorest of Belfast's poor were on the train, having scraped together by one means or another sufficient funds to take them out of the inferno. Others I was told had found the cost of the train journey to Dublin too much and were forced to walk across the border begging their way as they went.[86]

For many, it was only after the relief of managing to escape the immediate threatening situation wore off that the more difficult challenges began. After arriving in their new homes in Dublin, Liverpool or Glasgow, many refugees were viewed with suspicion and open hostility. In this vulnerable state, refugees became easy targets for exploitation and theft. Barbara McWhirter had all her belongings stolen shortly after she arrived in Dublin from Belfast, including all her clothes and the few mementoes she had managed to salvage from her burning house on the Shankhill Road.[87] Due to the politically charged and chaotic nature of the relief systems put in place, refugees were offered rich pickings to those offering fictional rooms to let or promises of a place at the overcrowded refugee centres. Lizzie Waters recalled giving all of her remaining money to a man who approached her shortly after arriving in Dublin and promised her and

---

[84] *Irish Independent*, 9 June 1922.
[85] *Irish Independent*, 16 June 1922. Maud Gonne MacBride herself made a similar angry comparison after her experience of the early stages of the crisis. See *Irish Times*, 7 April 1922.
[86] *Manchester Guardian*, 20 June 1922.   [87] *Irish Times*, 27 January 1923.

her three children refuge in a cottage in Wicklow. Despite travelling to a prearranged meeting place with the man on three consecutive nights, she never saw him again.[88] John Branagh from Lisburn, was promised a cheap room in Dundalk only to find that when he returned to the property the next night all his belongings had been stolen.[89]

The phenomena of the Belfast refugees in Dublin were a curiosity for many. When on 18 June 1922, the final 200 refugees left the Kildare Street Club for Marlborough Hall in three special trams, crowds turned up to watch the spectacle, taking photographs, held back by armed IRA guards and following the cumbersome procession several miles to their new home. What is most striking about reports of these refugees is how silent they themselves are. Numerous reporters tried to speak to them but most 'didn't want to talk about their experiences' or 'thought it best to stay silent', either through fear of reprisals against their remaining families in the North, trauma or their wish to retain some form of dignity.[90]

Their silence allowed for the projection of Southern stereotypes on to the refugees by playing into prevailing Southern prejudices about the nature of the average Northern Catholic. These stereotypes of Northerners saw them essentially as passive victims – 'slaves', 'filleted Catholics' or 'niggers on the average plantation in the Southern States of America'.[91] Certainly, as the historian Clare O'Halloran has perceptively observed 'the image of the northern minority held by southern nationalists was that of a subordinate, downtrodden and essentially passive people'.[92] Many saw the Northern refugees solely as victims or cowards, to quote one, Councillor French who, ironically, was for some time a leading light in the Irish White Cross organisation: 'Those people had no business coming here. It was creating bad morale. They should have stood their ground and faced their Gethsemane.'[93]

There is little doubt that such stereotyping in many instances gave way to active bigotry. Their distinctive dialects, as one press correspondent noted, 'speaking a language almost incomprehensible to the Southerner',[94] and retention of communal identity made the Northern Catholics easily identifiable. Many recount their experience of verbal and physical abuse. This was the case wherever they went – in Glasgow, for example, there were numerous reports of refugees being attacked, abused

---

[88] See, for example, Letter from Mrs Lizzie Waters, Department of Taoiseach files, NAI, S8289.
[89] *Irish Times*, 18 June 1924.   [90] *Irish Independent, Irish Times* 19 June 1922.
[91] O'Halloran, *Partition and the Limits of Irish Nationalism*, p. 61.   [92] Ibid, p. 60.
[93] *Irish Independent*, 13 June 1922.
[94] 'The Anti-Catholic Terror in Belfast: Sufferings of the Refugees', *Manchester Guardian*, 20 June 1922.

or robbed. Police reports state that over sixty such attacks occurred in the last two weeks of May alone. They also faced hostility from the Scottish establishment. It is no coincidence, for example, that it was in 1923 the Church of Scotland produced an infamous report about the 'growing menace' of Irish migration to the Scottish nation.[95]

The fact that the refugees arrived at a time of high unemployment and political and economic uncertainty added to the heightened tension. Due to lack of accommodation, they were highly visible in Ireland on the eve of the civil war, making them easy scapegoats. During the first week of June 1922, a number of demonstrations were held outside Marlborough Hall by unemployed Dublin workers demanding 'the same comforts given to the so-called Belfast Refugees'.[96,97] This was to be followed in early July when pickets staged a similar protest outside the South Dublin Union. They were only assuaged when one of the board members read out a statement on the steps of the building assuring them that the refugees were receiving no special treatment and would be returning home as soon as possible.

The outbreak of civil war in Dublin on 28 June 1922 was a turning point for the Northern refugees. The almost simultaneous end of the violence in Northern Ireland meant the refugee crisis slipped from the headlines as other priorities took over. Refugees found themselves side-lined and shunned as organised relief measures quickly faltered and then collapsed. In the early weeks of the civil war, refugees were moved out of Marlborough Hall, which was commandeered as a military hospital and convalescent home for wounded soldiers. The remaining refugees, around 900 of the neediest cases, were sent to various workhouses, the South Dublin Union, or to that at Ardee and other ad hoc accommodation. Again, the accommodation was to prove woefully inadequate for tackling the scale of the problem. While 342 Belfast refugees found a place in the Dublin workhouse, over three times that number were turned away. Despite calls for the government to occupy various schools and empty hotels around the city for the use of refugees, no other buildings were to be allocated to solve the problem. Indeed, if anything, the government intended to allow the situation to deteriorate – 'hoping it would solve itself' – and, certainly, by the end of August 1922 there were only eight refugees remaining in the Dublin Union.[98]

---

[95] *The Menace of the Irish Race to Our Scottish Nationality*, National Archives of Scotland, TD200/147g.

[96] *Irish Independent*, 10 September 1922.

[97] Belfast Refugees demonstration', *Irish Independent*, 4 June 1922.

[98] 'File on Belfast Relief', Department of Taoiseach files, NA Dublin, S1230.

Others were corralled into barracks and military installations under the care of the provisional government army and, as such, many were subject to attack and arrest. Certainly, it is one of the great ironies for Belfast refugees that, having fled to escape violence in the North, within weeks of their arrival they found themselves in the middle of another civil war. Many got caught up in the actual fighting itself. The fact that refugee relief has been put in the hands of the military (both republican and provisional government) meant that many of the buildings still occupied by refugees were those commandeered by republicans and were attacked by provisional government troops during the week-long fight for Dublin. For example, Fowler Memorial Hall still contained almost forty refugees when it was attacked on 28 June. In turn, Marlborough Hall itself was attacked by the IRA for the second time. Many of the houses the IRA had forcibly billeted refugees in during April and May were still occupied. They belonged almost exclusively to prominent Free State notables and, as such, were subject to attack. For example, one refugee, Robert Dennison, who had managed to get his wife and five children out of Belfast in early May was billeted by the IRA in a commandeered house in Dublin belonging to a key official from the finance department. In late June the house was blown up by the IRA, killing one of Dennison's daughters. It was a similar situation outside of Dublin. A large party of refugees under the care of provisional government troops at Killeshandra in Cavan, for example, were caught up in a republican attack on 29 October 1922 and were forced to flee into the streets in their nightclothes.[99] Similarly, at Castleshane Castle in Monaghan seventy refugees were arrested and imprisoned by provisional government troops as they were suspected of belonging to an IRA column, despite the fact that refugees from across the border had used the castle since March.[100] Furthermore, in November 1922 a fire broke out at the workhouse at Ardee, leaving over 150 refugees, many of them orphans, homeless.[101]

The outbreak of civil war, the collapse of public sympathy, the virtual end of organised relief and the new peace back in the North led the vast majority of Northern refugees to return home (this explains, particularly, the skewed inferences which have been made by historians about the census figures of 1926). The Northern government were surprisingly willing to allow the refugees back to Belfast. Many returned to unemployment or to find their old houses demolished. A study of the housing situation in the city shows that houses which were abandoned in 1922

[99] 'The Rat Plague', *Freeman's Journal*, 30 October 1922.
[100] *Freeman's Journal*, 31 August 1922.
[101] 'Ardee Workhouse Fire', *Irish Independent*, 24 November 1922.

were still empty one year later, most being either later demolished or occupied by Protestants, thus further delineating the city's sectarian divisions.[102]

From the autumn of 1922, as the refugees slipped from the political agenda, the issue morphed into a prolonged legal dispute between the three governments which was dominated by the question of financial responsibility. In Britain, the relief situation had been more straightforward than that which had prevailed in the chaotic atmosphere of Southern Ireland. In May 1922, in response to strident appeals from Sir Edward Carson and other leading unionist politicians, an Irish Distress Committee was formed under the chairmanship of Sir Samuel Hoare. The committee was given a budget of £10,000 and tasked with evaluating claims and providing financial relief in the form of loans of direct grants. By the end of 1923 the committee had received over 15,000 claims, made up almost equally of Catholics and Protestants, and paid out almost £30,000. It continued to sit in various guises until the summer of 1931 when it had paid out a sum of almost £1,000,000 in compensation and relief.

Both of the new partition governments had remarkably similar approaches to the financial claims surrounding the refugee crisis. They were both keen to maximise the suffering of co-religionists on the other side of the border, while minimising the claims put by members of their own minorities. This was demonstrated markedly in May 1922 when Reid Jameson, secretary to the Irish Distress Committee, personally wrote to both governments. To the Northern Irish minister of home affairs, Dawson Bates, he complained that the RUC had failed to endorse any of the 200 claims the London government had received from expelled Northern Catholics in Britain, despite the fact that his own investigations had shown that at least half of the applicants had valid cases. In response, Dawson Bates insisted that any further requests should be sent through the ministry rather than directly to the RUC, as 'it was leaving a bad impression'.[103] In the South, the provisional government argued that Southern loyalist claims of intimidation were 'largely invented' in order to undermine the new state. Jameson responded angrily that 'far from being a sham' thousands of people had arrived in Britain 'penniless and robbed of their homes'.[104] By the end of 1925, as part of the larger post-partition settlement between the three governments, it was decided to

---

[102] See Martin, *Migration within the Six Counties of Northern Ireland*, pp. 10–12.

[103] Dawson Bates memo, May 1922, Refugees from Northern Ireland, PRONI, CAB/9/Y/1.

[104] 'Reid Jameson to Minister of Local Government, 22 May 1922', 'Belfast Refugees: general file', Department of Finance FIN 1/924, NAI.

offset the various costs accrued in providing refugee relief. Despite numerous complaints from both parties, they both eventually paid up, with the Northern Irish government paying around £18,000 and the Free State £12,000. Later claims and expenses were finally dispensed with at the Imperial Conference of March 1926, which settled all outstanding financial matters from the partition period.[105]

Ireland's refugees were the most immediate victims of the unseemly haste with which partition was both planned and executed. While refugee numbers remain a subject of contention, there is little doubt that the partition period saw between 50,000 and 80,000 people forced to move from their homes as refugees. Certainly, far more people became refugees than ever died, were injured or took up arms to participate in the 'Irish revolution'. Despite this, their story remains a largely forgotten one, surfacing, if at all, only as a way of demonising the actions of one or other of the two partition states. However, a study of the refugee crisis in Ireland illuminates the study of partition in a number of important ways. Both of the new partition states failed to guarantee the safety of the refugees or that of the minorities from which they were drawn and their policies underline, despite the irredentist rhetoric, the basic partitionist assumptions which permeated their thinking. The refugees were a bad conscience to their would-be allies and an expensive embarrassment to the two new Irish governments. However, ironically, forced migration, rather than challenging partition, made it, if anything, more of a reality. The movement of people and the decisions they made reinforced pre-viously nebulous ideas of the new border and, for good or ill, painted the new states which emerged on either side as places of safety. It was thus the existence of the border itself which gave these movements both impetus and meaning and saw thousands of Irish people labelled as outsiders in what they had previously regarded as their own country; a country which with partition was unravelling and, unlike the new border, rapidly losing its significance.

---

[105] See 'Cabinet Conclusions', 13 January 1925, PRONI, CAB/4/85/4. For the Free State payments and later financial debate see Brennan, 'A Political Minefield: Southern Loyalists, the Irish Distress Committee and the British Government, 1922–1931'.

8   Holding the Line

Back in 1914, during the height of the Ulster Crisis, the British prime minister Herbert Asquith made a proposal that the problem of meeting minority aspirations in Ireland could be addressed by large-scale transfers of population, through the 'migration at state expense of Protestants and Catholics into and out of the excluded area'.[1] However, seven years later, in 1921, Article XII of the Anglo-Irish Treaty approached the problem from the opposite direction, attempting to meet such aspirations, not by moving people across the newly established frontier, but by moving the line itself through the mechanism of a boundary commission.

There was nowhere where the illogical nature of partition was most evident than in the new border. Lillian Spender recalled in her diary a tour of the frontier in 1923 during which her 'route corkscrewed about in the most bewildering manner through numerous small roads in a futile effort to avoid crossing over the border'.[2] The idea for a boundary commission to settle the extent of the new frontier between the two states, however, was an attempt to make partition appear natural and an authentic representation of the wishes of the population. Sean Connaughton, the Irish writer, crudely, but effectively, characterised the intractable problem of the Irish border when he had one of his characters say in his novel *The Run of the Country*:

The land was impervious to maps. What appeared plain on paper was on the ground an orgy of political and geographical confusion. Cavan and Monaghan in the South were locked into Fermanagh in the North, like two dogs trying to cover the one hot bitch.[3]

The Boundary Commission has been widely judged as a profound failure. Its final limited proposals barely touched the glaring incongruities of the border, enclosing hundreds of thousands of people who unambiguously preferred life in the other state. Despite this, however, the idea of drawing

[1] Hand, *Boundary Commission*, p. 72.
[2] Diary of Lady Lillian Spender, 25 June 1923, Spender Papers, PRONI, D/1633/2/26.
[3] S. Connaughton, *The Run of the Country* (Belfast, 1991), p. 2.

lines on maps as a way of satisfying contested communal identities retains a strong allure in the popular imagination. In such arguments a fairer redrawing of the boundary at the start of the partition process would have made it a more workable solution. By decreasing the size of the Northern minority, it is argued, the paranoia of the unionist government would have been lessened as would minority political opposition. This would have led to a far more stable and inclusive state and an avoidance of the collapse into civil and religious violence from the late 1960s.

Even in scholarly circles, this belief has retained some appeal, with a number of historians continuing to cite the mislocation of the border as one of the primary factors in explaining continued sectarian conflict. However, while many argued that the subsequent Irish border was in the wrong place, few, including the 'repartitionists' of the 1980s, have ever been able to put forwards a credible alternative frontier.[4] Such crude clean cuts were suggested at the time of partition itself. The Northern representative on the commission recommended that Craig call for a simple straight line from South Armagh running through to Fermanagh down to Newry, which would 'take in a fair share of the people we want and leave out those we don't want'.[5] For all its failings though, and in the light of such crudely expressed contemporary solutions, the Boundary Commission of 1925 must be seen as a genuine attempt to create a border more reflective of minority concerns. Actual change was attempted. Historical hindsight has certainly made the border appear fixed and solid. However, this was not either the perception or reality in the early years of partition.

Like so many aspects of the partition of Ireland, the idea for the setting up of a commission to settle the dimensions of the new frontier was an ad hoc response to a short-term political crisis. Emerging during the negotiations between the British government and Irish nationalists which led to the Anglo-Irish Treaty in the winter of 1921, the idea was suggested as a way of bypassing the vexed issue of Ulster and ending the tortuous treaty negotiations by leaving the border issue to be settled separately at a later date.[6] This was certainly the case with Collins, who displayed no belief in the Boundary Commission as a way of undermining Northern Ireland, relying instead on his typically conspiratorial methods of armed intimidation, non-cooperation and relentless propaganda.[7] In January 1922 he had even gone as far as to ditch the idea completely, agreeing with James

---

[4] See, for example, L. Kennedy, *Two Ulsters: A Case for Repartition* (Belfast, 1986).
[5] Fisher, quoted in Ervine, *Craigavon*, p. 481.
[6] Hopkinson, *Green Against Green*, p. 88.
[7] For an insight into Collins' thinking on the Ulster issue, see Woods to Mulcahy, 27 July 1922, Mulcahy papers, UCDAD, P7/B/77.

Craig that the two Irish leaders would settle the border issue between themselves without any British involvement. However, by the time the issue of the border re-emerged in 1924, Collins was long dead, as was his confrontational policy.[8] However, the expectation remained among many Irish nationalists that any future settlement would award them large swathes of Northern territory, amounting to something in the region of two and a half of the six existing counties, including major cities such as Newry and even Derry itself.

Detailed discussions about the extent of the new Northern Ireland had never taken place prior to the emergence of the Boundary Commission idea. Due to the fundamental significance of the border to the partition project, the issue had always been left as vague as possible. This served the purpose of allowing politicians to present the settlement as provisional and amendable, a central deception which lay behind the partition of Ireland, and a belief which persists to this day, even though Northern Ireland has existed for almost a century and is the one of the few states still surviving from the post-1918 redrawing of European boundaries.

For the first time in over a decade of active partitioning, real practical questions were to be posed to all parties involved, with their answers set to reveal their underlying attitude to the settlement. How close these would marry up with their ideological rhetoric remained to be seen. The boundary commission idea itself managed to survive largely because it was a way for all parties involved to abdicate their own responsibilities for partition, allowing someone else to make the inevitable compromise. The fact was that there was no fair border line that could be drawn which would meet everyone's expectations. Cosgrave later tellingly summed up this commission as an attempt 'to secure a divine solution by human agency'.[9] Indeed, so fanatical and utopian had been the ideological appeals of radical nationalists that they were now caught between the political need to placate their own supporters and their acceptance of partition.

This peculiar unreality of the problem was even clear in the very wording of the Boundary Commission clause itself in the Anglo-Irish Treaty. Article XII stated that, at an unspecified time in the future, a commission comprising one representative from each of the partition states and an independent chairman was to meet to 'determine in accordance with the wishes of the inhabitants, so far as may be compatible with economic and geographic conditions the boundaries between Northern Ireland and the rest of Ireland'.

---

[8] The change in provisional government policy on the north-east is dealt with in fascinating detail in Ernest Blythe's 'Memo on the North-East Ulster'.
[9] Cosgrave to MacNeill, 22 December 1925, MacNeill Papers, LA1/H/126.

The dangerous ambiguity of such an instruction was testament to the sheer impracticality of trying to define the parameters of a suitable mechanism for defining the frontier. Its lack of a definite timetable made it almost the ideal clause to cause even further friction and uncertainty in the Ulster border lands between and within both communities, raising as it did the hopes of many nationalists while, at the same time, causing further alarm in an already paranoid Protestant population. Furthermore, this lack of a clearly defined mechanism for dealing with partition allowed both sides to place radically differing interpretations on what the shape of any future settlement would look like.[10] Added to this was the problem that the Northern state was already up and running and had long established the foundations of its new institutions well before the commission actually sat.

In the end, this momentous decision would come down to one man, the South African judge Richard Feetham. The expectation that the two other Irish members of the commission would largely cancel one another out, it was Feetham who would have the casting vote. This was a fact that Craig himself was well aware of:

if I say I am not going to give away one inch of the soil of Fermanagh and Tyrone, does it not immediately mean that the destinies of these two counties rest in one hand in the hand of one man? Was there ever such a preposterous suggestion? If I cannot give way on the question of Tyrone and Fermanagh, and the other man [W. T. Cosgrave] will not by any sort or manner of means reduce his demand for the two counties, is there not a complete deadlock without a chance of success, and is not any Chairman, whoever he may be, in the position of having to decide the fate of these two places, and of Derry City?[11]

Despite the parliamentary debates, the violence, and involvement of millions of people in elections and mass movements, everything had devolved to this moment. There seems little doubt that if Southern nationalist propaganda, which claimed almost a third of Northern territory, came even close to being achieved, then Northern Ireland and the whole partition project would have been unsustainable. Despite his undeniable ability, Feetham faced a formidable task. He had never visited Ireland previously, which it was felt would make him a more impartial arbitrator, although his lack of sensitivity to the peculiarities of the Irish situation meant he was woefully out of touch.

---

[10] For the British perspective on the border issue see K. Matthews, *The Irish Boundary Crisis and the Re-shaping of British Politics, 1910–1925*. PhD thesis, London School of Economics, 2000; R. Fanning, 'Anglo-Irish Relations: Partition and the British Dimension in Historical Perspective', *Irish Studies in International Affairs*, vol. 2, no. 1 (1982), pp. 132–49.

[11] James Craig, NIHOC, 7 December 1922, vol. 2, cols 1151–2.

Even so, in the shape of the Irish Boundary Commission, he was being handed a poisoned chalice. Feetham realised this himself very early in the process, when he made negative comparisons with the more definitive terms present in the relevant clauses of the Treaty of Versailles.[12] The Irish boundary clause gave no definitive timetable for the sitting of the decision, a factor which had already led to a culture of rising expectations and fear in the most prominently discussed areas for transfer along the new border. There was no mention of exactly how the 'wishes of the inhabitants' were to be ascertained or how such ideological demands could ever be married with the practical 'economic and geographic conditions'.[13]

The clearest way for the commission to count the heads it needed for such deliberations was by use of the census. However, there had been no census in Ireland for thirteen years and, in the meantime, Ireland had been through a world war, revolution, partition and a variety of civil wars, all of which had led to voluntary or forced population movement, especially along the border where the most crucial decisions were to be taken.

The lack of reliable population statistics was only one problem and certainly not the most crucial. Right from the start, Feetham and the commissioners were bewildered by the lack of any reference in the treaty clause about which geographical unit would form the individual blocks to transfer. The most basic and archaic form of division in Ireland were townlands. These formed the basis of larger parochial areas such as baronies and parishes. While offering the possibility of rooting partition in a traditional and very Irish form of territory, townlands proved to be woefully inadequate for the demands of the commission. They were inconsistent in terms of area and did not reflect contemporary demographic realities. As Feetham himself observed, the townlands had 'no uniformity as regards area or population, and many of them are small, and have very few inhabitants, while some have none at all'.[14] Other areas such as poor law unions or electoral divisions proved unworkable due either to their size or their lack of any ongoing administrative function.

While the commission faced seemingly insurmountable practical problems, even if the tools it had to work with were ideal, the attitudes of the participants on both sides presented the biggest hurdle to a successful settlement. By this time, the commission was finally called in November 1924, after an earlier request by Cosgrave, Ireland itself had changed beyond all recognition and partition was a well-established

---

[12] Hand, *Boundary Commission*, p. ix.
[13] 'Final Text of the Articles of Agreement between Great Britain and Ireland', London, 6 December 1921, www.difp.ie/docs/1921/Anglo-Irish-Treaty/214.htm.
[14] Hand, *Boundary Commission*, p. 64.

fact. Less the beginning of a new nationalist crusade against partition, for Cosgrave the Boundary Commission was part of his government's wish to ensure that the treaty, on which their legitimacy largely rested was carried through in all its aspects.

Arguably, their uninspiring appointment of Eoin MacNeill, a sober academic and minister for education, whom one Ulster critic said 'should have restricted all his activities to the solutions of the problems in Gaelic grammar', was symptomatic of the Free State's more conservative approach to the vexing border issue.[15] The rather uncomfortable fact that Collins and Craig had both agreed to scrap the commission in January 1922 was itself quietly forgotten. Worse still, however, was the complete refusal of the Northern government to engage on any level with the scheme. As the commission was meant to involve representatives from each of the three parties involved, the refusal of the Belfast government to nominate a commissioner represented an embarrassing problem. In the end, the short-lived Labour government of Ramsay MacDonald were forced to pass a special amendment in parliament allowing them to make the appointment themselves. In the end, the man chosen was J. R. Fisher, a committed unionist and ex-newspaper editor, who would perform his role of defending Northern interests as ably as any representative of the Belfast government itself.

The commission was thus faced with irredentist and wholly incompatible campaigns from both unionists and nationalists. Unionists pledged themselves not to lose an inch of their promised land. Demonstrating how quickly partition foundation myths took hold, this new truncated 'Ulster', which they had been quite happy to carve out of the existing province, had been converted into a heartland to be zealously defended. Outside of the Free State cabinet, nationalist popular opinion veered between those who demanded the dismantling of the Northern state in its entirety and more moderate voices who, even so, wanted, not to say, expected, that the commission would award them a third of the Northern territory. Trying to marry up these conflicting aspirations would prove impossible. The most radical nationalist challenge to the North's right to exist was outlined in the handbook of the North-Eastern Boundary Bureau (NEBB), the provisional government-sponsored propaganda agency, headed by Kevin O'Shiel:

Even if the homogeneity of the greater portion of the four [majority Protestant] counties was established, it could not be held to justify a breach of the obvious national unity of Ireland, for there is a limit to the privileges which can be extended to national minorities. An examination of the elements which go to

[15] Ervine, *Craigavon*, p. 500. See also Hand, *Boundary Commission*, pp. vii–xxii.

the making of a nation has shown us that uniformity of race, religion, character and ideals is found in no modern nation whatsoever. Therefore, in arguing that there are two nations of this theory merely convict themselves of ignorance of the meaning of the national idea. A nation is the reconciliation of differences, not the assertion of uniformity.[16]

The NEBB had been formed shortly after the signing of the Anglo-Irish Treaty. However, it was only in the spring of 1923, 'the experimental year', with the Southern civil war finally coming to an end and the Free State government's attentions turning to its next showdown, this time with Ulster and Britain over the boundary, that it really moved into top gear. The focus of the bureau was to present a combination of propaganda and 'healthy persuasion' in the form of endless tables and statistics which would be used to reinforce its case before the commission. Under its umbrella were also all manner of anti-partitionist schemes, from strategising Northern Catholic non-recognition of the Belfast government, to commissioning reports on how best to manipulate excise duties along the frontier to gain political advantage. In this latter regard, it was argued that by lowering customs rates on some goods and raising them on others ('although care should be taken with tea as it is the national drink'), this 'political weapon' could be wielded to 'cripple . . . border towns such as Derry, Strabane, Enniskillen and Newry'. This, it was hoped, would

increase prices . . . add greatly to Northern unemployment . . . cause border towns to decrease in size and importance, so as to make Northerners discontented with partition, and mature amongst them a frame of mind compliant for opening up negotiations for Union with us.[17]

Aside from the fact that such 'suffering' would fall mostly on Northern Catholics, this notion of an economic war overestimated drastically the power of the Southern economy and the willingness of Northern Unionists to endure 'any means of privation, even death' rather than join willingly with the South. Furthermore, the keen hope expressed that the British would baulk at the expense of employing more customs officers to police the border against the proposed state-sponsored smuggling enterprise overlooked the vast expense they had been prepared to go to already in shoring up the unionist regime. It had also, of course, been tried, and failed, before with the Belfast Boycott. A final six-week-long scramble to improvise a last-minute strategy for the 'political use' of customs barriers, one of which involved 'fostering a great smuggling trade along the 240 miles of irregular and impossible border',[18] did not

[16] North-Eastern Boundary Bureau, *Handbook of the Ulster Question* (Dublin, 1923), p. 154.
[17] 'Memo on tactics, 23 March 1923', 'Customs barrier'.   [18] Ibid.

affect their imminent establishment on 1 April 1923. Once again, Southern nationalists not only underestimated the depth of unionist opposition, regarding it largely a matter of financial opportunism, but saw confrontation and compulsion as the best way to affect Irish unity. Typical of this attitude was Patrick McGoldrick, TD for Donegal, who wrote to Ernest Blythe in January 1923 concerning the importance of economic coercion:

Until the north east agrees to throw in its lot with us this [economic] weapon must be rigidly wielded. It is the main one in our armoury for securing national unity and no flummery about good will, will count as an iota in this game. There is nothing that will accelerate reunion more than leading those in the north east to the realisation, among all their other drawbacks, of their inferior status.[19]

It was clear, however, that, whereas the nationalist cupboard was bare when it came to finding strategies to combat partition, the NEBB and its energetic arguments generated a great deal of heat on the Boundary Commission, if little actual light.[20]

O'Shiel himself had presented his findings to the Free State cabinet two months after the end of the civil war. By his calculations, the South could expect significant transfers of territory. His expectations were alarming, although not untypical of those sharing his west Ulster background. Not only did he envision 'as a minimum' both Fermanagh and Tyrone, he also expected both Newry and Derry to be transferred to the South, including a large portion of their hinterlands in counties Down and Londonderry. This award would have certainly left a significant Catholic minority under the jurisdiction of the Belfast government, but it would have been reduced to a little under 30 per cent of the Ulster population. Overall, over 600,000 Irish people would change state, leaving less than one million people under the jurisdiction of the Belfast government. While this represented his most pessimistic hope for the commission, the demand which he felt the Dublin government could win were eye-watering. Northern Ireland would be now have only one intact county, Antrim, to which would be added a small portion of county Londonderry and parts of North Down. Perhaps most notable was that while such a change would have reduced the population of Northern Ireland by almost half, leaving it with barely 750,000 inhabitants, Catholics would still make-up over 20% of it. Even at these most minute of levels, partition failed to deliver the clean-cut that had been mooted in 1914. Over a quarter of a million people in Ulster would still be living in a state they regarded as an anathema.

---

[19] 'Customs barrier'.
[20] See 'Memo on Customs Barrier, Imperial Preference', in 'Customs barrier'.

It is little surprise then that Feetham, faced with such a maelstrom of irreconcilable demands, and furnished with such a moth-eaten set of tools to answer them, clung to the only reference point he had in the shape of the flawed wording of Article XII. Naturally, such a vague guide meant that the commissioners took a conservative line from the start, stating that 'it is not the duty of the Commission to start *de novo* on a reconstruction of the map without any regard for the existing boundary'.[21] The aspirations of local populations would only be met if the reality on the ground would not, in Feetham's words, 'cause economic or geographic inconvenience'.[22] Perhaps more fundamentally, Feetham demonstrated very early in the process that he had no intention of considering the more extreme nationalist demands that the Boundary Commission be used as a way of completely undermining Northern Ireland as a functioning entity. Not only did he argue that his job was to decide on the shape of the frontier and not 'whether there should be a boundary or not',[23] but also that the amendments could not be so radical as to make Northern Ireland 'unrecognisable as the same provincial entity' that had been defined under the Government of Ireland Act.[24]

The original moves to limit the state to six counties had been hard fought. While the British government had been prepared to offer the exclusion of the whole of the province, it was Ulster unionist opposition itself which had called for a contraction of that boundary. Taken as a nine-county unit, Protestants made up only a slim majority at 56.2 per cent of the population. Asquith confided that the rejection of the offer of the full province was fundamentally due to unionist fears that 'a big entire Ulster would gravitate towards a United Ireland'.[25] The six-county state, while changing the balance to a two-thirds majority, still contained an enormous minority population. No county was even close to containing a homogeneous population. Antrim had the largest Protestant contingent, with 79.5 per cent, followed by Down (68.4 per cent), Londonderry (58.5 per cent) and Armagh (54.7 per cent). Even more precarious were the Protestant populations in Fermanagh (43.8 per cent) and Tyrone (43.8 per cent). It was on these two counties that Catholic opposition had been long focused and the main forum for discussions about the making of a viable border line from the moment that Ulster exclusion was proposed. In July 1914 an

---

[21] Hand, *Boundary Commission*, p. 4.   [22] Ibid, p. 15.   [23] Ibid, p. 72.
[24] See T. White, *Kevin O'Higgins* (Dublin, 1957), pp. 248–9.
[25] Brock and Brock, *H.H. Asquith Letters to Venetia Stanley*, p. 97.

exasperated Asquith lamented 'that most damnable creation of the perverted ingenuity of man – the County of Tyrone'.[26]

Certainly, one of the most enduring features of debates about the shape of Northern Ireland was the concentration on the demographic characteristics of the Ulster counties. Thus, the decision of unionists to accept the sacrifice of the three other provincial counties of Donegal, Monaghan and Cavan was presented as an all-or-nothing decision. There is virtually no evidence of a serious proposition to partition the various counties to more reflect demographic realties. Carson himself expressed these frustrations as early as July 1914 during the abortive Buckingham Palace Conference, when he urged his fellow partitioners: 'let us have done with county limits, as if men in one county are going to abandon men in another county just because there may be a majority there'.[27] The consistent reference to county boundaries as offering some form of frontier has much to do with the level of denial that permeated the partition settlement; that exclusion as outlined in the Government of Ireland Act was only temporary and the border between the two jurisdictions a geographical expression of general political preference rather than a plan for a permanent division. Certainly, the county lines of Ulster, created in the seventeenth century were ill-suited to fulfilling their later role as an international boundary. Major urban centres such as Strabane, Newry and Derry city lay within only a few miles of the new frontier.

However, it is also true that the idea of partitioning the Ulster counties would have presented even more contradictions. Donegal, the most northerly county on the island, was perhaps the most peculiar omission from the six-county state. The county's main economic outlet was Derry city which now fell on the other side of the border. The county itself never managed to recover from the loss of Derry and remained a desperately poor region, isolated from the rest of Ireland. Fisher himself had written to Craig in February 1922 about the issue of Donegal: 'Ulster can never be complete without Donegal. Donegal belongs to Derry, and Derry to Donegal. With North Monaghan *in* Ulster and South Armagh *out*, we should have a solid ethnographic and strategic frontier to the South, and a hostile "Afghanistan" on our north-west frontier would be placed in safe keeping'.[28] Certainly, as the historian Ged Martin has observed, the case of Donegal's affiliation 'would have to be all or nothing as partition on

---

[26] G. Martin, 'The Origins of Partition', in M. Anderson and E. Bolt, eds, *The Irish Border* (Liverpool, 1995), p. 156.

[27] Lewis, *Carson*, vol. 2, p. 402.

[28] Joseph Fisher letter to James Craig, February 1922, quoted in Gwynn, *The History of Partition, 1912–1925*, p. 216.

sectarian lines would have shattered it into rocky fragments'.[29] The case of Donegal demonstrated that the partition plan was fundamentally incoherent. None other than Austen Chamberlain observed in 1922, 'partition was a compromise, and like all compromises indefensible and illogical'.[30]

The problem of Donegal was typical of a series of interlinked problems the commission faced in cutting up counties and thus dividing urban and rural populations. At the local level, there was a complex intermingling of Catholic and Protestant communities, meaning that no matter which area was chosen for transfer, substantial populations from each community would find themselves on what they viewed as the wrong side of the border. Dissatisfaction was thus hardwired into the process, and Feetham, therefore, argued that the commission should not come to 'rely on the verdicts of bare majorities'.[31] As such, he drew a fateful conclusion, interpreting the 'wishes of the inhabitants' as a way of ensuring the least discontent for existing populations, rather than meeting the demands of local majorities, no matter how defined. This was a negative, rather than positive, equation. The Southern demand for large-scale transfers was dealt a further blow by this decision, as Feetham himself explained, if the three and a half counties they demanded were transferred it would

gratify the wishes of 258,617 persons and be contrary to the wishes of 205,528 others . . . in order to achieve the net result of pleasing 53,089 persons, it would be necessary to transfer a total of 464,145 persons, or nearly nine times as many.[32]

Economic considerations further reinforced the conclusion that only limited small-scale changes would be considered. The 'economic conditions' of Article XII were interpreted largely with reference to the relation of urban centres to an imagined 'market area' stretching in five- to ten-mile bands around the numerous small towns that peppered Ulster's border counties. These market towns, it was decided, could only be transferred with their market areas intact so long as they conformed to the commission's other stringent criteria. Furthermore, many towns were so close together that their market areas overlapped and as such were deemed inseparable. Crucially, Feetham failed to understand that the development of newer forms of communication, transportation and urbanisation may make such economic units irrelevant in the future. The Irish border would lack flexibility for the future and there would be no mechanism whereby further change could be enacted. As one historian has perceptively

[29] Martin, 'The Origins of Partition', p. 94   [30] Ibid, p. 91.
[31] Hand, *Boundary Commission*, p. 51.   [32] Ibid, p. 76.

observed, the Boundary Commission 'designed a border for an Ireland that would virtually disappear within half a century'.[33]

Despite the attempt to establish a coherent set of principles on which to base their decisions, the sheer vagueness of their remit meant that in the end their decisions were made with reference to whichever reinforced their innate conservative caution. MacNeill plainly admitted:

> There was at no time any debate between the members of the Commission as to the principles of interpretation and no definite decision taken which could lead to an application of such principles and to their consistent application – to their application in the same way in different districts affected by the award. The details came before us in a very gradual and a very piecemeal manner.[34]

Indeed, the commission's final report demonstrated just how confused and contradictory the decisions were when placed against their criteria with MacNeill stating that

> in the Chairman's view, it was competent, in one part of our award, for us to make economic considerations dominant and, in another place, to make the wishes of the inhabitants dominant.[35]

The final decisions of the commission demonstrate the largely arbitrary and contradictory way with which the various problem areas were dealt with. The work of the commissioners involved vast amounts of statistical analysis, public meetings and statements from over one thousand local notables, including business leaders, politicians and church officials. The issue which took up the principal amount of the commission's deliberations were the fate of the numerous towns which lay perilously close to the new border. The demand for the transfer of Derry city had figured prominently in nationalist propaganda due both to its majority Catholic population and undeniably strong economic links with the county of Donegal. However, Feetham rejected the notion of cutting Derry out of the six counties as 'too serious a surgical operation'.[36] In fact, surprisingly, the commission, far from opting to transfer the city to the South and link it up with its natural hinterland, chose instead to come at the problem from the opposite direction, by proposing that parts of East Donegal with Protestant majorities should be appended to Northern Ireland. A solution which would ensure, it was felt, the city would retain a more cohesive market area, while still remaining within the territory of the Northern government. In such a proposal, the northern most part of Ireland, the peninsula of Inishowen, was only retained by the

[33] Martin, 'The Origins of Partition', p. 99.
[34] Dáil Éireann Debates, vol. 13, col. 802, November 1925.   [35] Ibid.
[36] Hand, Boundary Commission, p. 17.

Free State due to the existence of a single railway line linking it with the rest of Donegal.

Although not specifically referred to, Derry city's place in Ulster Protestant folklore may have played a role in the decision, and its Catholic majority was hardly overwhelming. Such considerations did not exist in other similar areas. Indeed, the most glaring example stood almost exactly at the other end of the 300-mile-long border in the shape of Newry. The city was three quarters Catholic (74.6 per cent) and was surrounded by substantial Catholic populations in South Armagh and South Down. As with Derry, economic criteria were pushed to the fore. However, in the case of Newry, exactly the opposite conclusion was reached, with Newry's strong links with South Down, it was argued, making it a poor candidate for transfer. So, if Derry was able to take its own perceived market area from across the border with it, the transfer of both Newry and South Down to the Free State would have seemed a similarly logical corollary. However, Feetham concluded:

In view of the above considerations the Commission has come to the conclusion that the change which would be involved in the separation of Newry and its surrounding area from the rest of Northern Ireland cannot be regarded as a change which is "compatible with economic and geographic condition." The two different sets of factors which the Commission is directed to take into account-the wishes of the inhabitants, and economic and geographic considerations – are thus found to be definitely in conflict with respect to this area, and under the terms of Article XII economic and geographic considerations must prevail.[37]

A similarly contradictory decision was taken at Strabane where there was reluctance to take a correspondingly sizeable chunk out of Northern Ireland that had been taken for Derry. In the case of Fermanagh, only minor transfers were advised principally due to the perceived problem of who was to control the vital waterways of the county. When it came to Monaghan, the substantial unionist population in the north of the county was a prime candidate for transfer. However, the existence of Catholic populations between them and the Tyrone border meant their claims were largely ignored. The most generous award was in South Armagh where the Catholic majority was overwhelming and couldn't be ignored. Even so, the eventual 84 square miles of territory recommended was the most conservative decision that could have been reached.

It was apparent that the commission, despite its veneer of legality, had considered the political impact of proposed changes of primary importance.

---

[37] Hand, *Boundary Commission*, p. 134.

MacNeill himself noted that politics became 'a dominant consideration' and their verdicts were designed principally so as not to

> produce a political effect on the Government of Northern Ireland, and so as to place the Government of Northern Ireland in a distinctly less advantageous position than it occupied under the Act of 1920 ... the political consideration was to override the wishes of the inhabitants. To that position I need not say I never assented.[38]

In the end, the Boundary Commission's tortuously compiled final report was completed in October 1925. Taken as a whole it involved only minor changes, effecting a rationalisation of the border rather than its wholesale dismantling. The border was to be reduced in length by some 51 miles, with 286 miles of territory awarded to the Free State and 77 square miles going the other way. However, the final report would never be seen by the generation who it was designed to appease. On 7 November, shortly before its release, the whole affair slipped into farce when details of the final award, including the fairly accurate pencil-drawn map, was published in the *Morning Post* after it was leaked, most probably by Fisher. There was a shocked public reaction in the South, whose population had been fed for years on the bombastic promises of the Free State leadership and the propaganda of the NEBB. Anger was particularly focused on the decision to award parts of East Donegal to the North and, in the confusion that followed, MacNeill tendered his resignation and the report was suppressed.

In the fall out from the failed commission, Free State ministers, led by the energetic minister for home affairs Kevin O'Higgins, engaged in all kinds of threats, including one to make a direct appeal to the League of Nations. At a hastily arranged meeting in London in early December, Free State officials were offered all manner of sweeteners to drop the matter, including the release of dozens of political prisoners held in Northern Irish gaols. These offer were rejected by O'Higgins who instead called very publicly for cast-iron protections for the rights of the Northern Catholic minority:

> If we could point to substantial improvement in the position of the Nationalists in Ulster, an emancipation of the minority, we [the Free State Government] might survive on the status quo. What are the disabilities? Special police, the coercion which would be necessary to hold Tyrone and Fermanagh, 45,000 special constables in a statelet of Six counties; abolition of proportional re presentation, changing of the Constitution in order to deprive Nationalists of their due place in Parliament and local administration ...[39]

---

[38] Dáil Éireann Debates, vol. 13, col. 801, November 1925.
[39] Jones, *Whitehall Diary*, p. 241.

Certainly, while border nationalists in West Ulster reacted to the collapse of the Boundary Commission with horror and dismay, those in East Ulster, whose transfer into the South was never a realistic prospect, saw it as an opportunity. Indeed, many now argued that if the Free State government did intend to abandon the Boundary Commission, they should extract a significant price for their acquiescence. The principal demand they made, along with the usual calls for the reduction in the power and number of the Specials, was for a reinstatement of PR, which had been hastily jettisoned by Craig in July 1922. Louis J. Walsh, the Ulster Sinn Féin leader, argued that 'such a settlement would be a hundred times better for northern Catholics than anything Mr. Feetham could have done for them'.[40]

Some British ministers were sympathetic to these calls. Lord Salisbury, hardly a noted friend of Catholic nationalists, went so far as to suggest that Belfast MP Joe Devlin be given a job as a liaison officer on a substantial salary. Craig, however, pointed out that incidents of sectarian discord had decreased dramatically since the dark days of 1922 and offered his own rather peculiar anecdotal evidence for the peaceful situation.

There had been a lot of unfounded charges against Ulster. Questions of unequal treatment were becoming fewer. He had got the ban against Roman Catholics in shipyards removed. A Protestant doctor had recently opened a Catholic bazaar and Lady Craig had been asked to a Catholic Whist Drive.[41]

In the end, however, it was the lure of money for the impoverished Southern state which won the day. Rather than his glib assurances of improved relations between both communities, and verbal promises of future interaction between the two states, it was Craig's suggestion that the government abrogate Free State responsibility for the British war debt as outlined in Article V of the treaty, which proved most appealing to all sides. The issue of minority rights was quickly dropped, with O'Higgins weakly claiming that financial recompense 'would act faster. Also it would spike de Valera's guns, for the latter had been saying that the Free State was going to be disappointed over its obligations under Clause V as it had been over the boundary award.'[42] The reality was that the Northern Catholic minority had been sold for the sum of a little over £8 million. It was clear that the Free State government, no longer feeling the need to appease its more radical anti-partitionist elements, as Collins had been forced to do in 1922, had chosen internal political hegemony over

[40] Quoted in E. Phoenix, *Northern Nationalism* (Belfast, 1994), p. 330.   [41] Ibid, p. 243.
[42] Ibid.

protection of the minority population in the North.[43] This shift towards accepting partition had long been gestating in the minds of moderate nationalist leaders. In early 1923, Charles McGleenan, a republican internee at the Curragh, struck up a friendship with an Ulster IRA man, now employed as his prison guard. During one of their daily chats, his prisoner mentioned the new Free State customs posts being erected on the new frontier.

> I said that erecting those huts was recognising the border as it was then. He said that the Boundary Commission would soon sit and define the border. I said that when they erected Customs huts they were recognising the border as it then was – that would be as far as it would ever go. He, however, maintained that when the Boundary Commission sits we will get the counties of Tyrone, Fermanagh, South Armagh and South Down. I then said: "Will you resign from the army if South Down doesn't get in seeing that you are a 'South Down Man'?" His reply was that he would not have to and after some further discussion in which he got a bit heated, he walked away and left me, and afterwards he never bothered about me again.[44]

Craig certainly emerged from the agreement as the victor from the debacle of the Boundary Commission. Not only did he manage to maintain the six-county border with no amendments, he had achieved this once again by using British money. The cherry on the top was the scrapping of the Council of Ireland which had been such a prominent part of the architecture of Long's proposals for the Government of Ireland Act six years earlier. Healy lamented that with the passing of the council 'the last hope of unity in our time' had gone. When Craig returned triumphant to the Belfast parliament, the unionist leader was presented with a silver trophy inscribed 'Not an Inch'. The most that the frankly relieved Cosgrave could offer the shell-shocked Northern minority was advice to both recognise and participate constructively in the Northern Irish parliament, a complete reversal of the policy nationalist governments had pursued since 1919.

Northern nationalists were far more stringent in their criticisms. Cahir Healy, the leading Sinn Féin nationalist in Fermanagh, only recently released from two years of internment, bitterly criticised the rumours that the Free State government were considering a financial offer in return for dropping its territorial claims in Ulster:

> I hope that a proposal so callous will not even be thought of by the Executive Council. We have made as many sacrifices for the Treaty as the people of any other part of Ireland. It is an amazing proposal that in order to free the people of

---

[43] Minutes of the Executive Council, 1 December 1925, NAI, Cab. 27/295. 1A (25) 9.
[44] Charles McGleenan statement, BMH, NAI, WS 829.

the Saorstat from the legal obligations they have incurred under Article 5, the liberties and rights guaranteed to the Nationalists by Article 12 should be scrapped, and the people sold into political servitude for all time. The Executive can surely find a manlier and more honourable way out.[45]

Northern nationalists were certainly devastated by the collapse of the commission. Healy later added with typical eloquence:

It is a betrayal of the Free State in its alleged support of our case since 1921. Time will decide if the betrayal will not bring its own retribution. John Redmond was driven out of public life for even suggesting partition for a period of five years. The new leaders agreed to partition for ever. We have been abandoned to Craig's mercy.[46]

This feeling of despair was especially true of those who lived in the west of the province whom, with the signing of the treaty and the very public rhetoric of their co-religionists in the South, were convinced that their short sojourn as citizens of Northern Ireland was soon to come to an end. As such, their political strategy remained largely one-dimensional and was based around abstention from the new Belfast parliament and a general policy of non-recognition, 'so as not give undue legitimacy to the Partitionist parliament'.[47] This policy had been fostered, and to a large extent funded, by Southern nationalist leaders during the partition period, despite its profoundly damaging impact on the Northern Catholic minority itself.

Subsequent Dublin governments would continue this strategy of supporting informal non-recognition, despite their own acquiescence in the partition plan in 1925. This would have far more to do with their own ideological concerns and their reluctance to accept with partition what Clare O'Halloran has called 'the limits of Irish nationalism', than any thought out strategy aimed at eventual Irish unity.[48] In 1922, Northern nationalists, firmly believing that their status as a minority would be brief, saw little need to develop a distinctive political ideology or organisation, something that was not to emerge for another forty years.

Indeed, Northern nationalist faith in the Boundary Commission was demonstrated markedly by their initial reaction to the treaty. On the day after its terms were published, a whole host of nationalist-controlled public bodies moved to repudiate the Northern government. These included the county councils of both Tyrone and Fermanagh and numerous other institutions, including poor law unions and local government

---

[45] Healy to editor of *The Irish Times*, 30 November 1925, Cahir Healy Papers, PRONI, D2991/B/1/10A.
[46] *Irish News*, 16 January 1925.   [47] See Collins Papers, PRONI, D921.
[48] O'Halloran, *Partition and the Limits of Irish Nationalism.*

bodies. This policy of outright non-recognition would lead to over twenty public bodies being dissolved by the Belfast authorities by the spring of 1922, including the Catholic-controlled Derry City Corporation.[49] With the decision to leave the border intact, the hollowness of Northern minority political strategy became apparent. Exactly one year after the final collapse of the Boundary Commission, Healy complained:

> The Free State leaders told us our anchor was Article XII: when the time of trial came they cut our cable and launched us, rudderless, into the hurricane without guarantee or security even for our ordinary civic rights.[50]

The impact of the Boundary Commission on Northern nationalist unity, and thus political effectiveness in subsequent years, cannot be under-estimated. It would lead to profound disillusion and lingering tension between nationalists in West and East Ulster. The willingness of the former to allow their co-religionists in Belfast to remain under unionist governance had caused bitter resentment. While some semblance of unity had been achieved by Collins, who managed to balance a covert policy of coercion with one of political agreement as a way of undermining Northern Ireland, his passing and the debacle of the Boundary Commission left deep wounds within the newly forming Northern minority. This division would fester in the Northern Catholic political culture, only being finally expunged in the crucible of the 'Troubles'. In the intervening years, the minority would find itself drifting towards the more irredentist policies of de Valera's Fianna Fáil, which, while certainly more strident, offered a barely less reasonable avenue to meeting minority aspirations than those blithely offered by Cosgrave in December 1925. In the 1970s, as the 'Troubles' entered their most devastating decade, Ernest Blythe candidly admitted that with the failure of the Boundary Commission, the Free State leadership

> felt that the broad prospect of national reunion had not been seriously injured, that if a wise policy were pursued, we might hope that in forty or fifty years the two parts of Ireland would be coming closer to reunion. Unfortunately, the great majority of Northern Catholics, egged on from the South, clung to a policy of barren recalcitrance which kept Protestants and Catholics in separate camps and prevented all political progress.[51]

The report itself was not publicly released at the time, only coming to light in the 1960s. Cosgrave's wish that 'in the interests of Irish peace it should

---

[49] P. Murray, 'Partition and the Irish Boundary Commission: A Northern Nationalist Perspective', *Clogher Record*, vol. 18, no. 2 (2004), pp. 181–217.

[50] Letter from Cahir Healy, December 1926, Cahir Healy Papers, PRONI, D2991/A/1/12.

[51] E. Blythe to T. Ryle Dwyer, 4 May 1970, Blythe Papers, P24/1528.

be burned or buried'[52] was matched by his opposite number James Craig who stated that he didn't even want to see the final report as on his return to Belfast:

he would be questioned on the subject and he preferred to be able to say that he did not know the terms of the proposed Award. He was certain that it would be better that no-one should ever know accurately what their position would have been.[53]

Perhaps most poignantly, on 9 December a delegation of Northern businessmen and political leaders arrived at the Dáil to plead their case, but were refused entry or the right to speak. Denial and collective forgetting was now government policy on both sides of the border.[54]

The shambolic failure of the Boundary Commission disguised the fact that hopes for its success were misguided in the first place. As with so much of the partition plan, it failed to accept the reality of the settlement. As O'Higgins himself mused, the reality was that the Boundary Commission was never

at any time was a wonderful piece of constructive statesmanship, the shoving up of a line, four, five or ten miles, leaving the Nationalists north of that line in a smaller minority than is at present the case, leaving the pull towards union, the pull towards the south, smaller and weaker than is at present the case.[55]

Certainly, as O'Shiel had realised, no matter how generous the award to the South may have been, it would still have left a substantial minority population in the North. However, in the immediate aftermath of the Boundary Commission, there appeared to be little concern over the potential trouble posed by the large minority Catholic population Northern Ireland had enclosed within its fiercely defended border. Overwhelmingly, the emotion was one of relief and deliverance. An editorial in the *Ulster Review* of January 1926 stated:

The signing of the border agreement wipes the political slate for us in Ulster ... We are like a garrison so surprised to find a prolonged siege suddenly raised, and the enemy quietly withdrawn, that we cannot quite believe our good luck.[56]

The process of turning the imagined Ulster envisioned in the original partition plan into a functioning state could now begin.

---

[52] Hand, *Boundary Commission*, p. ix.   [53] Ibid., p. 82.
[54] Dáil Éireann debate, 'Deputation of Northern Nationalists,' 9 December 1925.
[55] O'Higgins Memo to the provisional government, quoted in White, *Kevin O'Higgins*, p. 98.
[56] *The Ulster Review*, January 1926.

9   Brave New Worlds

In November 1916, barely six months after the Easter Rising, D. C. Maher's play *Partition* opened at the Abbey Theatre in Dublin. It told the story of Andy Kelly, a roguish ne'er do well, ever avoiding debt collectors and bailiffs, whose house is intersected by the 'border line of Eire and Northern Ireland'. Far from viewing this as an inconvenience, Kelly, who describes himself as 'a Siamese twin' draws a chalk line down the middle of his home, and is able to change his identity at will, shifting his belongings from one side of the house to the other in reaction to a knock on the door from bailiffs representing the Northern and Southern governments. Kelly continues this life 'as a kind of two in wan' quite happily, avoiding arrest and pledging allegiance to the agents of whichever state has not paid him a visit. The crisis comes for him, however, with the unexpected sight of the authorities on both sides of the border working together. The play's final scene ends with Kelly finally caught when bailiffs from both sides start knocking his front and back doors simultaneously. His final words are, 'Begobs, the Siamese twins will be kilt and buried in the wan coffin.'[1]

The denouement of Maher's alarmingly prophetic skit highlighted the significant question of how, and indeed if, the two new partition states would relate to one another. Certainly, the most lasting legacy of partition was the states themselves, both of which embodied oppositional ideologies that were both consciously and unconsciously articulated against one another. As Clare O'Halloran has insightfully observed, the border was treated by both sides as a kind of cordon sanitaire, separating and protecting each state from its ideological nemesis on the other side.[2] The border would prevent their opponents from interfering or in any way shaping the ongoing progress of state building and thus they and their nefarious traits were best kept out. In short, both states just wanted the other to go away. While they sought to keep each other at arm's length, each became the

---

[1] E. Bort, 'The Irish Border Play' in *The Irish Border* (Liverpool, 1999), p. 261.
[2] O'Halloran, *Partition and the Limits of Irish Nationalism*, p. xv.

great comparative framework for the other. In April 1934, James Craig stated in the Northern parliament in response to a question about the political direction of the Southern state under Eamon de Valera:

The honorable Member must remember that in the South they boasted of a Catholic State. They still boast of Southern Ireland being a Catholic State. All I boast of is that we are a Protestant Parliament and a Protestant State. It would be rather interesting for historians of the future to compare a Catholic State launched in the South with a Protestant State launched in the North and to see which gets on the better and prospers the more. It is most interesting for me at the moment to watch how they are progressing. I am doing my best always to top the bill and to be ahead of the South.[3]

Unspoken competition between the two states would continue to fester throughout the post-partition decades. Just as nationalists and unionists had championed their credentials with reference to the prospective poor performance of their rivals before 1922, both would seize on periods of crisis and poor performance as evidence of their own legitimacy. Political crisis in the South during the 1930s was compared unfavourably with the relative stability in the North as was both states differing reaction to the Second World War. The sectarian backwardness of Northern Ireland and its fatal collapse into squalid political violence during the 'Troubles' was contrasted with the emergence of a liberal, pluralist democracy in the South and the rise of the 'Celtic Tiger' economy.

So traumatic had been partition that mere existence seemed to become and end in itself and offer some form of victory. By 1925, a type of peace reigned in Ireland. There was to be no reconciliation either between the two partition states or within them. What replaced it was a collective forgetting and the construction of narratives of revolutionary deliverance or resistance. This failure to deal with the trauma of partition and the huge psychological damage that the violent process had left in its wake meant both states had to be formed around a self-justifying principle and were thus dysfunctional by definition. Paramilitaries, politicians, policemen, widows, orphans, refugees and the vast majority who had remained silent or complicit during the process now had to reorientate themselves to the new realities and make sense of the role they had played over the previous years. Their experience had made careers for some and reputations for many, but it also undid thousands of lives and crippled others psychologically, leaving tens of thousands in trauma. It would be left in the hands of this same generation, those who had experienced the violent upheavals and ideological dislocations of partition, to shape the new societies which emerged.

[3] Northern Ireland House of Commons Official Report, vol. 34, col. 1095, 24 April 1934.

The new governments used what little money they had to restyle the states in line with their revolutionary visions and ideologies. The focus was on a narrative of regeneration and a new beginning. Immediately on taking power, the new Irish Free State, in line with most emerging nations of the period, worked to promote and preserve their chosen culture and national language. Gaelic, dubbed 'Irish' by its supporters, was to be the official first language of the Southern Irish state, a decision confirmed in the new constitution of 1937. Many were critical of the cost and end result of this project if successful, seeing in it the addition of a further cultural partition of the island to add to the political one. So central, however, had been the language issue to the character of Irish nationalism since the late nineteenth century that the advocates of this linguistic evangelicalism were bullish. Louis J. Walsh, nationalist politician and author, argued rather illogically that, opposed to further dividing the island, the Gaelic project would act as a force for Irish unity:

> of all the fallacies of *The Irish Times* and its likes, the most glaring is that the pushing of Irish will tend to stabilize Partition. I know my Ulster as well as any man in Ireland and I say in all sincerity that the surest way of breaking the barrier between us and the six counties would be to make the Free State Irish-speaking. When the Belfast commercial traveller has to learn Irish in order to do business in Cork or Dublin, he will have learned to respect us at last; and until he does that, he will always be the ignorant bigot that he now is.[4]

By contrast, J. L. Garvin, editor of *The Observer*, wrote to Stephen Gwynn in September 1922: 'The atavistic *chinoiserie* of the Gaelic Revolution can never unite any part of Ireland but can only organise the real and lasting partition in a way that is going on now.'[5]

Indeed, the reality of the state-sponsored furtherance of the Gaelic project would spread further division between and within the new states. Ironically, the Free State government established yet another border in Ireland, this time a cultural one. This new partition involved the creation of a 'Gaeltacht' commission whose job was to cordon off majority Gaelic-speaking areas, predominantly in the west, and enhance and protect the national language in these areas. Outside of the protected areas of the Gaeltacht, where English remained overwhelmingly the language of choice, the Dublin government faced a formidable challenge and were forced to rely on duress and compulsion. A thorough grounding in Gaelic was made compulsory for employment in the civil service and the military, both areas which central government exerted direct control over and represented key vehicles for the spread of state power. In education, Gaelic was given first priority, with the numbers of

---

[4] Louis Walsh, *The Leader*, 2 October 1926.
[5] J. L. Garvin letter to Stephen Gwynn, Gwynn Papers, NLI, MS8600.

trained Gaelic-speaking teachers increasing at all levels from only 1,107 in 1922 to over 9,000 by 1943, amounting to two-thirds of all qualified teachers in the Southern state. Teachers were awarded financial incentives and grants for retraining and the students themselves received extra credit for answering questions in the written national language. Horace Plunkett, founder of the Irish Dominion League and Irish Protestant Senator, noted in 1925 the regressive impact which the Gaelic project had on Irish education:

In my field, I have serious complaints to make. I had something to do with building up a system of practical [technical] education and you can imagine my feelings at the treatment of the College of Science and of the whole system of vocational education at which I was at the head. Yesterday I heard of a county council which had voted a sum of £1,400 for the teaching of Irish and only £200 for technical education. I give it up.[6]

Despite its advocacy and funding from the state, the Gaelic project proved to be an expensive and divisive failure. It was clear that outside of its use as a propaganda tool during the national struggle, its immediacy and relevance to everyday life diminished. The language never became the conversational norm for the vast majority of people in the twenty-six counties, remaining almost exclusively a language for official and state use. The failure of the new nationalist state to reignite the fervour of cultural nationalism dismayed many of its chief evangelists. Eamon de Valera, later to become Taoiseach and president of the new state, himself a language enthusiast, called for individuals themselves to embrace the language as a way of demonstrating their personal patriotism:

Only one person can save the Irish language and that is the individual citizen ... If they could see the language as Pearse saw it, as the very breath of Irish liberty, they would themselves ensure, without more ado, its survival and its perpetuation.[7]

In Northern Ireland, the minority language was neither supported or suppressed by the new state, but rather allowed to die. Only decades later during the 'Troubles' and another period of radical nationalist protest did the language once again assume its prominence in the nationalist propaganda toolkit. While often painted as a benign expression of cultural diversity, the reality was that the language issue became politicised, spreading a further division between communities, and one that excluded unionists deliberately. Gerry Adams, the Sinn Féin leader, wrote in the 1990s, that 'for the Protestant people to embrace the Irish language today would be for them to reject Loyalism'.[8]

---

[6] Letter from Horace Plunkett to John Dillon, 11 January 1925 (Dillon papers, TCD).
[7] Quoted in Anderson and Bolt, eds, *The Irish Border*, p. 185.
[8] G. Adams, *Free Ireland* (Dingle, 1995), p. 43.

Exactly seventy years earlier in December 1924, just after the calling of the Boundary Commission, Stephen Gwynne reflected on the barrier that the policy of Gaelicisation was having on hopes for eventual Irish unity:

The matter is complicated, at present, by the question of Gaelic. Our Constitution has affirmed that Gaelic is the national language. Yet there is scarcely one person in a thousand throughout Ireland who cannot speak English and scarcely one in ten who can speak Irish easily. The theorists are at present attempting to spread the use of Irish by all means at the command of Government, and Ulstermen, who in the main are not descended from Gaelic speakers even in a remote past, resent this: they think it an attempt to secure jobs for Catholics by setting up a test which will disqualify most Protestants. But already in the Free State itself there is a reaction against what somebody called 'Gaelic on forced draught." And here also time may remove a good deal that today makes against union. The problem of actual symbols may be more difficult: it will not be easy to combine the Union Jack and the tricolour, and I cannot conceive that either party would surrender its flag. Thus the obstacles to union in the main are ideals, symbols, pretences or pretensions, and prejudices: and no one who knows Irish human nature will underrate their stubbornness.[9]

While the new Irish Free state sought to situate its identity at as far a distance away from Britain as possible, the Northern Ireland government made a similar effort to create a historical, cultural and geographical gulf between itself and its Southern neighbour. The assumption underlying these projects was that the more distance both new Irish governments placed between themselves and their respective antithetical states, the more Irish or Ulsterised their populations would become. By contrast with Irish nationalists, whose well-entrenched ideological mythologies of the pre-partition era were welded on to the framework of the new state, those of Northern Ireland were only given full form after the boundary issue had been finally settled in 1925. The fact that Ulster resistance to Home Rule had never envisioned a separate devolved state, and not accepted one until barely two years before its creation, meant that the practical task of state formation had to be achieved at the same time as these ideological justifications were being sought. When it came to Northern Ireland, it was to be imagined after, rather than before, the fact.

This unenviable project was taken up most notably by the influential figure of E. Estyn Evans. Hailing from Wales, with not even a tenuous link to Ulster, Evans arrived in Belfast in 1928 to take up a lectureship in geography at Queen's University where, among others, he built a strong friendship with a fellow academic, none other than Thomas Jones, one-time private secretary to Lloyd George and a key instigator of the

[9] Gwynn, 'Ireland, One and Divisible'.

Boundary Commission plan in the Anglo-Irish Treaty of 1922. Under Evan's tutelage a whole host of eminent geographers, archaeologists and historians set to work constructing a distinctive six-county Ulster identity, seeking to give a more scientific, academic solidity to a boundary that ironically was one of the most artificial in the history of partition.[10] The many histories of Ulster published in the wake of partition, bypassed the turmoil, violence and artificiality of the recently drawn border, imagining instead permanence and inevitability.[11]

In this enterprise, Evans, who acted as a mentor to Heslinga, later writing the foreword to his influential book, was to play a vital role in what Mary Burgess has called 'the rural theme-parking of the province'.[12] Through the use of government patronage, the geography department at Queen's became one of the largest in the British Isles and sought to inculcate a form of 'cultural patriotism' for the new northern state.

These attempts to naturalise Northern Ireland, while not overtly political, focused instead on uncovering, preserving and classifying the material culture of a distinctive Ulster folklore. Much like the Gaelic revival of the 1890s, it explored a whole raft of traditional rural pursuits and practices on which was placed a distinctly partitionist spin. Mirroring the work of the Irish Folklore Commission, established in the South in 1935, the Committee on Ulster Folklife and Traditions created twenty years later under Evans' chairmanship, published its findings in a new journal, *Ulster Folklife*, and culminated in the creation of the Ulster Folk Museum in 1958.[13] It was also a project which sought to map and differentiate the physical space of the new Northern territory. At times this enterprise fell into absurdity. For example, in the 1930s Evan's archaeological team published a whole raft of findings which claimed that ancient monuments on the Northern side of the new border were distinctive from those being found in the South. These millennium-old burial mounds, the so-called Horned Cairn-Tombs, it was argued closely

---

[10] These efforts even led to a failed attempt to rename 'Northern Ireland' as 'Ulster' in the 1920s. For details see Heslinga, *Cultural Divide*, p. 36.

[11] Along with Chart's *A History of Northern Ireland*, see also J. Logan *Ulster in the X-Rays* (Belfast, 1924); C. J. C. Street, *Ireland in 1921* (London, 1922); H. S. Morrison, *Modern Ulster, Its Character, Customs, Politics and Industries* (London, 1920); F. H. Crawford, *Why I Voted for the Six Counties 1920* (Belfast, 1920), McNeill, *Ulster's Stand for Union*; Falls, *The History of the 36th (Ulster) Division* and his *The Birth of Ulster* (London, 1936); Henry Maxwell, *Ulster Was Right* (London, 1924); D. J. Owen, *History of Belfast* (Belfast, 1921); and H. C. Lawlor, *Ulster: Its Archaeology and Antiquities* (Belfast, 1928).

[12] Burgess, 'Mapping the Narrow Ground', p. 125.

[13] A similar journal exploring Southern folklife, *Bealoideas*, was established in the Irish Free State in 1927.

resembled those found in Scotland and were thus somehow foreign, being more British than Irish.[14]

Such assertions were not difficult to lampoon. In his play *Lost Belongings*, for example, Stewart Parker has one of his characters, an Orangeman, recite a view of the geology of partition which would have made Heslinga proud:

> The bedrock of Ulster is just a continuation of the bedrock of Scotland. The rocks stretching across under the sea . . . Now along the southern edge of Ulster bedrock there's what they call a fault. South of that fault there's an entirely disconnected type of a bedrock altogether. That's the foundations of the Free State. So the two parts of this island, you see, are different and separate right down in their very bones. You can't join together what God has set apart. We've got British rocks under the very soil of this province.[15]

There was certainly a distinctive defensiveness about many of the interpretations placed on this work and the narrow statist narratives which underpinned it. Clearly, throughout its century-old history, the Ulster of Northern Ireland remained insufficiently imagined. As the historian Oliver MacDonagh has observed: 'One cannot very well write Protestant supremacy onto a map.'[16] Ironically, in the wake of the 1998 Good Friday Agreement and the growth of widespread cross-border collaborative initiatives, there were signs that these statist attempts to manufacture cultural difference between the two Irelands were becoming increasingly anachronistic. However, with the current uncertainty about the effects of Brexit on Ireland, the border and all of its wider meanings have once again risen to the fore. Political leaders are now forced to deal with the same problem as that faced by the original partitioners back in the 1920s, namely that of defining exactly what the Irish border is and what it represents. While successive British and Irish governments have managed, in modern parlance, to 'kick the can down the road' for generations, there is little sign that political elites are any closer to offering definitive answers. Century-old ideas such as imperial federalism and the Council of Ireland have been replaced by 'backstops' or fanciful technological solutions, none of which resolve the fundamental and seemingly insoluble issues which lie at the heart of partition.

There was certainly a stubborn refusal on both sides to come to terms with the ambiguous realities of partition. Its inherent contradictions were

---

[14] This affair actually led to a short-lived, but lively, dispute with Ruaidhri de Valera, the son of the Free State leader. See 'Disputing with De Valera' in E. E. Evans, ed., *Ireland and the Atlantic Heritage* (Dublin, 1996).

[15] Stewart Parker, *Lost Belongings* (London, 1987), p. 50.

[16] O. MacDonagh, *States of Mind: Two Centuries of Anglo-Irish Conflict, 1780–1980* (London, 1992), p. 20.

shown particularly in regards to monuments and remembering. Despite its profound impact on the shape of modern Ireland, there are no monuments to partition, only those which reflect other state-sponsored narratives of revolution and resistance. This is doubly ironic, as the immediate post-partition period in the 1920s was very much the age of remembrance and commemoration. In the 1920s, sixty-two public war memorials were opened in towns across Northern Ireland in parks, schools, churches, hospitals, sports clubs and Orange halls, most of them funded locally. The first war memorial was opened in July 1918, and 1922, the partition year itself, was the peak year for the opening of public memorials. For Ulster Protestants, it was these memorials, as opposed to any attempt to commemorate the birth of the state, which became the centre of remembrance parades on 11 November each year.

This lack of public commemoration does not mean that partition has been forgotten. Politically, for nationalists partition remained an ongoing, reversible state of affairs. Ensconced for sixty years in Articles 2 and 3 of the Irish constitution, the pledge to end partition has become a nationalist shibboleth, with generations of Southern politicians espousing the idea of a future united Ireland, while in reality doing very little to bring it about. Despite recent shifts in the wake of the 'Troubles' towards increased cross-border cooperation, the unrelenting reality of the formation of the two states has been mutual hostility and suspicion.

Partition certainly spread far more division and resentment than that which it was designed to address. It shaped the rather draconian defensiveness of the unionist government which emerged in its aftermath, and a state which never got over the torrid experience of its birth. When the Troubles erupted in 1968, perhaps the least surprised people on the planet were Ulster unionists themselves. Such a development was long expected and planned for, shown by the Belfast government's refusal to disband its auxiliary police forces or dismantle its coercive epical powers legislation. In such a view, the IRA wasn't so much reborn in the early 1970s, it merely emerged from the shadows where it had been hiding all along. The sense, which had developed both before and during partition, that its Southern neighbour sought to undermine and overwhelm it, never went away, but instead became a cornerstone of Northern Ireland's political culture. Such paranoia was fed by generations of Southern politicians who, much like the politicians of Weimar, interwar Italy or those of the French Third Republic and the unredeemed lands of Alsace-Lorraine, cynically used the Northern issue as a way of shoring up its electoral support, while initiating very little in the way of practical policy.

The experience of partition also led to a huge amount of disunity among the Northern Catholic minority, not only between nationalists and republicans, but also between border and Belfast nationalists, something which would cripple minority politics for decades to come. It would also create profound divisions between Northern and Southern nationalists which have been slow to heal. The backdrop to this has been the almost adolescent way that both new Irish states themselves have done their best to ignore each other, meaning that they engaged only with cartoonish and occasionally demonic images of one another. While money was not spent on remembering partition, there was a huge amount of money and time spent in disseminating sanitised memories of the period to their new citizens. Generations of Irish children were not furnished with a nuanced story of how partition came about or the way polarisation occurred between Irish Protestants and Irish Catholics reinforced through strong alliances between nationalist state builders and radical sectarian militants. Instead, they were fed on a rich diet of patriotic pieties. In the South, public history presented a simple, sanitised story about the perfidy of British imperialism and partition the story of how Northern Ireland was retained by the British out of some kind of colonial vindictiveness. In such retellings, therefore, Northern Ireland is characterised largely by its artificiality and illegitimacy, born out of its reluctance to be part of the progressive, liberal nation-state born in Dublin. Northern Irish history, by comparison, gloried in the part it played in British imperial history. Ulster was painted as the ideal British state, retaining values lost even on the mainland. Surviving an unprecedented assault by a Catholic conspiracy which took the name of nationalism, it had pulled itself from the fire in 1922.

If partition did have a concrete memorial, it was the border itself. The actual boundary between the two new states would remain a surreal, much neglected grey area between the two Irelands. Perhaps surprisingly, the line itself was never heavily policed or given any concrete form. Its most obvious manifestation would be in the creation of customs posts on both sides which were to be seen on most, but not all, major roads crossing the frontier. The incursions of paramilitaries were replaced by those of smugglers. Due to the important revenue stream customs duties offered the Belfast government in the limited Government of Ireland Act, the Northern Ireland ministry of commerce, with a small staff of less than fifty, fought an energetic, but ultimately futile, battle against smuggling.[17] In Sean Connaughton's novel *Run of the Country*, one of the characters voices the common culture of border smuggling between the two Irelands:

---

[17] See Ministry of Commerce files, PRONI, COM/62.

To live decent it was necessary to smuggle. Living well came with practice. In Prunty's house there was always chocolate, sweet cake, butter, and in the big kitchen bin, bottles of whiskey and razor blades. Blades fetched good money in Dublin. In the recess of the kitchen window sat a television.[18]

The lack of permanent marking of the border was one of many peculiar paradoxes of partition. While some major routes were patrolled by customs officials and occasional police patrols, it proved difficult for strangers, as it does today, to locate the much fought over boundary. The border remains porous and unrecognised, a symbolic abstraction rather than a physical barrier. Despite its evident impracticality, there was never any serious attempt made to address these oddities.

The border itself would be a line painted in blood. The violence of the partition period has become deeply sanitised, with little focus on the suffering of ordinary Irish people who stood on either side of the line. Popular portrayals of the period are characterised by much hackneyed nationalistic posturing and an adoration of the sanctity of militarism and the righteousness of the militias who furthered the goals of freedom and independence. The public hounding of the late Peter Hart in the 1990s for his pointing out the savage reality of rural violence, not to mention the rather shameful silence of so many Irish historians about the matter, revealed the powerful delusion that still permeates large parts of nationalist Ireland about this period. While violence in the north is often painted as the work of hooligans or extremists, the reality was, much like in the south and west, it was carried out in collusion with the very founding fathers that the states have come to sanctify. After partition, both states worked tirelessly through the creation of state symbols and smoothed over biographies to create a revolutionary heritage industry which worked to erode the confusion, savagery and chaos of partition, replacing it with a sanitised story of an ordered transition carried out by newly respectable statesmen.

Partition has been largely lost and squeezed out in such retellings. It is presented paradoxically both as the end of one set of distinct historical stories, in this case the culmination of the period of national struggle, and the start of another-the struggle to end colonial British rule has become one narrative and the tale of heroic state-building efforts another. Partition is thus the tipping point, the grey area between these two monolithic phases in the national story. With reference to another later, eerily similar partition to that of Ireland, twenty five years later, Nehru, the new Indian prime minister perceptively described partition as a line 'dividing the past from the future'.[19]

---

[18] Connaughton, *The Run of the Country*, p. 2.
[19] Nehru speech quoted in H. Nisid, *Midnight's Furies: The Deadly Legacy of India's Partition* (London, 2015), p. 244.

It is the dominance of nationalist mythology and its teleological impera-
tive which has caused this problem. While generations of subsequent Irish
politicians have participated in anti-partition campaigns, lobbying international statesmen and raising money through the Irish–American lobby,
their efforts have failed largely because of the pervasive reluctance to
accept that partition is an Irish problem, and its undoing not in the gift
of British or American politicians. As John J. Horgan, the Cork nationalist
wrote in 1950:

Neither the British nor the Americans are likely to batter the North out of the
British Empire into a Papist Republic. Our politicians will not face these obvious
facts and prefer to go on with their rabble rousing tactics which make neither
statesmanship nor common sense.[20]

In short, it has proved easier to blame the British, a contrivance
which has not only fostered a dreary and all-pervasive culture of anti-
English bigotry in nationalist Ireland and the diaspora, but as
O'Corrain has insightfully argued became 'a form of escapism
which absolved southern politicians from reuniting Ireland by their
own creative efforts'.[21] The fact remains that, despite the many
changes of identity Southern Ireland has gone through, the border
has not shifted one inch. Ulster's survival in 1922 was painted as the
culmination of long years of resistance and refusal to surrender, that
of the South of generations of struggle to make the independent Irish
nation a reality. The anachronisms, ambiguities and sheer confusion
which characterised the process have found little place in the national
story. Neither have the people partition left behind. The voices of
those who did not fit into these pre-packaged accounts or had different experiences and expectations have been largely silenced. Despite
the power of hindsight and the tendency to view Irish history through
a rear view mirror, there was nothing inevitable about the partition of
Ireland. There were many other possible outcomes and huge
amounts of differing expectations and uncertainty. We have become
too hamstrung by the images and mythologies of these states that
they have become concrete things almost willed into existence by
history itself.

For good or ill, regardless of state mythologies and the rhetoric of their
apologists, partition endures and remains an unavoidable reality in Ireland.
Partition is not a relic of the past, it remains a troubling going concern.

---

[20] Horgan to Blythe, 3 November 1950 quoted in O'Corrain, '"Ireland in His Heart North
and South": The Contribution of Ernest Blythe to the Partition Question'.
[21] O'Corrain, '"Ireland in His Heart North and South": The Contribution of Ernest Blythe
to the Partition Question', p. 69.

Despite the more recent attempts to build links between the two Irelands through shared cross-border cultural exchange and confidence-building measures, the fact remains that Irish people have been locked into imagined communities of their own making for almost a century. In a telling passage, Edward Said once noted:

Just as human beings make their own history, they also make their own cultures and ethnic identities. No one can deny the persisting continuities of long traditions, sustained habitations, national languages, and cultural geographies, but there seems no reason except fear and prejudice to keep insisting on their separation and distinctiveness, as if that was all human life was about. Survival in fact is about the connections between things. It is more rewarding-and more difficult-to think concretely and sympathetically about others than only about 'us'. But this also means not trying to rule others, not trying to classify them or put them in hierarchies, above all, not constantly reiterating how 'our' culture or country is number one (or not number one, for that matter.)[22]

Partition cut a jagged line across Ireland. Far from the clean surgical cut promised by its architects, Ireland was hastily sawn apart leaving an open wound. In this sense the partition of Ireland can only be viewed as a profound failure. While the notion of dividing up geographic space and resources between apparently incompatible populations retains a wearying appeal as a solution to ethnic conflict in the modern world, Ireland's experience demonstrates that as a solution partition is an answer to a wholly different type of question. The vast majority of Irish people never viewed or accepted partition as rational or legitimate, both at the time and subsequently. Indeed, partition in Ireland went horribly wrong. The lack of clarity, planning and the sheer haste of it all left fundamental flaws and little reassurance or security for those minorities left outside its borders. It would quickly become apparent that the key question of Irish identity was bypassed and can more fairly be viewed as not answering the 'Irish Question', but rather transforming it into a new even more intractable 'Ulster Question'. The story of Ireland's partition is a pressing one as it shows up the dangers implicit in both colonialism and the nationalisms which emerge to challenge it.

Partition remains the most vital and dynamic force in modern Ireland. Almost exactly one hundred years after the event, the problem of the Irish border remains as insoluble as it did in the aftermath of the First World War. Despite this, it remains a woefully misunderstood and under-researched area of Irish history. In addressing this deficit, historians, rather than aiming for a master narrative of Ireland's experience between

---

[22] E. Said, *Culture and Imperialism* (New York, 1994), p. 402.

1912 and 1925, need to work to transcend such simplistic frameworks and replace it with an understanding of the tensions between the assumptions which underlay the constructions of identity and the aspiration to the creation of meaningful communities. Only by doing this will a narrative emerge which will include both the causes and consequences of partition, and its bitter legacies that Ireland is still living with today.

Appendices

The Government of Ireland Act (Extracts)

(1) On and after the appointed day there shall be established for Southern Ireland a Parliament to be called the Parliament of Southern Ireland consisting of His Majesty, the Senate of Southern Ireland, and the House of Commons of Southern Ireland, and there shall be established for Northern Ireland a Parliament to be called the Parliament of Northern Ireland consisting of His Majesty, the Senate of Northern Ireland, and the House of Commons of Northern Ireland.

(2) For the purposes of this Act, Northern Ireland shall consist of the parliamentary counties of Antrim, Armagh, Down, Fermanagh, Londonderry and Tyrone, and the parliamentary boroughs of Belfast and Londonderry, and Southern Ireland shall consist of so much of Ireland as is not comprised within the said parliamentary counties and boroughs.

2. Constitution of Council of Ireland.

(1) With a view to the eventual establishment of a Parliament for the whole of Ireland, and to bringing about harmonious action between the parliaments and governments of Southern Ireland and Northern Ireland, and to the promotion of mutual intercourse and uniformity in relation to matters affecting the whole of Ireland, and to providing for the administration of services which the two parliaments mutually agree should be administered uniformly throughout the whole of Ireland, or which by virtue of this Act are to be so administered, there shall be constituted, as soon as may be after the appointed day, a Council to be called the Council of Ireland.

(2) Subject as hereinafter provided, the Council of Ireland shall consist of a person nominated by the Lord Lieutenant acting in accordance with instructions from His Majesty who shall be President and forty other persons, of whom seven shall be members of the Senate of Southern Ireland, thirteen shall be members of the House of Commons of Southern Ireland, seven shall be members of the

Senate of Northern Ireland, and thirteen shall be members of the House of Commons of Northern Ireland.

The members of the Council of Ireland shall be elected in each case by the members of that House of the Parliament of Southern Ireland or Northern Ireland of which they are members . . .

3. Power to establish a Parliament for the whole of Ireland. –

(1) The Parliaments of Southern Ireland and Northern Ireland may, by identical Acts agreed to by an absolute majority of members of the House of Commons of each Parliament at the third reading (hereinafter referred to as constituent Acts), establish, in lieu of the Council of Ireland, a Parliament for the whole of Ireland consisting of His Majesty and two Houses . . .

(2) On the date of Irish union the Council of Ireland shall cease to exist and there shall be transferred to the Parliament and Government of Ireland all powers then exerciseable by the Council of Ireland, and (except so far as the constituent Acts otherwise provide) the matters which under this Act cease to be reserved matters at the date of Irish union, and any other powers for the joint exercise of which by the Parliaments or Governments of Southern and Northern Ireland provision has been made under this Act . . .

4. Legislative powers of Irish Parliaments. –

1 Subject to the provisions of this Act, the Parliament of Southern Ireland and the Parliament of Northern Ireland shall respectively have power to make laws for the peace, order, and good government of Southern Ireland and Northern Ireland with the following limitations, namely, that they shall not have power to make laws except in respect of matters exclusively relating to the portion of Ireland within their jurisdiction, or some part thereof, and (without prejudice to that general limitation) that they shall not have power to made laws in respect of the following matters in particular, namely: –

(1) The Crown ... or the Lord Lieutenant, except as respects the exercise of his executive power in relation to Irish services as defined for the purposes of this Act . . .

(2) The making of peace or war, or matters arising from a state of war . . .

(3) The navy, the army, the air force, the territorial force . . .

(4) Treaties, or any relations with foreign states, or relations with other parts of His Majesty's dominions . . .

(5) Dignities or titles of honour;

(6) Treason, treason felony, alienage, naturalization, or aliens as such, or domicile ...

(7) Trade with any place out of the part of Ireland within their jurisdiction, except so far as trade may be affected by the exercise of the powers of taxation given to the said parliaments, or by regulations ...

(8) Submarine cables;

(9) Wireless telegraphy;

(10) Aerial navigation;

(11) Lighthouses, buoys, or beacons ...

(12) Coinage; legal tender; negotiable instruments ...

(13) Trade marks, designs, merchandise marks, copyright, or patent rights; or

(14) Any matter which by this Act is declared to be a reserved matter, so long as it remains reserved. Any law made in contravention of the limitations imposed by this section shall, so far as it contravenes those limitations, be void ...

8. Executive Power. –

(1) The executive power in Southern Ireland and in Northern Ireland shall continue vested in His Majesty the King, and nothing in this Act shall affect the exercise of that power ...

Source: Acts Parliament, UK, 1920 (10 & 11 Geo V, Cap. 67)

The Anglo-Irish Treaty (Extracts)

Extracts from the final text of the Articles of Agreement for a Treaty between Great Britain and Ireland as signed in London, 6 December 1921

ARTICLE 1. Ireland shall have the same constitutional status in the Community of Nations known as the British Empire as the Dominion of Canada, the Commonwealth of Australia, the Dominion of New Zealand, and the Union of South Africa with a Parliament having powers to make laws for the peace order and good government of Ireland and an Executive responsible to that Parliament, and shall be styled and known as the Irish Free State.

ARTICLE 2. Subject to the provisions hereinafter set out the position of the Irish Free State in relation to the Imperial Parliament and Government and otherwise shall be that of the Dominion of Canada, and the law, practice and constitutional usage governing the relationship of the Crown or the representative of the Crown and of the Imperial Parliament to the Dominion of Canada shall govern their relationship to the Irish Free State.

ARTICLE 3. The representative of the Crown in Ireland shall be appointed in like manner as the Governor-General of Canada and in accordance with the practice observed in the making of such appointments.

ARTICLE 4. The oath to be taken by Members of the Parliament of the Irish Free State shall be in the following form:-

I ... do solemnly swear true faith and allegiance to the Constitution of the Irish Free State as by law established and that I will be faithful to H.M. King George V., his heirs and successors by law, in virtue of the common citizenship of Ireland with Great Britain and her adherence to and membership of the group of nations forming the British Commonwealth of Nations ...

ARTICLE 5. The Irish Free State shall assume liability for the service of the Public Debt of the United Kingdom as existing as the date hereof and towards the payment of War Pensions as existing at that date in such proportion as may be fair and equitable, having regard to any just claim on the part of Ireland by way of set-off or counter claim, the amount of such sums being determined in default of agreement by the arbitration of one or more independent persons being citizens of the British Empire ...

ARTICLE 12. If before the expiration of the said month, an address is presented to His Majesty by both Houses of the Parliament of Northern Ireland to that effect, the powers of the Parliament and the Government of the Irish Free State shall no longer extend to Northern Ireland, and the provisions of the Government of Ireland Act, 1920, (including those relating to the Council of Ireland) shall so far as they relate to Northern Ireland, continue to be of full force and effect, and this instrument shall have effect subject to the necessary modifications. Provided that if such an address is so presented a Commission consisting of three persons, one to be appointed by the Government of the Irish Free State, one to be appointed by the Government of Northern Ireland, and one who shall be Chairman to be appointed by the British Government shall determine in accordance with the wishes of the inhabitants, so far as may be compatible with economic and geographic conditions the boundaries between Northern Ireland and the rest of Ireland, and for the purposes of the Government of Ireland Act, 1920, and of this instrument, the boundary of Northern Ireland shall be such as may be determined by such Commission.

(Signed)

On behalf of the British Delegation	On behalf of the Irish Delegation
D. LLOYD GEORGE	ARTHUR GRIFFITH
AUSTEN CHAMBERLAIN	MICHAEL COLLINS
LORD BIRKENHEAD	ROBERT BARTON
WINSTON S. CHURCHILL	EAMON DUGGAN
L. WORTHINGTON-EVANS	GEORGE GAVAN DUFFY
HAMAR GREENWOOD	

Further Reading

Abbott, R., *Police Casualties in Ireland, 1919–1922* (Dublin, 2000).

Adams, G., *Who Fears to Speak . . .? The Story of Belfast and the 1916 Rising* (Belfast, 1991).

Akenson, D., *Education and Enmity: the control of schooling in Northern Ireland, 1920–50* (Newton Abbot, 1973).

Andrews, C .S., *Dublin Made Me: An Autobiography* (Dublin,1979).

Augusteijn, J., *From Public Defiance to Guerrilla Warfare: The Experience of Ordinary Volunteers in the Irish War of Independence 1916–1921* (Dublin, 1996).

    ed., *The Revolution in Ireland* (London, 2002).

Ballymacarrett Research Group, *Lagan Enclave: A History of Conflict in the Short Strand 1886–1997* (Belfast, 1997).

Bardon, J., *A History of Ulster* (Belfast, 1992).

Beckett, J. C., *The Making of Modern Ireland, 1603–1923* (London, 1966).

Bowyer, Bell, J., *The Secret Army: A History of the IRA, 1916–70* (London, 1972).

Boyce, D. G., *Englishmen and Irish Troubles: British Public Opinion and the Making of Irish Policy, 1918–22* (London, 1972).

    Nationalism in Ireland (London, 1982).

    ed., *The Revolution in Ireland, 1879–1922* (Dublin, 1988).

Brady, C., ed., *Interpreting Irish History: The Debate on Historical Revisionism* (Dublin, 1994).

Breen, D., *My Fight for Irish Freedom* (Dublin, 1924).

Buckland, P., *Ulster Unionism and the Origins of Northern Ireland 1886–1922* (Dublin, 1973).

    A History of Northern Ireland (Dublin, 1981).

Budge, I., and O'Leary, C., *Belfast: Approach to Crisis: A Study of Belfast Politics, 1603–1970* (London, 1973).

Clark, W., *Guns in Ulster: A History of the 'B' Special Constabulary in part of County Derry* (Belfast, 1967).

Coogan, T. P., *The IRA* (London, 1970).

Cunningham, J., 'The Struggle for the Belleek-Pettigo Salient, 1922', in *Donegal Annual*, 34 (Ballyshannon, 1982).

Dangerfield, G., *The Damnable Question: A Study in Anglo-Irish Relations* (London, 1977).

Denman, T., *Ireland's Unknown Soldiers: The 16th (Irish) Division in the Great War* (Dublin, 1992).

Doak, J. C., *Rioting and Civil Strife in the City of Londonderry during the 19th and Early 20th Centuries*, MA thesis, Queen's University Belfast (1978).

Dooher, J., *Tyrone Nationalism and the Question of Partition, 1910–25*, MPhil thesis, University of Ulster (1986).

Earl of Longford and O'Neill, T. P., *Eamon de Valera* (London, 1974).

Elliott, S., *Northern Ireland Parliamentary Election Results 1921–1972* (Chichester, 1973).

English, R., *Ernie O'Malley: IRA Intellectual* (Oxford, 1998).

English, R., and Walker, G., eds, *Unionism in Modern Ireland* (Dublin, 1996).

Fanning, R., *Independent Ireland* (Dublin, 1983).

Farrell, M., *Northern Ireland: The Orange State* (London, 1980).
  Arming the Protestants: The Formation of the Ulster Special Constabulary and the Royal Ulster Constabulary 1920–1927 (London, 1983).

Fitzpatrick, D., *The Two Irelands, 1912–1939* (Oxford, 1998).

Forester, M., *Michael Collins – The Lost Leader* (London, 1972).

Foster, R. F., *Modern Ireland, 1600–1972* (London, 1988).

Fox, C., *The Making of a Minority: Political Developments in Derry and the North, 1912–1925* (Derry, 1997).

Garvin, T., *1922: The Birth of Irish Democracy* (Dublin, 1996).

Gaughan J., ed., *Memoirs of Senator Joseph Connolly* (Dublin, 1996).

Greaves, D. G., *Liam Mellows and the Irish Revolution* (London, 1971).

Griffith, K. and O'Grady, T., *Curious Journey: An Oral History of Ireland's Unfinished Revolution* (Dublin, 1982).

Hand, G., 'MacNeill and the Boundary Commission' in F. X. Martin and F. J. Byrne, eds, *The Scholar Revolutionary: Eoin MacNeill, 1867–1945, and the Making of the New Ireland* (Shannon, 1973).

Harbinson, J. F., *The Ulster Unionist Party, 1882–1973: Its Development and Organisation* (Belfast, 1973).

Harkness, D., *The Restless Dominion* (London, 1969).
  Northern Ireland since 1920 (Dublin, 1983).

Harris, M., *The Catholic Church and the Foundation of the Northern Irish State* (Belfast, 1993).

Hart, P., 'Michael Collins and the Assassination of Sir Henry Wilson', Irish Historical Studies, vol. xxviii, no. 110 (November 1992), pp. 150–170.

Hepburn, A. C., ed., *Minorities in History* (London, 1978).

Hezlet, Sir. A., *The 'B' Specials: A History of the Ulster Special Constabulary* (London, 1973).

Hopkinson, M. A., 'The Craig–Collins Pacts of 1922: Two Attempted Reforms of the Northern Irish Government', Irish Historical Studies, vol. xxvii, no. 106 (November 1990), pp. 145–158.
  The Irish War of Independence (Dublin, 2002).

Kelly, B., ed., *Sworn to Be Free: The Complete Book of IRA Jailbreaks 1918–1921* (Tralee, 1971).

Kennedy, D., *The Widening Gulf: Northern Attitudes to the Independent Irish State, 1919–1945* (Belfast, 1988).

Kleinrichert, D., *Republican Internment and the Prison Ship Argenta 1922* (Dublin, 2001).

Laffan, M., *The Resurrection of Ireland: The Sinn Fein Party 1916–1923* (Cambridge, 1999).

Lee, J., *The Modernisation of Irish Society, 1848–1918* (Dublin, 1973).

Ireland, 1912–1985: Politics and Society (Cambridge, 1988).

Lyons, F. S. L., *Ireland since the Famine* (London, 1971).

MacDonagh, O., *Ireland: The Union and Its Aftermath* (London, 1977).

MacEoin, U., *Survivors* (Dublin, 1980).

Maguire, G., *The Political and Military Causes of the Division in the Irish Nationalist Movement, January 1921–August 1922*, DPhil thesis, University of Oxford (1985).

Mansergh, N., *The Irish Free State* (London, 1934).

The Government of Northern Ireland: A Study in Devolution (London, 1936).

McColgan, J., *British Policy and Irish Administration 1920–22* (Dublin, 1983).

McDermott, J., *Northern Divisions: The Old IRA and the Belfast Pogroms, 1920–22* (Belfast, 2001).

McGarry, F., *Eoin O'Duffy: A Self Made Hero* (Oxford, 2005).

Mercer, E., 'For King, Country and a Shilling a Day: Belfast Recruiting Patterns in the Great War', History Ireland, vol. 11, no. 4 (Winter 2003).

Miller, D., *Queen's Rebels: Ulster Loyalism in Historical Perspective* (Dublin, 1978).

Mitchell, A., *Revolutionary Government in Ireland: Dáil Éireann, 1919–22* (Dublin, 1995).

Labour in Irish Politics, 1890–1930 (Dublin, 1973).

Monaghan, A., 'Monaghan-1920' in *The* Capuchin Annual *1970* (Dublin, 1969).

Morgan, A., *Labour and Partition: The Belfast Working Class and the Belfast Labour Movement, 1868–1920* (London, 1991).

Murphy, R., 'Walter Long and the Making of the Government of Ireland Act, 1919–20', *Irish Historical Studies*, vol. 25, no. 97 (1986), pp. 82–96.

Murray, C., *The 1918 General Election in the Three Derry Constituencies*, thesis, Queen's University Belfast (1990).

Murray, P., *The Irish Boundary Commission and Its Origins 1886–1925* (Dublin, 2011).

O'Broin, L., *Michael Collins* (Dublin, 1983).

O'Donnell, P., *The Gates Flew Open* (London, 1932).

O'Donoghue, F., *No Other Law* (Dublin, 1954).

O'Drisceoil, D., *Peadar O'Donnell* (Cork, 2001).

O'Halpin, E., *The Decline of the Union: British Government in Ireland, 1892–1920* (Dublin, 1987).

O'Mahoney, S., *Frongoch: University of Revolution* (Dublin, 1987).

O'Malley, E., *On Another Man's Wound* (London, 1936).

Patterson, H., *Class, Conflict and Sectarianism: The Protestant Working Class and the Belfast Labour Movements, 1868–1920* (Belfast, 1980).

Quinn, R. J., *A Rebel Voice: A History of Belfast Republicanism, 1925–1972* (Belfast, 1999).

Regan, J., *The Irish Counter-Revolution, 1921–1936* (Dublin, 1999).

Rumpf, E., and Hepburn, A. C., *Nationalism and Socialism in Twentieth Century Ireland* (Liverpool, 1977).

Shearman, H., *Northern Ireland, 1921–1971* (Belfast, 1971).

Simkins, P., *Kitchener's Armies: The Raising of the New Armies, 1914–16* (Manchester, 1988).

Staunton, E., *The Nationalists of Northern Ireland 1918–1973* (Columbia, 2001).

Stewart, A. T. Q., *Edward Carson* (Dublin, 1981).

Sweeney, J., 'Donegal and the War of Independence' in *The Capuchin Annual 1970* (Dublin, 1969).

Towey, T., 'The Reaction of the British Government to the 1922 Collins–De Valera Pact', *Irish Historical Studies*, vol. xxii, no. 85 (March 1980).

Townshend, C., *The British Campaign in Ireland, 1919–1921: The Development of Political and Military Policies* (Oxford, 1975).

'The Irish Republican Army and the Development of Guerrilla Warfare, 1916–21', *English Historical Review*, vol. xciv, no. 371 (April 1979).

Political Violence in Ireland (Oxford, 1983).

Urquhart, D., *Women in Ulster Politics, 1890–1940* (Dublin, 2000).

Walker, B. M., *Parliamentary Election Results in Ireland, 1801–1922* (Dublin, 1978).

Younger, C., *Ireland's Civil War* (Fontana, CA, 1982).

Bibliography

Adams, G., *Free Ireland* (Dingle, 1995).

Adamson, Ian, *The Identity of Ulster: The Land, the Language and the People* (Belfast, 1982).

Anon, 'The Denial of North-East Ulster', *The Irish Review (Dublin)*, vol. 2, no. 17 (July 1912), p. 230.

Ansari, Sarah, 'The Movement of Indian Muslims to West Pakistan after 1947: Partition-Related Migration and Its Consequences for the Pakistani Province of Sind,' in Judith M. Brown and Rosemary Foot, eds, *Migration: The Asian Experience* (Oxford, 1994), 149–68.

Auger, Martin F., 'On the Brink of Civil War: The Canadian Government and the Suppression of the 1918 Quebec Easter Riots', *Canadian Historical Review*, vol. 89 (2008), p. 4.

Baruah, Sanjib, *India Against Itself: Assam and the Politics of Nationality* (New Delhi, 1999).

Baumann, A. A., *Persons and Politics of the Transition* (London, 1916).

Bew, P., *Ideology and the Irish Question* (Oxford, 1994).
    'Against Partitionist History', in *Ideology and the Irish Question: Ulster Unionism and Irish Nationalism, 1912–1916* (Oxford, 1998).
    'Moderate Nationalism and the Irish Revolution, 1916–1923', *Historical Journal*, vol. 42, no. 3 (Sept. 1999), p. 748.
    Churchill and Ireland (Oxford, 2016).

Bew, P, Gibbon, P., and Patterson, H., *The State in Northern Ireland 1921–72: Political Forces and Social Classes* (London, 1995).

Bogdanor, Vernon, *Devolution in the United Kingdom* (Oxford, 2001).

Bort, E., 'The Irish Border Play', in *The Irish Border* (Liverpool, 1999).

Bowman, John, *De Valera and the Ulster Question, 1917–1973* (Oxford, 1982).

Boyce, G., and O'Day, A., eds, *The Ulster Crisis, 1885–1921* (London, 2005).

Boyd, E., 'Ireland: Resurgent and Insurgent', *Foreign Affairs*, vol. 1, no. 1 (15 September 1922), p. 90.

Brennan, N., 'A Political Minefield: Southern Loyalists, the Irish Distress Committee and the British Government, 1922–1931', *Irish Historical Studies*, vol. xxx, no. 119 (May 1997), pp. 406–19.

Brewer, J., *The Royal Irish Constabulary: An Oral History* (Belfast, 1990).

Brock, Michael, and Brock, Eleanor, eds, *H.H. Asquith: Letters to Venetia Stanley* (Oxford, 1995).

Brook, Sydney, 'The Problem of Ulster', *The North American Review*, vol. 198, no. 696 (November 1913), pp. 617–29.

Buckland, P., *Irish Unionism* (Belfast, 1973).

The Factory of Grievances: Devolved Government in Northern Ireland 1921–39 (Dublin, 1979).

James Craig (Dublin, 1980).

Irish Unionism 1885–1921 (Dublin, 1988).

'Carson, Craig and the Partition of Ireland, 1919–1921', in Peter Collins, ed., *Nationalism and Unionism: Conflict in Ireland, 1885–1921* (Belfast, 1994).

Bulfin, W., *Rambles in Eireann*, vol. 2 (Dublin, 1905).

de Búrca, Marcus, *The GAA a History* (Dublin, 1980).

Burgess, M., 'Mapping the Narrow Ground: Geography, History and Partition', *Field Day Review*, vol. 1 (2005), pp. 121–132.

Bury, R., *Buried Lives: The Protestants of Southern Ireland* (Dublin, 2017).

Carville, A., 'The Impact of Partition Proposals on County Monaghan', *Clogher Record*, vol. 14, no. 1 (1991), pp. 37–51.

Chambers, I., *The Chamberlains, the Churchills and Ireland, 1874–1922* (New York, 2006).

Chart, D. A., *A History of Northern Ireland* (Belfast, 1928).

Chatterji, Joya, *Bengal Divided: Hindu Communalism and Partition, 1932–1947* (Cambridge, 1995).

Chesterton, G. K., *Irish Impressions* (London, 1918).

Clark, G., *Everyday Violence in the Irish Civil War* (Cambridge, 2017).

Coleman, M., *County Longford and the Irish Revolution, 1910–1923* (Dublin, 2002).

Colles, R., *A History of Ulster* (London, 1919).

Connaughton, S., *The Run of the Country* (Belfast, 1991).

Coogan, T. P., *De Valera: Long Fellow, Long Shadow* (London, 1993).

Michael Collins (London, 1991).

Copland, Ian, 'The Further Shores of Partition: Ethnic Cleansing in Rajasthan, 1947,' Past and Present, vol. 160 (1998), pp. 203–39.

Craig, Frederick, *British General Election Manifestos, 1918–1966* (London, 1970).

Crawford, L., *The Problem of Ulster* (Toronto, 1920).

Crawford, F. H., *Why I Voted for the Six Counties 1920* (Belfast, 1920).

Crosby, T., *Joseph Chamberlain: A Most Radical Imperialist* (London, 2018).

Delaney, P., 'D. P. Moran and the Leader: Writing an Irish Ireland through Partition', *Eire-Ireland*, vol. 38, no. 3 (Fall/Winter 2003), p. 194.

The Churches and Irish Emigration to Britain, 1921–60', *Archivium Hibernicum*, vol. 52 (1998), pp. 102–4.

Dooley, T., 'Monaghan Protestants in a Time of Crisis, 1919–1922' in R. V. Comerford, Mary Cullen, J. R. Hill and Colm Lennon, ed., *Religion, Conflict and Coexistence in Ireland* (Dublin, 1990).

Doyle, L., *An Ulster Childhood* (Dublin, 1921).

Earl of Oxford and Asquith, K. G., *Memories and Reflections, 1852–1927*, vol. 2 (1928).

Elliott, M., *The Catholics of Ulster* (London, 2000).

Ervine, St. John, *Craigavon: Ulsterman* (London, 1949).

Evans, E. E., ed, 'Disputing with De Valera' in *Ireland and the Atlantic Heritage* (Dublin, 1996).

Evans, N., 'Across the Universe; Racial Violence in the Post War Crisis in Imperial Britain 1919–1925' in D. Frost, ed., *Ethnic Labour and British Imperial Trade: A History of Ethnic Seafarers in the United Kingdom* (London, 1995), pp. 59–88.

'The Personality of Ulster,' *Transactions of the Institute of British Geographers*, no. 51 (November 1970), p. 3.

Falls, C., *The History of the 36th Ulster Division* (London, 1922).

Fanning, R., 'Anglo-Irish Relations: Partition and the British Dimension in Historical Perspective', *Irish Studies in International Affairs*, vol. 2, no. 1 (1982), pp. 132–49

Arming the Protestants: The Formation of the Ulster Special Constabulary and the Royal Ulster Constabulary 1920–1927 (London, 1983).

Farry, M., *Aftermath of Revolution: Sligo 1921–23* (Dublin, 2000).

Fazila-Yacoobali Zamindar, Vazira, *The Long Partition and the Making of Modern South Asia* (New York, 2007).

Finnan, J., *John Redmond and Irish Unity, 1912–1918* (Syracuse, NY, 2004).

Fitzpatrick, D., *Politics and Irish Life, 1913–21: Provincial Experience of War and Revolution* (Cork, 1998).

'The Orange Order and the Border', *Irish Historical Studies*, vol. 33, no. 129 (May 2002), pp. 52–67.

Follis, B., *A State under Siege: The Establishment of Northern Ireland 1920–1925* (Oxford, 1995).

Foster, R., *Vivid Faces: The Revolutionary Generation in Ireland, 1890–1923* (London, 2015).

Foster, R. F., *Lord Randolph Churchill: A Political Life* (Oxford, 1988).

Fox, C., *Marx, Engels and Lenin on Ireland* (New York, 1940).

Foy, M., 'Ulster Unionist Propaganda against Home Rule, 1912–1914', *History Ireland*, vol. 4, no. 1 (Spring 1996), pp. 49–53.

Fraser, T. F., *Partition in Ireland, India and Palestine: Theory and Practice* (London, 1984).

Gallagher, F., *The Indivisible Island* (Cork, 1957).

Gannon, Patrick J., 'Studies', *An Irish Quarterly Review*, vol. 11, no. 42 (June 1922), pp. 279–95.

Garvin, T., *The Evolution of Irish Nationalist Politics* (Dublin, 2005).

Gilbert, M., *Winston S. Churchill: Years of Turmoil* (New York, 2015).

Green, A., 'Homage to Heslinga', in *Forging the Smithy: National Identity and Representation in Anglo-Irish Literary History* (Amsterdam, 1995).

Greer, A., 'Sir James Craig and the Construction of Parliament Buildings at Stormont', *Irish Historical Studies*, vol. 31, no. 123 (May 1999), pp. 373–88.

Griffith, A., *The Resurrection of Hungary* (Dublin, 1904).

Griffith, Arthur, 'Sinn Fein and Ulster', *Notes from Ireland* (Irish Unionist Alliance, 1917), vol. 26, no. 4, p. 74.

Gwynn, D., *The History of Partition, 1912–1925* (London, 1950).

A History of Partition, 1911–1925 (Dublin, 1950).

Gwynn, S., 'Ireland, One and Divisible' *Foreign Affairs*, vol. 3, no. 2 (15 December 1924), pp. 183–98.

Hand, G. J., Report of the Irish Boundary Commission 1925 (Dublin, 1969).

Hart, P., *The IRA and Its Enemies: Violence and Community in Cork, 1916–1923* (Oxford, 1998).

The IRA at War (Oxford, 2003).

Healy, T. M., *The Great Fraud of Ulster* (Dublin, 1917).

Hennessey, T., *Dividing Ireland: World War One and Partition* (Abingdon, 1998).

Hepburn, A. C., *A Past Apart: Studies in the History of Catholic Belfast, 1850–1950* (Belfast, 1996).

Catholic Belfast and Nationalist Ireland in the Era of Joe Devlin, 1871–1934 (Oxford, 2008).

Heslinga, M. W., *The Irish Border as a Cultural Divide: A Contribution to the Study of Regionalism in the British Isles* (Assen, 1962).

Hood, Susan, *Royal Roots, Republican Inheritance – The Survival of the Office of Arms* (Dublin, 2002), pp. 119–20.

Hopkinson, M., *Green Against Green* (Dublin, 1988).

Hyde, D., *The Religious Songs of Connacht* (Dublin, 1906).

Hyde, Montgomery, H., *Carson: The Life of Sir Edward Carson, Lord Carson of Duncairn* (Portsmouth, NH, 1953).

Inoue,Keiko, 'Sinn Féin Propaganda and the 'Partition Election', 1921', *Studia Hibernica*, no. 30 (1998/1999), pp. 47–61.

Jackson, A., *The Irish Party: Ulster Unionists in the in the House of Commons, 1884–1911* (Oxford, 1989).

Jenkinson,J., 'Black Sailors on Red Clydeside: Rioting, Reactionary Trade Unionism and Conflicting Notions of Britishness Following the First World War' *Twentieth Century British History*, vol. 19, no. 1 (January 2008), pp. 29–60.

Johnson, D. J., 'The Belfast Boycott, 1920–22', in J. M. Goldstrom and J. A. Clarkson, eds, *Irish Population, Economy and Society: Essays in Honour of the late K.H. Connell* (Oxford, 1981).

Jones, Thomas, *Whitehall Diary* (Oxford, 1969).

Keogh, Dermot, *Twentieth Century Ireland: Revolution and State Building* (Dublin, 2005).

Kendle, John, *Ireland and the Federal Solution: The Debate over the United Kingdom Constitution, 1870–1920* (Montreal, 1989).

Walter Long, Ireland and the Union (Montreal, 1992).

Kenna, G. B. (Father John Hassan), *Facts and Figures of the Belfast Pogrom, 1920–22* (Dublin, 1922).

Kennedy, L., *Two Ulsters: A Case for Repartition* (Belfast, 1986).

Kennedy, L. and Ollrenshaw, P., eds, *An Economic History of Ulster, 1820–1939* (Manchester, 1995).

Kenny, James, 'The Catholic Church in Contemporary Ireland', *The Catholic Historical Review*, vol. 18, no. 2 (July 1932), p. 166.

Kettle, T. M., *The Open Secret of Ireland* (Dublin, 1912).

Kiely, B., *Counties of Contention* (Cork, 1945).

Kinsella, A., '"Goodbye Dublin": The British Military Evacuation 1922', *Dublin Historical Record*, vol. 51, no. 1 (Spring, 1998), pp. 4–24.

Laffan, M., *The Partition of Ireland 1912–1925* (Dublin, 1983).

Lawlor, H. C., *Ulster: Its Archaeology and Antiquities* (Belfast, 1928).

Lawlor, S., *Britain and Ireland 1914–1923* (Dublin, 1983).

The Burnings, 1920 (Cork, 2009).

Lewis, G., *Carson: The Man Who Divided Ireland* (London, 2005), p. 227.

Logan, J., *Ulster in the X-Rays* (Belfast, 1924).

Lynch, R., 'Explaining the Altnaveigh Massacre, June 1922', *Eire-Ireland*, vol. 38, no. 3 (Fall/Winter 2003), pp. 184–210.

The Northern IRA and the Early Years of Partition, 1920–1922 (Dublin, 2006).

'The People's Protectors? The Irish Republican Army and the "Belfast Pogrom, 1920–1922"', *Journal of British Studies*, vol. 47, no. 2 (April 2008), p. 391.

Revolutionary Ireland, 1912–1925 (London, 2015).

Lyons, F. S. L., 'Ulster: The Roots of Difference', in *Culture and Anarchy in Ireland, 1890–1939* (Oxford, 1979).

Macardle, Dorothy, 'The Manifesto of Sinn Féin as Prepared for Circulation for the General Election of December, 1918', in *The Irish Republic: A Documented Chronicle of the Anglo-Irish Conflict and the Partitioning of Ireland, with a Detailed Account of the Period 1916–1923* (London, 1937), pp. 919–20.

MacDonagh, O., *States of Mind: Two Centuries of Anglo-Irish Conflict, 1780–1980* (London, 1992).

MacKnight, T. *Ulster as It Is*, vol. 2 (London, 1896).

Mansergh, N., *The Unresolved Question: The Anglo-Irish Settlement and Its Undoing, 1912–1972* (New Haven, CT, 1991).

Martin, D., *Migration within the six counties of Northern Ireland with Special Reference to the City of Belfast, 1911–37*, MA thesis, Queen's University of Belfast (1977).

Martin, G., 'The Origins of Partition', in M. Anderson and E. Bolt, eds, *The Irish Border* (Liverpool, 1995).

Matthews, K. *The Irish Boundary Crisis and the Reshaping of British Politics, 1910–1925*. PhD thesis, London School of Economics, 2000.

Maume, P., 'Nationalism and Partition: The Political Thought of Arthur Clery', *Irish Historical Studies*, vol. 31, no. 122 (November 1998), p. 230.

Maxwell, Henry, *Ulster Was Right* (London, 1924).

May, R. and Cohen, R., 'The Interaction between Race and Colonialism: A Case Study of the Liverpool Race Riots of 1919' *Race and Class*, vol. 16 (1974), pp. 111–26.

McDowell, R. B., *The Irish Convention, 1917–18* (Abingdon, 1980).

McGarry, F., *The Rising: Easter 1916* (Oxford, 2011).

McKnight, T., *Ulster as It Is* (London, 1896).

McNeill, Ronald, *Ulster's Stand for Union* (New York, 1922).

The Birth of Ulster (London, 1936).

Meleady, D., *John Redmond: The National Leader* (Merrion, 2018).

Middlemass, K., eds, *Thomas Jones, Whitehall Diary: Vol. III: Ireland 1918–1925* (Oxford, 1971).

Moneypenny, W., *Two Irish Nations* (London, 1913).

Morrison, H. S., *Modern Ulster, Its Character, Customs, Politics and Industries* (London, 1920).

Muldoon, Paul, 'The Boundary Commission', in *Why Brownlee Left* (London, 1980).

Murray, C., 'Partition and the Irish Boundary Commission: A Northern Nationalist Perspective', *Clogher Record*, vol. 18, no. 2 (2004), pp. 181–217.

Myers, K., *Ireland's Great War* (Dublin, 2014).

Nisid, H., *Midnight's Furies: The Deadly Legacy of India's Partition* (London, 2015).

North-Eastern Boundary Bureau, *Handbook of the Ulster Question* (Dublin, 1923).

O'Brien, C. C., *The Shaping of Modern Ireland* (London, 1970).

O'Brien, W., *The Irish Revolution and How It Came About* (London, 1923).

O'Corrain, D., '"Ireland in His Heart North and South": The Contribution of Ernest Blythe to the Partition Question,' *Irish Historical Studies*, vol. xxxv, no. 137 (May 2006), 61–80.

O'Halloran, C., *Partition and the Limits of Irish Nationalism* (Dublin, 1987).

O'Hegarty, P. S., *The Victory of Sinn Fein* (Dublin, 1924).

O'Malley, E., *The Singing Flame* (Dublin, 1978).

Ogg, Frederic A., 'Proportional Representation in Ireland', *The American Political Science Review*, vol. 14, no. 2 (May 1920), pp. 323–4.

Orr, P., *The Road to the Somme: Men of the 36th Ulster Division Tell Their Story* (Belfast, 2008).

Owen, D. J., *History of Belfast* (Belfast, 1921).

Parker, Stewart, *Lost Belongings* (London, 1987).

Phoenix, E., *Northern Nationalism* (Belfast, 1994).

'Political Violence, Diplomacy and the Catholic Minority in Northern Ireland, 1922' in J. Darby, N. Dodge and A.C. Hepburn, eds, *Political Violence: Ireland in a Comparative Perspective* (Belfast, 1990).

'Michael Collins: The Northern Question 1916-22' in G. Doherty and D. Keogh, eds, *Michael Collins and the Making of the Irish State* (Cork, 1998).

Pringle, D. G., *One Island, Two Nations: A Political Geographical Analysis of the National Conflict in Ireland* (Letchworth, 1985).

Pseudonymous, 'Light on Ulsteria', *The Irish Review*, vol. 2, no. 16 (June 1912), pp. 220–1.

Ulster on Its Own (Belfast, 1912).

Rahman, M. and Schendel, W., 'I Am Not a Refugee': Rethinking Partition Migration, *Modern Asian Studies*, vol. 37, no. 3 (2003), pp. 551–84.

Rose, A. J., *Partition and Ireland* (Dublin, 1955).

Rowe, M., 'Sex, Race and Riot in Liverpool, 1919', *Immigrants and Minorities*, 19 (July 2000), pp. 53–70.

Russell, G., *The Inner and Outer Ireland* (Dublin, 1921).

What's the Matter with Ireland? (Ulan, 1920).

Said, E., *Culture and Imperialism* (New York, 1994).

Shaw, Fr. F., 'The Canon of Irish History', *Studies*, vol. 61 (1972), p. 151.

Sheehan, M., Hamilton, D., and Munck, R., 'Political Conflict, Partition, and the Underdevelopment of the Irish Economy', *Review of Radical Political Economics*, vol. 30, no. 1 (1998), pp. 1–31.

Sheridan, P. J., 'At the Irish Junction', *The Irish Review*, vol. 4, no. 37 (March 1914), pp. 12–15.

Stewart, A.T.Q., *The Ulster Crisis: Resistance to Home Rule, 1912–14* (London, 1969).
  The Narrow Ground: Aspects of Ulster, 1609–1969 (London, 1977).
  The Ulster Crisis (Belfast, 1997).
Street, C. J. C., *Ireland in 1921* (London, 1922).
Taylor, P. *Heroes or Traitors?: Experiences of Southern Irish Soldiers Returning from the Great War 1919–1939* (Liverpool, 2015).
Townshend, C., *Easter 1916: The Irish Rebellion* (London, 2015).
de Valera, E., *Ireland's Claim to the Government of the United States of America for Recognition as a Sovereign Independent State* (Washington, 1920).
White, J., 'The Summer Riots of 1919' *New Society*, vol. 57 (13 August 1981), 260–1.
White, T., *Kevin O'Higgins* (Dublin, 1957).
Wilson, P. W., 'The Irish Free State', *The North American Review*, vol. 215, no. 796 (March 1922), p. 324.
Winder Good, James, *Ulster and Ireland* (Dublin, 1919).
  Ireland and Unionism (Dublin, 1920).
  'British Labour and Irish Needs', *Irish Quarterly Review*, vol. 9, no. 36 (December 1920), pp. 557.
Yates, P., 'Oh What a Lovely War! Dublin and the First World War', *History Ireland*, vol. 19, no. 6 (November/December 2011), pp. 22–4.

Index